Managing Human Resources in Small and Mid-Sized Companies

Second Edition

Diane Arthur

American Management Association

New York • Atlanta • Boston • Chicago • Kansas City • San Francisco • Washington, D.C.
Brussels • Mexico City • Tokyo • Toronto

This book is available at a special
discount when ordered in bulk quantities.
For information, contact Special Sales Department,
AMACOM, a division of American Management Association,
135 West 50th Street, New York, NY 10020.

Library of Congress Cataloging-in-Publication Data

Arthur, Diane.
    Managing human resources in small and mid-sized companies / Diane
Arthur. — 2nd ed.
        p.   cm.
    Includes bibliographical references and index.
    ISBN 0-8144-0277-1
    1. Personnel management. 2. Small business—Personnel management.
I. Title.
HF5549.A955   1995
658.3—dc20   95-412
                                                                           CIP

Printing number

10   9   8   7   6   5   4   3   2   1

To
Warren, Valerie, and **Victoria**
my favorite human resources

Contents

Appendixes

Preface to the Second Edition

As more organizations grow from family-run businesses, where everyone is on a first-name basis, to companies with staffs numbering several hundred, the need for a professionally run human resources (HR) function increases. (The more encompassing designation "human resources" is now used almost exclusively rather than "personnel.")

Since the first edition of this book was published in 1987, much has changed with respect to the HR function in small and mid-sized companies. The 1986 $520,000 median expenditure for human resources activities and staffs reported by the Bureau of National Affairs rose as high as $651,000 in 1991, only to drop to a projected 1994 figure of $535,000.* Of the organizations that participated in the SHRM-BNA survey, 66 percent have fewer than 1,000 employees.

Despite this roller-coaster ride, the HR departments of small and mid-sized businesses are currently being given increasing authority in areas that transcend such traditional human resources activities as recruiting, interviewing, compensation, and benefits. For example, 68 percent of the surveyed HR departments reported overseeing one or more general service functions, such as security, food services, public relations, travel services, and purchasing, with many small companies giving HR additional responsibility for administrative services. HR departments are also increasingly in charge of new functions, such as environmental compliance and dependent care resources.

As HR responsibilities in small and mid-sized companies continue to escalate and diversify, so does reliance on human resources specialists. Of the smallest companies surveyed (fewer than 250 employees), 15 percent reported employing HR specialists; 46 percent of organizations with 250 to 499 workers and 55 percent of those with 400 to 999 employees hire HR

*Society for Human Resource Management—Bureau of National Affairs, *Bulletin to Management*, Survey 59 (Washington, D.C., June 30, 1994), p. 11.

practitioners. Additionally, these companies, striving to remain competitive, are adjusting HR staff salaries and benefits accordingly. The median proportion of HR costs represented by salaries and benefits reveals a steady increase: 69 percent in 1993, up from 60 percent in 1992, 57 percent in 1991, and 54 percent in 1990.

These figures signify that small and mid-sized companies are addressing human resources issues but not necessarily in the same way as large corporations. Organizations with fewer than 1,500 employees have unique HR needs not adequately addressed in general human resources publications. This book is written specifically for such companies; it serves as an overall guide to developing an effective human resources function or improving an established HR department. Its contents pertain to corporate and nonprofit environments alike and will benefit both human resources professionals and non-HR practitioners responsible for human-resources-related activities.

Although the basics of establishing an HR function suitable for a small or mid-sized business have not changed since 1987, other factors in our society have, warranting the revisions made in this edition. These begin with a new chapter (Chapter 1) that looks to the future by exploring human resources challenges for the twenty-first century. An entire chapter is also devoted to the subject of human resources and the law (Chapter 3), previously discussed as part of employee relations. This is necessitated by changes in, and additions to, equal employment opportunity legislation, as well as the increasing importance of other employment-related factors such as negligent hiring and retention. Similarly, due to the growing focus on various types of testing, such as drug tests, and concerns about the ramifications of using tests that have not been validated, a new chapter on preemployment and employment testing (Chapter 5) is included.

Other chapters have been expanded and revised to encompass recent HR developments, such as the growing popularity of variable pay and other nontraditional compensation programs, alternative dispute resolution in grievance matters, the use of CD-ROM for employee training and development, and the increasing reliance on computerized human resources information systems for record keeping.

Many of these revisions have affected the appendixes appearing in the original edition. Consequently, in this edition several forms have been updated, such as the application form.

Readers are cautioned on two points. First, any reference made to specific publications, services, or institutions is for informational purposes only and is not meant as an endorsement. Second, this book is not intended to provide legal advice. If such advice is required, the services of an attorney specializing in human resources or employment law should be sought.

By analyzing just what the human resources function entails and by assessing its various components, this book will enable any small or mid-sized organization to become more productive and profitable through full utilization of its most valuable asset: its employees.

D.A.

Acknowledgments

I wish to express special appreciation to Adrienne Hickey, AMACOM's Senior Acquisitions and Planning Editor, for her invaluable insights and suggestions. I am also indebted to Barbara Horowitz, Associate Editor, for her masterful editing. Adrienne and Barbara are two significant reasons I have been an AMACOM author for the past ten years.

In addition, thanks to my clients, colleagues, friends, former employers, and the hundreds of students from my training programs, for the opportunities and experiences they have provided. All will forever be counted among my human resources.

1

Human Resources Challenges for Small and Mid-Sized Companies in the Twenty-First Century

How well a small business copes with the expanding role of human resources depends largely on its willingness to embrace HR as one of its primary responsibilities.

Attend a workshop or read an article about the human resources (HR) function in the twenty-first century and you are likely to come across terms such as: alternative work arrangements, balancing work and family issues, business-education partnerships, changing workforce, cross-cultural awareness, employee dependent care needs, glass ceiling, global corporate culture, multiculturalism, telecommuting, and workplace diversity. Keeping up with these issues and their impact on business, while managing the wide range of traditional human resources tasks, is enough to keep several HR practitioners in a major corporate setting busy on a full-time basis; the effect on small and mid-sized companies, many struggling just to remain afloat and competitive, may seem nothing short of overwhelming. And yet, ready or not, the twenty-first century is almost here, bringing with it more HR-related responsibilities and change requiring the attention of all companies, regardless of size, than ever before.

Recruitment Challenges

One of the greatest areas of change in the next century is certain to be in recruitment. To begin with, there is expected to be a shortage of adequately trained employees. The flood of baby boomers entering the labor market since the mid-1960s has not been matched in recent years because of lower birthrates, with the possible exception of California, where, according to the Center for Continuing Study of the California Economy, 1994 birthrates were 20 percent above those of the rest of the nation. This means that companies must become more aggressive in their recruitment efforts by tapping populations of women (many of whom will have young children), minorities, immigrants, persons with disabilities, older workers, and dwindling numbers of youth. Unfortunately, many of these workers will be unskilled and require training, and in some instances retraining, even for many entry-level jobs. The most basic jobs will demand new, more complex skills; even simple clerical work will necessitate computer knowledge. The greatest demand will be in jobs that require independent thinking, reasoning, logic, and the ability to diagnose and take action. Many experts are concerned that these skills are not being adequately taught in our schools.

A shortage of properly trained employees is one trend that will shape the employment picture of the future. Another has to do with where job opportunities are anticipated. According to the Bureau of Labor Statistics, one of the fastest-growing industries will be computer services. With the introduction of high technology in the workplace—for example, networked information systems, online services, and CD-ROM—employees with a combination of business and computer skills will be in greater demand. Three other growth areas are projected to be personnel services, such as temporary agencies, miscellaneous business services such as credit reporting, and health care. The last is expected to generate a particularly wide range of jobs for several decades: gerontologists, physical therapists, medical assistants, home health aides, pharmacists, health care financial advisers, and occupational therapists, to name but a few occupations. Other fast-growing jobs will be paralegals, data processing equipment repairers, and computer systems analysts. Significantly, these openings are in service industries, as opposed to manufacturing, the traditional source of most jobs in the United States.

Many also predict that jobs will be generated by government entities, as well as private companies, concerned about conforming to future environmental laws or building new, environmentally sound residences, hospitals, and other structures.

The Department of Labor forecast is that fast-growing positions at the turn of the century will be in the professional, technical, service, and sales fields, requiring the highest levels of education and skill. Engineering jobs are expected to increase by more than 165,000, and there will be an anticipated 85,000 additional managerial positions available.

Essentially, then, employers may anticipate the following changes:

- Because of the overall shortage of labor, employers can no longer be as selective as in years past when they could afford to seek out the ideal candidate. Indeed, for some positions, finding any qualified applicants at all may be a challenge.
- Employers can no longer rely on traditional forms of recruitment, such as word of mouth, to find suitable workers.
- As the percentage of women, minorities, immigrants, persons with disabilities, and senior citizens in the workforce continues to increase, employers must extend fair thinking and behavior well beyond the minimal standards required by equal employment opportunity laws and affirmative action programs.
- Since the fastest-growing industries will require higher levels of skill and knowledge than in years past, greater emphasis must be placed on education and training.

Preparing now for the changes predicted for the next century will better enable employers to look forward to recruitment challenges rather than recruitment problems.

The Literacy Crisis

In 1983, the National Commission on Excellence in Education published *A Nation at Risk*. This report described an educational foundation that is "being eroded by a rising tide of mediocrity that threatens our very future as a nation and a people. If this mediocrity were thrust upon us by an unfriendly nation, we could call it an act of war."

More specifically, we are talking about a country where, according to the National Alliance of Business, more than 25 percent of all teenagers drop out of high school (Los Angeles, Chicago, and Boston have much higher rates). That translates into almost 3,800 teenagers dropping out of school daily! Of those who do graduate, many are not prepared for even entry-level jobs.

The U.S. Department of Education offers equally disturbing statistics with regard to illiteracy in adults. One in every seven American adults is a functional illiterate, unable to read, write, calculate, or solve basic problems. In 1991, functionally illiterate people comprised 30 percent of unskilled workers; 29 percent of semiskilled workers; and 11 percent of all managers, professionals, and technicians. Another 47 million adults were categorized as borderline illiterates. In addition, one-half of our nation's industrial workers read at or below the eighth-grade level, and, according to the Business Council for Effective Literacy, one out of every eight employees in the United States reads at no more than a fourth-grade level. Meanwhile, 85 percent of material read on the job is written at the ninth-grade level or above.

Add to this Department of Labor statistics indicating that 2.5 million illiterate Americans reportedly seek employment each year in a job market where 80 percent of all available jobs require at least a high school education, and it becomes clear that American businesses are facing an educational crisis.

The impact of illiteracy on business is far-reaching: lost profits, lowered productivity, declining international competitiveness, reduced promotability, workers who cannot read instructions, illiterate customers who cannot read advertisements, and illiterate consumers who cannot read instructions.

Some experts believe our schools' approach to education needs to be systemically changed. Janice Hird, director of corporate public involvement for Portland, Maine–based UNUM Life Insurance Co., stated in 1991, "We're educating students for the 1950s. Both the subject matter we teach and the way in which we teach it is for an industrialized society, and as our society has changed to an information-based society, the subject matter and the way we teach haven't changed with it. Children are still receptacles of information given to them by teachers, rather than thinkers who learn to process information, interpret and think critically about information and then express it in a creative way. In the year 2010, we'll be preparing students for the 1980s and 1990s. Schools have to deliver education in a fundamentally different way to stay in touch with the workforce and societal needs."

Preventing illiteracy from infiltrating business is the first line of defense. Preemployment screening offers an opportunity for employers to identify job applicants with skill deficiencies who may require remedial training. Unfortunately, recruiters and interviewers often assume that a high school, business school, or college graduate can automatically master basic reading, writing, and math skills. This, sadly, is not always so. It has been found that many college graduates cannot write a coherent business letter, and many are deficient in critical reasoning skills.

Some human resources departments actually help illiterate applicants to hide their deficiencies by allowing them to take employment applications home to complete. Such illiteracy may remain concealed when employers shy away from preemployment tests out of fear of discrimination charges. In addition, employment and educational reference checks are increasingly difficult to conduct, and many employers do not even at-tempt them. Consequently, employees are placed on the payroll even though their literacy levels are unknown.

Many employers concerned with screening potential employees for basic literacy have found the following techniques helpful:

- Applicants should be required to complete the employment appli-cation form by themselves, at the time of the interview.

- Job descriptions, defining both the requirements for the job and pri-mary duties and responsibilities, should be shown to the applicant during the course of the interview. Sufficient time should then be allotted for the applicant to read the contents and ask questions.

- Job-related, validated tests may be used as one of the selection cri-teria.

- Thorough employment and educational reference checks should be conducted whenever possible.

- In-depth, face-to-face interviews should be conducted by trained interviewers. The emphasis should be on open-ended questions so that the interviewers can evaluate such factors as the applicant's word use, clarity of thought, organization of information, and analytical ability rele-vant to a given job opening.

Some companies choose to get directly involved with basic skills edu-cation—a step that often turns out to be a win-win situation for everyone. In 1991, more than 200,000 businesses, both large and small, reported some form of partnership with educational institutions, according to the National Association of Partners in Education. These efforts range from short-term, local projects, such as adopt-a-school, and long-term efforts that are broadly based and likely to involve several businesses and com-munity groups. The latter are usually referred to as coalitions, compacts, or alliances. In Chicago, for instance, a coalition of more than 120 groups organized to support Chicago's Corporate/Community Schools, an inno-vative, year-round educational program.

Some companies choose to send management representatives to local schools to observe firsthand what the students are learning. This is also an opportunity for them to describe to the students the skills required for various jobs in their companies, as well as the benefits of working for them. The Los Angeles Unified School District's Partnership Office exem-plifies this approach.

Others become deeply committed to a business-education partnership. One such company is Weber Metals, a manufacturer of aluminum and titanium forgings in Paramount, California, with 200 employees of all ethnic and age groups. In 1989, it developed a partnership with the adult education division of Paramount's Unified School District. The school provided instructors and computers, and Weber paid for books and other instructional materials, as well as providing telephone line connections and upkeep for computer software covering more than 130 courses. This voluntary educational program, attended by employees on their own time, produced significant educational improvements that translated into increased work skills, bolstered self-esteem, and resulted in several promotions within just two years.

The human resources function in an organization is an important component of the school-business partnership. HR staff usually understand the needs of the workplace as well as knowing the skills, interests, and limitations of the employees. They can explore different educational and training opportunities, presenting senior management with options.

In the past, businesses left education completely up to the schools, a mistake that more companies need to rectify. Organizations interested in learning more about entering partnerships with educational institutions can contact the following organizations:

Council for Aid to Education
51 Madison Avenue, Suite 2200
New York, N.Y. 10010
212/689-2400

National Association of Partners in Education, Inc.
209 Madison Street, Suite 401
Alexandria, Va. 22314
703/836-4880

National Alliance of Business
1201 New York Avenue, N.W.
Washington, D.C. 20005
202/289-2888

The Conference Board, Inc.
845 Third Avenue
New York, N.Y. 10022
212/759-0900

Committee for Economic Development
477 Madison Avenue
New York, N.Y. 10022
212/688-2063

The Business Roundtable
200 Park Avenue
New York, N.Y. 10166
212/682-6370
or
1615 L Street, N.W.
Washington, D.C. 20036
202/872-1260

Workplace Diversity

How well a small business copes with the expanding role of human resources depends largely on its willingness to embrace HR as one of its
primary responsibilities. This begins simply with understanding that any
business, regardless of size, requires the support of well-trained, properly
placed, motivated employees in order to prosper. In the twenty-first century, this means recruiting, and being responsive to the needs of, an increasingly diverse workforce.

Women

According to the Department of Labor, by the year 2000, half the entire
U.S. labor force will consist of women. Many of these women, it is anticipated, will strive to penetrate the "glass ceiling" and enter the ranks of
senior management, although according to one report, it will take 475
years for women to reach equality with men at the upper levels.* Significantly, many of the women in the workforce will be mothers who are either
financially unable, or unwilling, to choose either child rearing or employment. Since more and more women are delaying the start of families until
their thirties or forties, considerable numbers are certain to be valued professionals with established track records and lengthy careers. Many will
require alternative work arrangements from the traditional eight-hour day,
five-day week to balance home and work responsibilities.

Minorities

It is projected that the term *minority* will soon disappear from our vocabu-
lary when we refer to employment in the twenty-first century. How can

*Feminist Majority Foundation, *Empowering Women in Business* (Washington, D.C.).

we label "minority" a group of people who, according to the Department of Labor, will account for nearly one-third of the labor force by the year 2000 and, by some government estimates, nearly half of the U.S. population by 2050? Although workplace attitudes toward minorities in general, and blacks in particular, are more accepting—a 1994 nationwide Gallup Poll reported 97 percent of white Americans said that they think blacks and whites deserve equal employment opportunities—there is still cause for concern. Subtle discrimination and racist beliefs continue to exist, including the notion that the best employees are those who most resemble the (white male) members of the upper echelon in terms of skills, interests, background, and appearance.

Immigrants

Foreign-born employees are expected to account for some 23 percent of the change in the labor force by the turn of the century, according to the Department of Labor. These "new Americans" include trained professionals, such as nurses from the Philippines, college professors from Europe, and scientists and engineers from Asia and the Middle East. Others will arrive lacking concrete job skills or the ability to speak English, seeking any kind of work.

Finding immigrants who want to work is not likely to be a problem, since the Immigration Act of 1990, effective as of October 1991, raised legal immigration levels to approximately 700,000 persons per year. This is a 35 percent increase over the maximum allowed prior to the act. Under the act, individuals are permitted to enter the United States, regardless of educational or skill level, ability to speak English, or the labor market they wish to enter. Since the demand for labor increasingly is for highly trained workers with advanced verbal, mathematical, scientific, engineering, and linguistic skills, the continued mismatch between large numbers of immigrant workers and jobs is a growing concern.

Expatriates

Global expansion is going to be a reality for many businesses, large and small, in the twenty-first century. As a result, human resources specialists will be entering an international work environment with varying employment procedures. Companies like Powersoft, a software company in Burlington, Massachusetts, with about 190 employees; FMC Gold, a precious-metal mining company with about 500 employees based in Reno, Nevada; and Gupta Corp., a 260-employee software company located in Menlo

Park, California, are examples of small businesses that have hired expatriates—employees for assignment (usually temporary) in another country. Such companies have come to understand that finding the right employee to handle operations thousands of miles away can be quite a challenge. Careful consideration must be given to understanding the culture, labor market, laws, and customary benefits and compensation packages of the host country. Companies are advised to develop a comprehensive expatriate policy manual outlining the terms and conditions of placement.

People With Disabilities

The term *disabilities* refers to a wide range of impairments. According to a nationwide survey conducted by the International Center for the Disabled and the National Council on the Handicapped in Washington, D.C., 45 percent of people with disabilities have physical disabilities, such as orthopedic impairments, memory loss caused by stroke or brain injury, or neurologic conditions such as multiple sclerosis; 32 percent suffer from heart disease, cancer, diabetes, or respiratory disease; 13 percent have visual, hearing or speech impairments; and 6 percent have mental disabilities.* The Americans with Disabilities Act of 1990 identifies over one thousand different impairments as disabilities and is believed to embrace an estimated 43 million Americans. Yet this well-intentioned law has thus far failed to eliminate a lingering reluctance on the part of employers to hire people with disabilities. A 1994 survey conducted for the National Organization on Disabilities reports only 31 percent of disabled persons ages 16 to 64 were working part time or full time; in 1986, that number was 33 percent.

Older Workers

As 76 million baby boomers (people born from 1946 to 1964) reach age 50 and beyond, Ken Dychtwald, the "guru of aging," and founder/chairman of Age Wave Inc.,† views us as being on the brink of a "senior boom"; that is, we are rapidly refocusing from youth orientation to a mature population of healthier Americans who are living and working longer than ever before. Dychtwald reports that 100 years ago only 3 million Americans were over age 65—a mere 4 percent of our population. Now, as we ap-

---

*Reported in "The Diversity Challenge," special supplement to *The New York Times* (October 23, 1994), p. 10.
†Patricia Galagan, "The Age Wave," *Training and Development Journal* (February 1990), pp. 22–30.

proach the next century, there are more than 30 million over-65 Americans, or 12 percent of our population. Many want to work, for economic reasons, because it makes them feel useful and needed, enables them to stay in touch with current developments, provides structure to their days, or enables them to retain a sense of productivity and worth. Older workers reportedly have fewer avoidable absences from work than do younger workers, exhibit less stress on the job, and have a lower rate of illegal drug use. In addition, with the exception of a slight decline in productivity in jobs requiring a great deal of physical exertion, many studies indicate that older workers perform at least as well as, and in many instances better than, younger workers.

Youth

According to Census Bureau figures, the number of people between the ages of 20 and 29 will shrink to 34 million by the turn of the century, down from 41 million in 1980, and representing only 13 percent of the population. This group, referred to as "baby busters," "generation X'ers," "yiffies" (young, individualistic, freedom minded, and few), "twenty-somethings," "twenty-nothings," and 13ers (in reference to the fact that they are the thirteenth generation to know the U.S. flag and the Constitution), born from 1961 to 1981, bring with them high levels of skill and education. Collectively, they have a keen interest in new technology, equipment, and strategies. For this group, financial success takes a back seat to intangibles such as rewarding family lives, the opportunity to help others, and the chance for leisure and travel.

Gender, ethnicity, national origin, physical and mental fitness, and age are not the only traits altering the composition of tomorrow's labor pool. Workplace diversity can also encompass religious affiliation, political views, economic class, military experience, sexual orientation, personality, culture, value systems, appearance, attire, grooming, and learning, communication, work, and leadership styles. Indeed, any characteristic that differentiates one person from another contributes to a diverse workplace. Depending on an organization's perspective, these differences can either be detrimental or enhance the overall work environment.

Multiculturalism in the Workplace

In order for workplace diversity to be effective, employers must commit to valuing the skills of a wide range of employees and let go of any lingering traditional views that certain jobs are appropriate for men or women only, unsuitable for older people, undesirable for minorities, or cannot be accomplished by people with disabilities. Such views may be not only discriminatory and in violation of certain equal employment opportunity laws but impractical and self-defeating from the standpoint of productivity and profitability.

Employers also must work toward developing an environment that is suitable and comfortable for all employees. This includes implementing flexible work schedules, job sharing, at-home work arrangements, and on-site child care facilities, to name but a few alternatives to the traditional nine-to-five, Monday-through-Friday schedule.

The term often used to describe an environment that encompasses a diverse workforce and offers something for everyone is *multicultural* or *cross-cultural.* Depending on the perspective of the employer and the level of knowledge about the issue, multiculturalism can have positive meaning or a highly negative connotation, stemming from discrimination, fear, or past experiences with ineffective diversity programs.

For those threatened by diversity, answering a series of questions about one's own biases can be the first step in developing greater cultural awareness and sensitivity:

- Do you feel that your culture has something positive or special to offer others? If so, what is it?
- Do you sometimes view people from other cultures as less capable? If so, is it because they cannot express themselves clearly in your language?
- Do you prefer to avoid people who do not share your cultural views?
- Are you uncomfortable working around people who look different, perhaps because of a disability?
- Do you feel uneasy when dealing with someone from another culture who behaves and acts differently from you?

Multiculturalism is part of the inevitable change of the twenty-first century that will promote an interactive, interdependent society. Consequently, employers have an obligation to ensure a workforce that is willing to accept diversity. This means providing ongoing training to foster appreciation, respect, and tolerance of differences rather than fear and rejection.

Two means for helping any organization value and manage diversity are *awareness-based multicultural training* and *skill-based diversity training.* Described by Anthony Carnevale and Susan Stone, awareness-based training is designed to increase employee knowledge, understanding, and sensitivity to diversity issues.* It also reveals and examines people's tendencies to stereotype by assessing prevailing attitudes and values. The approach is founded on the assumption that people tend to respond to situations according to their cultural beliefs as to what is correct or acceptable behavior. Our reaction to people who operate from a different set of cultural beliefs is often biased, which in a work setting can result in misunderstandings that may undermine performance, impair employee and customer relations, or create safety risks. Ultimately, the goal of an awareness-based diversity training program is more effective multicultural interaction, improved employee morale, greater productivity, and increased creativity, all of which point toward an improved organizational competitive position.

Examples are an important aspect of this type of training, since they encourage workers to view one another as individuals rather than images of what a group of people are thought to be like. Examples exemplifying the business necessity for awareness training and anecdotes may also help to ensure understanding on the part of participants.

Assuming awareness-based training succeeds in heightening trainees' knowledge, awareness, and sensitivity, what then? Skill-based training picks up by going beyond awareness and providing employees with suggested methods and techniques for dealing effectively with diversity. The ultimate goals are the same as those for awareness-based training (improved morale, productivity, creativity, and improving a company's competitive edge), but the focus is on adaptability rather than understanding.

Not surprisingly, there are different approaches to implementing an effective multicultural environment.† According to Ann M. Morrison, five major steps are required:

1. Identifying the diversity problems in an organization
2. Strengthening management commitment
3. Establishing meaningful numerical goals
4. Revisiting goals to ensure their continued relevance
5. Maintaining momentum

---

*Anthony Carnevale and Susan Stone, *The American Advantage: Our Diverse Workforce* (New York: American Society for Training and Development and McGraw-Hill, 1995).
†The following books are highlighted in this section: Ann M. Morrison, *The New Leaders* (San Francisco: Jossey-Bass, 1992); Lawrence M. Baytos, "Launching Successful Diversity Initiatives," *HR Magazine* (March 1992); R. Roosevelt Thomas, *Beyond Race and Gender* (New York: AMACOM, 1992); Renee Blank and Sandra Slipp, *Voices of Diversity* (New York: AMACOM, 1994).

Lawrence M. Baytos offers a somewhat different model. He identifies the following five steps:

1. Establishing a clear business reason for the program
2. Seeking employee input
3. Converting employee input into action steps
4. Setting the timing and focus of training
5. Preparing to sustain the momentum

In his book *Beyond Race and Gender,* R. Roosevelt Thomas emphasizes that managing diversity is not a specific program but a process for developing an environment that works for *all* employees (including white males). He offers an action plan, an extended case study of diversity initiatives at Avon Products, Inc., and a list of penetrating questions and answers to stimulate thinking about how best to use the human talent available in an organization.

Yet another perspective is offered by diversity specialist Kay Iwata. First, she urges companies to distinguish between "buy-in commitment," the kind expressed by managers who feel compelled to carrying out diversity directives but do not really believe in it, and "leadership commitment," which is action oriented. Next, Iwata expresses caution against proceeding without leadership commitment. Third, if leadership commitment is missing, she recommends doing what is necessary to obtain it.

A unique perspective is offered by Renee Blank and Sandra Slipp in their book, *Voices of Diversity.* The book discusses nine "groups" that make up the diverse workforce: African-Americans, Asian-Americans, Latinos, recent immigrants, disabled workers, gays and lesbians, younger and older workers, women, and white males. Subtitled *Real People Talk About Problems and Solutions in a Workplace Where Everyone Is Not Alike,* the book features candid comments from members of each group, background on the group's culture and values, and scenarios of typical on-the-job management and communications problems, with advice on what to do and say if you are faced with similar situations.

Finally, Jeffrey Goldstein and Marjorie Leopold suggest these guidelines for employers in promoting multiculturalism:

- Do not avoid the issue of diversity.
- Discuss how everyone comes to the workplace with a unique combination of background influences.
- Insist on tact and respect in discussions of ethnic, cultural, racial, or gender differences.

- Stay within the boundaries of equal employment opportunity laws.
- Distinguish between personal and professional needs.
- Explain unwritten company rules pertaining to behavior, attitude, and style.
- Suggest employees talk to coworkers about the organization's culture.

Cynthia F. Barnum, cofounder of Diversity Publications in New York City, additionally recommends that employees have discussions about what they have read, thereby enhancing the learning process. Following are some suggested categories and titles by Barnum:

- *About women: The Revolution of Little Girls* by Blanche McCrary Boyd
- *About African-Americans: Baby of the Family* by Tina McElroy Ansa, *Middle Passage* by Charles Johnson, and *On the Eve of Uncertain To-morrows* by Neil Bissoondath
- *About disabilities: Touching the Rock* by John M. Hull and *What's That Pig Outdoors?* by Henry Kisor
- *About Hispanic-Americans: Los Gusanos* by John Sayles, *The General in His Labyrinth* by Gabriel Garcia-Marquez, and *Woman Hollering Creek and Other Stories* by Sandra Cisneros
- *About Asian-Americans: The Incorporation of Eric Chung* by Steve C. Lo, *Typical American* by Gish Jen, and *The Clay That Breathes* by Catherine Browder*

Multiculturalism is becoming a vital element of every business in this country as the U.S. population becomes more diverse and cross-cultural communication is no longer an issue just for people who travel overseas. In 1993, according to *The New York Times,* 40 percent of American companies provided some form of diversity training.[†] By the year 2000, that figure should be closer to 100 percent, as more companies come to embrace differences among employees and use diversity to create a competitive advantage. Ultimately, and ideally, diversity training should not be necessary at all, as employers come to understand that success in tomorrow's economy hinges on getting along with our multicultural neighbors.

---

*Cynthia F. Barnum, "A Novel Approach to Diversity," *HR* magazine (May 1992), pp. 69–73.
[†] As reported in Patricia A. Galagan, "Navigating the Differences," *Training & Development Magazine* (April 1993), p. 30.

Work and Family Issues

It was long assumed that one would enter the U.S. labor market, work a forty-hour week, five days a week for approximately forty years, and then retire to a life of relaxation. However, today's workers are starting to protest, in an increasingly louder voice, that an arrangement committing much of the first half of their lives (we are now living to age 80, 90, and beyond) to an inflexible schedule, with little time for familial activities and other interests, is no longer acceptable. The focus on improving the balance between work and family is due largely to the increase of women and aging baby boomers in the labor market, as well as the changed focus of today's youth. These groups bring with them a desire to reevaluate how careers, relationships, and life in general should be approached. Since the labor pool is shrinking and companies must become more creative and competitive in their recruitment and retention efforts, employers have little choice but to try to accommodate their workers' desire to integrate work and family.

Work-and-Family Programs

More companies are moving in the direction of institutionalizing work-and-family programs, integrating them with the corporate culture and the corporate strategic plan. A wide range of services, including courses for expectant mothers, new parents, single parents, parents of children with special needs, blended families, nursing mothers, mothers experiencing anxiety about returning to work after childbirth, parents of preschoolers, school-age children, preadolescents, and adolescents, may be offered. Some companies conduct separate segments for parents and children, then bring them together for a final session. Special workshops may be provided for fathers, encouraging them to play a more participative role in raising their children. Sometimes private rooms for nursing mothers are provided. In addition, information covering a wide range of child-related materials may be found in parent resource libraries; parenting support groups may be organized; field trips for fathers and their children may be sponsored; and employees may be loaned beepers in the event of a potential family emergency. A newsletter focusing on family and work-related matters may be published, providing employees with up-to-date news on parenting and other family issues.

These activities and services need not be costly. Many of the courses and support group sessions are generally run during lunchtime, require minimum staff, and often may be integrated with community resources such as the adult education department of a local school district. Courses may even be made available on videocassette. Books and resource materials are often donated by employees, a local library, or a bookstore. Sometimes employees pay a nominal fee, say for a field trip, to cover transportation costs or any other fees. And newsletters can be prepared by the employees themselves.

Rona Greenstadt, a Los Angeles parent-educator since 1981, believes that parents who participate in these projects become more productive and confident in their relationships with their children as they apply the practical tools acquired. She maintains that parenting education can reduce stress and absenteeism and increase productivity. Additionally, the communication skills learned in parenting classes often work well with colleagues, thereby helping employees deal with on-the-job stress.

Small and mid-sized businesses interested in the impact that work-and-family programs can have on employee performance may wish to develop a program similar to the one at Fel-Pro, an Illinois-based manufacturer of automotive-sealing products. The company has approximately 2,000 employees and provides numerous family-related benefits, including summer day camp and college scholarships for employees' children. Cost of a work/family benefits package at Fel-Pro is $700 per employee per year. A study of the program revealed that Fel-Pro employees participating in the program have the highest job performance evaluations and the highest level of commitment to the company. In fact, the more that workers use Fel-Pro's work/family benefits, the greater is their support for company efforts toward total quality improvement. A whopping 92 percent praise Fel-Pro's benefits and boast of how the company has improved the balance of their work and personal lives.

At SAS Institute, a 1,700-employee computer software developer in Cary, North Carolina, the results are similar. Employees attribute a low turnover rate to work-and-family initiatives, including a policy of providing nutritious take-home dinners. Far below the computer industry average of approximately 20 percent, SAS's turnover rate is about 5.9 percent.

Companies with work-and-family programs also project concern for their employees' needs outside the workplace. For employees with children, these programs can be a valuable part of their benefits package. Even applicants without children are bound to be impressed with the organization's commitment to its workers.

Employers interested in obtaining additional information about work-and-family programs may contact the following organizations:

Families and Work Institute
330 Seventh Avenue
New York, N.Y. 10001
212/465-2044

Catalyst
250 Park Avenue South
New York, N.Y. 10003-1459
212/477-4252

Paradigm Group
75 Livingston Street
Brooklyn Heights, N.Y. 11201
718/643-0156

Child Care Programs

Employers nationwide are slowly yet steadily beginning to respond to the undeniable need for a greater balance between work and family by heeding the increasing need for child care programs. In its June 1993 issue, *Working Woman* magazine reported that one-tenth of 1 percent of all U.S. companies—an estimated 5,600 businesses—have formal programs to assist employees with child care needs.* This may seem like a very small number, yet it represents a tenfold increase over the past decade.

The specific level and extent of care offered depends on several factors, including an organization's financial resources. Services may include assistance in locating local day care, preschools, and camps; financial aid to supplement child care; and support for near-site care centers and on-site care facilities.

A company considering child care benefits for its workers should remain flexible and adjust its offerings according to employee need. For example, even though a company is 55 percent female, one-third with children under the age of 12, it would be presumptuous for a business to assume that on-site child care would be appreciated and utilized. Depending on the length of the employees' commutation, it might not be feasible to have their children make the trip to and from work on a daily basis. In such instance, a better option might be to help find suitable, affordable care near the employees' homes.

The Stride-Rite Corp., a manufacturer and retailer of shoes, is the earliest, and probably the best-known, champion of child care in the work-

---

*As reported in Jennifer Laabs, "Family Issues Are a Priority at Stride-Rite," *Personnel Journal* (July 1993), p. 49.

place. In 1971, the company opened the first on-site child care facility for employees and community members in the United States. Later, when the company moved its headquarters from Boston to Cambridge, it opened a day care center there as well. While it is unable to provide on-site day care for its workers at every location, the company strives to provide such options as resource and referral services. Although Stride-Rite has built a new distribution center in Louisville, Kentucky, and closed its Boston facility, it has committed to continue funding a community-based child care center in Boston with a Stride-Rite capital grant. Stride-Rite reports that its child care facilities are used equally by both mothers and fathers and by single and married employees.

Stride-Rite continues to make day care a priority. It is considered to be an employer of choice, due, in part, to its caring environment, and consequently, it can recruit from a more-qualified pool of candidates. In 1991, Stride-Rite was named one of the five most socially responsible corporations in the United States, by Franklin Research and Development. In addition, the company enjoys low absenteeism and a high retention record, with many employees staying on even after they no longer need the child care program.

Some companies, like John Hancock Financial Services, offer supplemental day care by permitting employees to bring their children to work on school holidays and during school vacations. Their Kids-to-Go program extends far beyond being a baby-sitting service and includes exposure to cultural events and field trips.

Small and mid-sized companies can pattern themselves after Stride-Rite and John Hancock, developing child care programs tailored to their particular needs and budgets. In general, setting up a child care program consists of seven components:

1. Assessment of needs
2. Analysis of program feasibility
3. Employee communication
4. Program implementation
5. Program management
6. Measurement of program results
7. Reassessment of needs

According to Kathy Hazzard, family care issues consultant for John Hancock and coordinator of the Kids-to-Go program, "The lovely thing about this [child care] program is it can be sculpted to whatever a company needs or wants to do."*

Collaboration among businesses, nonprofit organizations, and community agencies is a popular trend in child care. An example of this cooperative effort is the American Business Collaboration for Quality Dependent Care. It currently brings together 137 organizations, funding them with $26.3 million. Many of these businesses, like Scitor Corp., a Silicon Valley software company with 180 employees, are small. The effort is expected to increase both the quality and supply of child care in twenty-five states.

Ellen Gannett, the associate director of the School-age Childcare Project at the Wellesley College Center for Research on Women in Wellesley, Massachusetts, advocates that "this kind of leadership should be applauded. It's visionary. Although research may not be able to quantify these programs as an effort-equals-output one-to-one correlation, these aren't altruistic efforts; they're business issues. A community that's healthy, where families and children—and employees—are thriving because they feel aided by services, supports business. Where there's violence, poor education, fear and a sense of helplessness, businesses don't do well. Healthy communities are where businesses thrive.†

Elder Care Programs

Another growing area of concern that greatly affects the relationship between work and family relates to the care of our nation's elderly population. According to the Older Women's League, elder care is the number 1 workplace issue of the 1990s. As long as ten years ago, the Travelers Insurance Company surveyed employees age 30 and over and found that one in five cared for an elderly relative. Today, according to *Helping Yourself Help Others*, written by former First Lady Rosalynn Carter, 80 percent of all caregivers are women and more than 20 percent of that group have had to quit their jobs to provide elder care.‡ This translates into an average loss of nearly $30,000 in personal income a year. Those who continue working full or part time devote an additional forty hours a week providing care to an elderly relative. In addition, more than 50 percent of caregivers have

---

*Joyce E. Santora, "Kids-to-Go," *Personnel Journal* (March 1991), p. 70.
†Charlene Marmer Solomon, "Work/Family's Failing Grade," *Personnel Journal* (May 1994), p. 79.
‡As reported in *Newsday* (November 8, 1994), p. B3.

asked other family members for help, but 66 percent reported that their requests were ignored.

An elder care facility is designed to help workers face a growing national concern: taking care of elderly dependents while having a full-time job. Those responsible for two generations of dependents (children and parents) are known as the sandwich generation.

Workers responsible for the care of an elderly relative need both financial and emotional support from their employers. According to the National Council on Aging, more companies recognize that employees torn between responsibilities to their loved ones and their jobs may be less effective on the job.

In 1990, Stride-Rite added to its list of accomplishments the expansion of the Cambridge child care center into an intergenerational center for both children and elder dependents. The program is the first of its kind in American business; as of July 1993, it served fifty-five youngsters and thirty elders. To qualify, elders must be at least 60 years of age and capable of taking care of their personal needs with a minimum of assistance. Once accepted, they must attend the center for a minimum of two days a week, six hours a day. Much like the company's child care fee schedule, enrollees fall into one of three fee scales: the center's set fee, a state-subsidized rate for low-income elders, or fully Stride-Rite-subsidized care for low-income elders not qualifying for state funding. The program is staffed by twenty-seven professionals, many of whom have training in such areas as gerontology, rehabilitation, social services, and recreational therapy. Activities and discussion groups focus on the participants' social, physical, and emotional developmental needs. If they desire, the elders can participate in activities with the children at the center.

At Stride-Rite's other locations, elder care resources and referral services are provided. Small and mid-sized companies considering limited elder care services might want to start with a similar program limited in services and cost—perhaps putting employees in touch with a social worker specializing in geriatric concerns. Thought might also be given to offering seminars and sharing books and articles about the common concerns experienced by caregivers to the elderly. More ambitious businesses interested in a full-scale elder care program should consider the following basics before proceeding:

1. Determine current elder care arrangements. How many employee elder dependents require care? What type of living arrangements do they have (are they living alone or in a group facility)? What is the geographic

proximity of the current residence to the proposed elder care site? How much do employees pay for elder care? What services are the dependents accustomed to receiving? What services are deemed to be the most essential? What are some of the problems connected with current elder care arrangements?

2. Prepare a report reflecting the results of the study, adding to it management's objectives for establishing an elder care program and its specific offerings.

3. Survey various care providers, dependent care consultants, or nonprofit groups in an effort to match services with your organization's needs. Determine how much outside help you require or desire.

4. Upon deciding on the scope of elder care to be provided, publicize and explain the program to employees, describing the benefits, costs, and other aspects.

5. Monitor the fiscal impact of the program to determine its cost-effectiveness. Be certain this analysis includes the impact of elder care problems on turnover, absenteeism, and productivity, as well as the effect of the program on employee morale.

Changing Work Arrangements

It is evident that alternatives to the traditional workweek and work schedule must be offered if companies hope to attract and retain talented individuals, as well as to maintain competitive levels of productivity. As employees become increasingly vocal about their commitments, needs, and interests outside the workplace, greater latitude must be provided in determining when, how often, and, in some instances, where they can work most effectively. While many of these alternative work arrangements, such as part-time employment, have found limited use for a long time, now such options are being considered for different levels of employees and with some creative twists. Other options, such as telecommuting, are relatively new and will, no doubt, receive mixed reviews. And, of course, not all arrangements will work equally well in every environment. It is significant, however, that increasing numbers of organizations are testing different work options and reporting positive results. (A comprehensive examination of this trend is offered in *Creating a Flexible Workplace: How to Select and Manage Alternative Work Options*, by Barney Olmsted and Suzanne Smith (AMACOM, 1994).

Before adopting flexible work arrangements, employers need to consider a number of important elements. Salary for part timers, for example, is usually prorated, based on the amount of time worked on either an annual or, more typically, a weekly basis. Benefits, too, may be prorated, in terms of the company's contributions to the benefits plan, with the employee picking up the remaining costs; some businesses provide employees working more than twenty hours a week with full benefits, while others offer separate benefit packages to less-than-full-time employees. Job requirements and responsibilities, areas of accountability, lines of authority, work flow, scheduling logistics, impact on peak periods, client needs and preferences, arrangements for overtime, and payroll and human resources record keeping are other factors to be weighed. Additionally, for any flexible arrangement to be successful, communication is vital. When coworkers and customers clearly understand how the arrangement is to be implemented, as well as daily responsibilities and schedules, greater cooperation is achieved.

As the trend toward varying work schedules becomes more widespread, it is projected that by the turn of the century, the typical American company will employ workers from entry levels all the way up to the highest levels of management in various work arrangements. In fact, it may very well be that at some point in the future, regular, full-time employment will be the exception.

Telecommuting

This alternative work arrangement refers to employees who work at home or in a satellite office linked to the home office electronically. The concept of telecommuting has been around since the 1970s, but it did not gain popularity until some ten years later with the explosive growth of personal computers and facsimile machines. Today the home-based workforce is one of the fastest-growing components of the labor market. The U.S. Department of Labor reports that now, in the mid-1990s, there are more than 15 million full-time and part-time at-home workers as compared with approximately 5 million during the late 1980s. These employees perform virtually any job, or part thereof, that involves work independent of other people.

The advantages of hiring people who work out of their homes are numerous. From a cost standpoint, businesses save on utility and office leasing costs. If they hire independent contractors or consultants, there are savings in health benefit costs as well. As a recruitment tool, telecommuting not only attracts employees; it allows employers to expand their recruiting base beyond the geographic area. In addition, organizations are able to utilize the services of disabled and elderly individuals who cannot commute to an office. Working parents caring for their children can more readily balance both tasks. At-home workers additionally are capable of performing their duties without the typical office interruptions and enjoy the freedom of working during "off-hours." Other benefits include commutation time and cost savings, the ability to wear casual clothes while working, and savings on dry cleaning bills and clothing purchases.

Naturally, employers may be concerned about the lack of direct control over a telecommuting employee's work. Jane Sandler, president of Support Our Systems (SOS), a Red Bank, New Jersey, producer of user guides for computer systems, offers a method for lessening these concerns. As reported in May 1991 by *Inc.* magazine, her sixty home workers (mostly writers) so appreciated the telecommuting arrangement that they had no objection to the monitoring system she devised: multiple means of electronic communication, checking in with SOS several times a day, detailed design statements, frequent deadlines, and personal meetings with each employee at least four times a year, to name but a few of the conditions.

Managers concerned about not being able to supervise the work of telecommuting employees directly should be encouraged to practice performance management; that is, managers are committed to evaluating employees based on how well mutually agreed-upon goals are achieved, as opposed to what they observe on a daily basis.

Some employers express concern over unsupervised access to data and theft of equipment, while some employees complain of a sense of isolation and worry about being self-disciplined enough to meet deadlines.

Companies that want to offer telecommuting work arrangements to some employees should consider the following guidelines:

- Determine what kind of equipment will be needed, who will pay for it, and who is responsible for its maintenance.
- Make certain security programs are in place to protect data.
- Ensure the safety of workers at home by providing adequate furniture, lighting, and electrical outlets.
- Set compensation and benefits to reflect the requirements and duties of the job, not where the job is performed.
- Formulate telecommuting policies, including eligibility, arrangements, and reporting requirements.
- Provide training for employees who are new to telecommuting, covering such topics as time management, dealing with interruptions by family members, organizational skills, safety, and security.
- Develop a telecommuting agreement form, to be signed by the em-

ployee and manager, outlining the details of the telecommuting arrangement.

Employers considering telecommuting are also advised to consult with legal and tax experts regarding employee classifications, local zoning regulations, and insurance requirements.

Part Time

Traditionally, part-time employment meant schedules of up to twenty hours per week and limited benefits for nonexempt-level employees—usually women with child care responsibilities or students. As times continue to change, so does the term *part time*. Now it encompasses male and female employees, at varying levels, entitled to many of the privileges and benefits available to full-time workers, but who work reduced weekly, annual, or slow-season hours or who have project-based part-time work.

Job Sharing

Job sharing means that two employees share or equally divide the responsibilities of one full-time job. It is distinguishable from part-time employment in its application to positions that cannot be separated into two definitive part-time jobs. Initially, it was viewed as a female-related issue; now, job sharing is seen as a solution to the needs of many employees, including parents and older workers.

Numerous benefits are reportedly derived from job sharing, including the broader range of skills brought to the position, retaining valuable workers who might otherwise leave, a higher level of energy, and reduced absenteeism. In addition, job sharing virtually eliminates the need for employees to take care of personal business while on the job. Also, any time one partner terminates, the job is still half filled.

Naturally, there are some drawbacks. Twice as much payroll and human resources record keeping is required; an overlap in scheduling can create logistics problems; and clients or customers may complain about an inability to deal with the same person consistently.

Flextime

The classic definition of flextime requires each worker to put in the same number of hours each day, with identical core hours but varying starting and quitting times. Employers may vary the amount of flexibility granted workers in establishing their schedules according to the specific needs of the organization and the employees concerned.

Flextime allows employees to better balance work demands with those of home, school, and outside activities. It also helps relieve commuting congestion. In addition, given a voice in the scheduling of their workday, employees tend to feel involved in the company's decision-making process, which, in turn, may strengthen employer-employee relations. Employees are able to schedule work more in tune with their own biological clocks; that is, they can choose to work during the hours when their own skill and response levels are most keen.

Benefits to the employer include extended hours of coverage or service, reducing or eliminating the need for overtime; reduced tardiness, absenteeism, and turnover; an expanded and improved recruitment pool; and improved work performance attributable to enhanced employee morale. As a system, it is also adaptable to many situations and can easily be implemented, although it tends to function best in work environments that promote independence and self-motivation and is least effective in situations when work must be accomplished in a short time span.

The number 1 problem with flextime appears to have less to do with the employees than with supervisors uncomfortable with having workers on the job, unsupervised, during noncore hours. A sufficient level of discomfort may compel some supervisors to put in longer hours in order to make certain that work is being accomplished. Other concerns include difficulty in scheduling meetings, not always having key employees available when needed, and employee abuse of flextime. In addition, overhead costs are increased by keeping facilities open for longer periods of time.

Compressed Workweek

This alternative arrangement allows employees to work the required forty hours in less than five days. The most popular schedule is four ten-hour days.

The compressed workweek has received mixed reactions from both employees and management. Positive votes come from employees, who react favorably to the longer periods of personal time the compressed workweek provides. Also appreciated is commuting during nonrush hours and costs saved by not working a fifth day. In addition, many workers reportedly accomplish more in a day during those hours when telephone calls from customers or clients are less likely to cause interruptions. Employers have reported that the compressed workweek works well as a recruitment tool. Some improvements in rates of absenteeism, tardiness, and turnover have also been reported.

On the other hand, workers and managers alike have complained abut excessive fatigue brought by the length of the ten-hour workday. This fatigue is troublesome to older employees, young singles with active social lives, and employees with families. Long-term effects on health are also of concern. Both factors can adversely affect productivity.

Companies considering this alternative work arrangement should ascertain whether applicable state laws preclude a compressed workweek. Some states require the payment of overtime compensation for hours worked in excess of eight hours per day.

Temporaries

Temporaries represent one of the largest areas of job growth in the United States today. Previously this flexible workforce was almost exclusively clerical in composition. Now it consists of a wide range of nonexempt and professional positions, often used by small companies that cannot afford to hire regular employees and by large companies that have downsized or want to avoid inflated payrolls. Some organizations have established their own temporary pools, staffed with former employees and retirees.

Supplemental Workforce

These are employees recruited through conventional means, then trained in job- and industry-specific matters. They are then placed in a standby pool for work as needed, with the company committing to weekly or longer work assignments. This program provides a consistency and level of skill not usually found in temporary employees.

Independent Contractors

These are self-employed workers in a variety of fields in exempt and nonexempt capacities. Companies may employ independent contractors for short- or long-term assignments, without any of the obligations that accompany an employer-employee relationship. Generally there is a written contract outlining the services to be provided, the approximate or specific period of time for the services, and the schedule of payment. Conditions governing severance of the agreement may be outlined in the contract as well.

Employee Leasing

This is a somewhat unique work arrangement popular with small and mid-sized companies wanting to avoid some of the headaches of human resources administration. The system allows for an entire group of employees to be fired from a company, hired by a leasing agency, and then contracted back to the original employer. The leasing company prepares the company's payroll, pays payroll taxes, and assumes responsibility for compliance with various state and federal reporting requirements. Additionally, it provides fringe benefits to the employees. These services typically cost the employer approximately 20 to 35 percent above gross payroll.

Leasing is not without risks. Organizations considering leasing should consult an attorney; check references; study the contract for costs, fees, and a description of who is responsible for what; assess the company's financial statements; and ask for regular updates on the leasing agencies from the National Staff Leasing Association.

Additional Changes

Besides these specific programs and techniques, what else can companies do to attract and motivate tomorrow's workers? To begin with, recognize that, unlike generations before, this new workforce is more interested in opportunity than security, more willing to take risks, and less concerned with financial security. Hence, employers must provide challenging and varying work assignments. In addition, participative management, involving employees at all levels in at least some aspect of the decision-making process, is of importance to tomorrow's workers. Workers have expressed the need to be recognized and rewarded for specific contributions. Furthermore, they are seeking greater autonomy in a structure with fewer levels of management.

Flexibility will be a key element in the near future, with regard to both work schedules and work arrangements. Flexible benefits plans are increasingly being sought. Also growing in significance is an interest in the fostering of relationships among coworkers off the job. Managers will need to promote social activities and sponsor company outings. The continuing interest in physical fitness will also affect employment, as more employees seek out employers that provide workout rooms or gym memberships.

Summary

The twenty-first century promises to offer numerous human resources challenges for small and mid-sized companies. The shortage of adequately trained employees, a shift in where job opportunities are expected to exist, and the alarmingly high rate of illiteracy in American businesses signify that organizations must form closer alliances with schools to produce a better educated, more qualified labor pool. In addition, there is a trend toward an increasingly diverse workforce consisting of women, minorities, immigrants, expatriates, disabled people, older workers, and youth. In order to attract and retain members of these groups, employers must create a multicultural environment that is suitable for all employees. This new workforce will place a high value on integrating work and family. Accordingly, more companies are moving to develop work-and-family instructional programs, as well as on- and off-site child and elder care programs. Finally, if companies hope to attract and retain talented workers to maintain effective, competitive levels of productivity, alternatives to the traditional workweek and work schedule must be offered. These options include telecommuting, part-time employment, job sharing, flextime, a compressed workweek, temporary assignments, developing a supplemental workforce, hiring independent contractors, and employee leasing.

2

The Human Resources Function in Small and Mid-Sized Companies

Often it is not until a company has grown to the point where managers have more to do than they can comfortably handle that certain functions are designated as human resources functions and "given away."

Whether it has a staff of 50 employees or 5,000, every company must concern itself with basic human resources–related issues. The following topics represent the major HR areas that all organizations should deal with on a regular basis:

- Equal employment opportunity
- Recruiting, interviewing, and hiring employees
- Orienting new employees
- Workplace diversity
- Performance appraisals
- Salary reviews and increases
- Health benefits
- Records maintenance
- HR policies and procedures
- Employee handbooks
- HR planning
- Training and development
- Grievance and disciplinary action

Companies may concern themselves with additional human resources–related topics, including:

- Child and elder care programs
- Labor relations
- Employee publications
- Recreation programs
- Employee assistance programs
- Employee attitude surveys
- Food services
- Health and medical services
- Preemployment and employment testing
- Retirement-preparation programs
- Suggestion programs
- Travel services
- Alternative dispute resolution

All companies have these and other human resource–related areas in common, but there are several major factors that differentiate small and mid-sized from large organizations, factors that directly affect the way these areas are handled. These differences contribute to determining when human resources should be established as a formal, separate entity; who should be assigned responsibility for the various human resource–related areas; how the human resources function relates to other departments within a company; and the respective responsibilities of HR and non-HR practitioners.

Human Resources in Small and Mid-Sized Companies vs. Large Companies

There are ten primary factors that distinguish the human resources function of large companies from that of small and mid-sized organizations:

1. Degree of specialization
2. Number of geographic locations
3. Unionization
4. Variety of jobs
5. Hierarchy of reporting relationships
6. Grievances and disciplinary problems
7. Equal employment opportunity and affirmative action
8. HR policies and procedures manual

9. Benefits
10. Compensation

Degree of Specialization

Because of their size, large organizations require more specialized human resources functions than smaller companies. HR generalists well versed in several areas of the field are usually sufficient for very small companies, and a handful of specialists in such broad human resources areas as employment, compensation, employee relations, and training is generally adequate for mid-sized companies. However, large organizations require specialists in many more aspects of human resources, such as career planning, employee assistance programs, employee attitude surveys, and suggestion programs.

Although organizations with fewer than 1,500 employees usually do not require specialists in these areas, growing companies would do well to consider incorporating some of these categories into their human resources functions. For example, career development and human resources planning can help an organization build a solid foundation of employee skills and talents as well as create a highly motivating environment in which to work. Employee assistance programs can often prevent minor employee concerns from blossoming into more serious problems. Employee attitude surveys can help workers feel that their opinions are valuable, and they often reveal correctable problems management may not have been aware of. And suggestion programs can result in creative, cost-effective ways for the company to expand and develop. All these areas will be discussed in greater detail in subsequent chapters.

Number of Geographic Locations

Most large organizations have more than one location. Some have one central human resources department responsible for the HR activities of all the different locations. More commonly, however, organizations with more than one location have auxiliary HR functions in addition to the central unit. The responsibilities of these satellite departments range from records maintenance to a full scope of HR responsibilities, such as recruitment, interviewing, compensation, benefits administration, and employee relations. Accordingly, even though everyone is working for the same parent company, some of these units operate quite independently. Indeed, simply monitoring the workflow from the several different human resources units of some large companies can be a full-time job.

Unionization

Generally, the larger an organization is, the more likely it is to be unionized. In fact, many large companies must contend with several unions. There is a growing trend for job categories traditionally classified as nonunion to become unionized.

The existence of unions within a company automatically means added responsibilities for those in the human resources area. For example, labor relations experts skilled in the art of contract negotiations and preventing further unionization are essential. Employee relations experts capable of handling union-related grievances and disciplinary matters are needed. Recruiters and interviewers must be aware of the union status of various openings and be prepared to describe accompanying union responsibilities to applicants, exercising care not to express any personal opinions about unions. And training and development specialists must be prepared to train nonunion personnel in the specific tasks ordinarily performed by union employees in the event of a walkout or strike.

The entire structure and emphasis of an organization's human resources function can be altered by the presence of unions. Small and mid-sized organizations are less likely to be similarly affected.

Variety of Jobs

Not surprisingly, large organizations have the greatest number and variety of jobs. An increase in both generic and specialized positions means that more job descriptions are needed. It also means that grades and salary ranges must be established for more jobs. Of course, there are also more openings to fill. In addition, more employees must be trained, supervised, and dealt with in all HR-related matters. Hence there is an increase of responsibilities in the areas of compensation, employment, training, and employee relations.

Hierarchy of Reporting Relationships

The larger the organization is, the more layers of reporting relationships there are between the bottom and top positions. With regard to human resources, this means:

- It often takes a very long time to get decisions, policies, and procedures approved, changed, or implemented.

- Numerous signatures are often required before a seemingly simple matter is resolved.
- Employees near the lower end of the hierarchy in human resources often hesitate to express their views to those higher up.

In addition, in a multitiered environment, the person ultimately in charge of making critical human resources decisions is often not an HR specialist. Rather, an executive in charge of several different functions will rely on the expertise of lower-level human resources experts reporting to him or her and make decisions accordingly.

A complex hierarchy can also mask the use of human resources as a "dumping ground" for employees who, for one reason or another, cannot perform adequately at their own jobs. Instead of being trained, counseled, or terminated, they are placed in HR.

Grievances and Disciplinary Problems

Grievances and disciplinary problems in large organizations usually require more steps and the involvement of more people. The list of infractions leading to disciplinary action is usually longer in a larger company. Also, if unions are involved, matters become that much more complicated.

One specific issue relating to grievances and discipline that large companies often face, and smaller companies are less likely to, is making sure that employees understand acceptable and unacceptable on-the-job behavior. It seems that the larger the company is, the poorer the lines of communication are. Hence employees may find themselves being verbally warned or written up for violating rules they were not even aware of. In smaller companies, with fewer employees and reporting levels, it is more likely that management will clearly communicate company procedures and what constitutes an infraction.

Open communication can also preclude the necessity for grievances, since employees will have a clearer understanding of what is expected of them and what they in turn have the right to expect from their employer.

EEO and Affirmative Action

Large companies are subject to virtually every piece of legislation relating to EEO and affirmative action. This is not necessarily the case with smaller companies. For example:

- To be covered by Title VII of the Civil Rights Act of 1964, a company must have at least fifteen employees and do business in the United States.
- To be covered by the Age Discrimination in Employment Act of 1967 (ADEA), a company must have at least twenty employees.
- The Rehabilitation Act of 1973 applies only to recipients of federal financial assistance and to contractors and subcontractors whose federal government contracts exceed $2,500.
- Executive Order 11246 of 1965 (amended by Executive Order 11375 of 1967) requires a written affirmative action plan by employers with at least 100 employees and $100,000 in federal government contracts.
- The Americans with Disabilities Act of 1990 covers employers with 15 or more employees.
- The Civil Rights Act of 1991 limits the amount of compensatory and punitive damages any one claimant can receive according to the size of the business being sued.

Since large companies are obliged to abide by more EEO and affirmative action laws than smaller companies, and since they have a greater applicant flow and more employees, it is not surprising that they also have a greater number of discrimination charges brought against them. This means that the human resources departments of large companies must have specialists in the areas of EEO and affirmative action, both to answer charges of discrimination and to ensure full EEO and affirmative action compliance companywide, thereby precluding future violations or charges of violations. Large firms must also frequently retain attorneys specifically skilled in these areas.

Although small and mid-sized organizations may not be affected by EEO laws to the same extent as large companies, or involved in as many lawsuits, human resources staff members and managers in all organizations must have a thorough understanding of EEO and affirmative action requirements. The areas of EEO and affirmative action will be dealt with more specifically in Chapter 3.

HR Policies and Procedures Manual

The primary purpose of any HR policies and procedures manual is to assist managers in the uniform interpretation and application of organizational practices. In addition, it should answer many of the questions managers may have in their day-to-day interaction with employees, thus making some of their decision making less taxing.

As a company grows in size and complexity, it becomes more difficult to interpret and comply with management objectives uniformly. Accordingly, a policies and procedures manual designed for a larger company is likely to cover more areas and go into greater detail than one designed for a smaller organization. For example, regardless of size, every organization's HR policies and procedures manual should contain a policy statement regarding EEO. In the manual of a larger company, however, an entire section might be devoted to this topic.

Since the policies and procedures manuals of large companies are more complex, they require full-time attention—that is, one or more employees whose specific responsibility is to research, develop, implement, monitor, and revise the organization's manual. In contrast, small and mid-sized companies can treat this as a part-time task and readily delegate it either to someone responsible for other HR-related functions or to a committee consisting of human resources representatives and selected managers.

Benefits

Benefits administration has become an increasingly complex area. In both small and large companies, experts are clearly needed to interpret and implement detailed, complex health insurance plans as well as other types of benefits.

All organizations require benefits administration, but some of the benefits offered by larger companies simply do not exist in small and mid-sized organizations. Hence a smaller and less specialized benefits staff is usually sufficient. For example, many large companies offer business travel accident insurance, which provides benefits for employees required to conduct business for their organization somewhere away from their usual worksite. Also, many large companies offer profit-sharing plans, designed to provide a supplement to the benefits received after retirement.

A detailed discussion of the recommended structure for benefits administration in small and mid-sized organizations appears in Chapter 8.

Compensation

As with benefits, compensation programs for large companies are generally more complex than those for smaller companies. In large organizations, elaborate position evaluation programs and complicated compensation schedules require the attention of full-time salary experts. This is not necessarily the case in smaller firms. Conducting salary surveys; comparing various compensation programs; and designing, implementing, and monitoring an appropriate system need not be a complicated, highly specialized, or excessively expensive venture. Salary surveys can usually be conducted for little or no cost, information on different compensation formats is readily attainable, and it is not difficult to develop a basic system that can expand as the company grows.

Chapter 6 will discuss these and other important components of compensation for small and mid-sized organizations.

When to Establish a Human Resources Function

When a company starts out, it does not really need a separate HR function. The duties eventually to be performed by human resources experts are handled by selected staff in addition to their other duties. For example, managers may fill their own job openings, set starting salaries, decide when to grant increases, and so on. Consequently, there is rarely any uniformity or consistency between the different units of an organization at the early stages of its development. Programs such as performance appraisal, tuition reimbursement, career planning, and other areas commonly associated with human resources do not exist at all.

Often it is not until a company has grown to the point where managers have more to do than they can comfortably handle that certain functions are designated as human resources functions and "given away." Not surprisingly, responsibilities viewed as burdensome or time-consuming are among the first. Processing the paperwork necessary to place new employees on payroll, assigning benefits, and maintaining necessary employee records are the most common tasks defined early on as human resources functions. Since these duties are clerical, the employees chosen to perform them usually have a clerical background.

Establishing a human resources function because managers simply have too much to do may work—for a while. Even when it operates at an optimum level, however, a human resources function based on clerical responsibilities discarded by management is going to make a limited contribution to the organization. More important, as the organization continues to grow, the HR department will be unable to grow along with it.

A far more successful and logical approach to determining when it is appropriate to establish a human resources function is to think in terms of

HR staff ratios. According to the most recent survey available,* the median number of individuals in the HR department per number of employees on company payroll is currently one per 100; this number represents the total HR staff size, including the professional, technical, secretarial, and clerical employees. The number of professional and technical HR employees for every 100 workers is 0.7; this includes top human resources executives and all other management-level people within the department. Nonmanufacturing environments reported a slightly higher ratio of HR staff to total workforce: 0.8 professional and technical employees and 1.3 total staff members for every 100 employees. These numbers were exceeded slightly by banking and financial institutions, which reported a median ratio of 1.5 total staff per 100 employees and 1.0 professional and technical employees. Health care organizations reported the lowest staff ratios, with 0.4 professional and technical employees and 0.6 total HR staff per 100 workers.

The figures in this survey are based on responses from organizations throughout the United States. Geographically, 29 percent of these companies are located in the North Central states, 35 percent in the South, 18 percent in the Northeast, and 18 percent in the West. Thirty-six percent of the companies are manufacturing, 36 percent are financial and other nonmanufacturing businesses, and 28 percent are nonbusiness. Eighty-four percent of the companies that responded had fewer than 2,500 employees.

It is significant to note that the smaller the company is, the higher is the ratio between HR staff and total number of workers. For example, in companies of fewer than 250 employees, the median total HR staff per 100 employees is 1.5. For companies with between 250 and 499 employees, the median per total HR staff is 1.2 per 100 employees. In companies with between 500 and 999 employees, the ratio is 1.0 for every 100 employees. Companies with over 1,000 employees (up to 2,499 employees) reported a ratio of 0.7. Thus, as the size of the workforce increases, the total HR staff ratio decreases, from 1.5 per 100 employees in the smallest companies to 0.7 in firms with 1,000 or more employees. The professional and technical staff ratios also drop accordingly as organizational size increases, ranging from 1.0 individuals per 100 employees in firms with fewer than 250 employees to 0.4 in companies with 1,000 or more employees.

Small and mid-sized organizations that plan on establishing or revamping a human resources function should view these statistics as a

Society for Human Resource Management—Bureau of National Affairs Bulletin to Management (Washington, D.C.: June 30, 1994), pp. 1, 5, 8, 9.

guide. They should consider their own environment, present needs, projected growth, and budget, and then proceed accordingly.

Choosing Your Company's First Human Resources Professional

As mentioned earlier, transferring an employee with a clerical background to a company's first human resources position is not the wisest way to proceed. Of course, a current employee is already familiar with how the organization operates, understands its philosophy, and probably knows most of the employees on a first-name basis. However, unless this person has a background in the field of human resources, it generally makes more sense to bring in someone from the outside who has HR experience and/or training. In this way, as the company grows, the individual selected can help the human resources function expand accordingly.

When you seek the best candidate for this important position, be careful not to establish excessively rigid requirements that will draw resumes and phone calls from HR "heavy hitters" who possess far more knowledge and expertise than you need at this stage—and who may expect a higher salary than you are prepared to offer. Ideally, an organization's first human resources person should be experienced with the primary facets of the HR function: employment, compensation, benefits, records maintenance, employee relations, training and development, and other employee activities. One to two years' experience, preferably in an environment comparable to your organization's, is usually adequate. A degree, preferably in human resources, is desirable but not essential. Even more ideal would be someone who served as another company's "start-up" HR person.

What's in a Name?

Human resources professionals go by many different titles. Some of the most common are:

General Human Resources Job Titles

- Director of human resources
- Assistant director of human resources
- Human resources manager
- HR consultant
- Human resources specialist

- HR assistant
- HR officer
- HR generalist
- Vice president, human resources
- Human resources coordinator
- Human resources manager

- Senior HR representative
- HR administrator
- Assistant HR administrator
- Human resources executive
- Manager, industrial relations
- Corporate director of human resources

Specialized Human Resources Titles

- Labor relations manager
- Labor relations hearing officer
- Benefits manager
- Benefits assistant
- Benefits coordinator
- Benefits administrator
- Benefits writer
- Benefits specialist
- Recruiter
- Employment assistant
- Employment coordinator
- Recruiting department assistant
- Job evaluation analyst
- Salary administrator
- Wage and salary manager
- Compensation administrator
- Skills trainer
- Training supervisor
- Training manager
- Manager, training and development
- Executive recruiter

- Interviewer
- Employment coordinator
- Assistant recruiter
- Nonexempt recruiter
- Exempt recruiter
- College recruiting coordinator
- Manager, employment
- Compensation analyst
- Senior compensation analyst
- Survey analyst
- Compensation officer
- Job evaluation administrator
- Hiring administrator
- Senior trainer
- Assistant director of career development
- Director of organizational and management development
- Employee relations coordinator
- Senior research assistant
- Human resources information systems analyst

Trying to select the most appropriate titles for human resources employees from this list can make one dizzy. However, two simple guidelines should help. First, make certain that the title selected accurately reflects the duties to be performed. At the same time, allow room for expansion, so that as the job grows, it does not become necessary to change the title. Second, make certain that the title is consistent with the titles of other positions of comparable skill and responsibility within the company. This will help establish the credibility and importance of the HR function from the outset.

You might narrow your list to the following, which are the most commonly used titles for first-time human resources positions:

- Human resources manager
- Director of human resources
- Human resources administrator
- Human resources representative
- Human resources officer
- Human resources specialist

Note that the term "human resources" has replaced "personnel" for each of these titles. The latter reflects a more traditional reactive function, primarily concerned only with employee utilization. "Human resources," on the other hand, connotes a commitment to making the most of human resources potential and is concerned with examining future needs, that is, management by anticipation.

The Human Resources Function in Relation to Other Departments

Every aspect of an organization is affected by the human resources function. Matters concerning policies and procedures, budgets, employee communication, hiring, compensation, performance appraisals, insurance, employee records, planning, and all areas of employer-employee relations require knowledge about human resources. Whether this means HR experts or department managers depends, to a large extent, on each organization's unique environment as well as the skill level of its managers and human resources staff. A clear definition of who should do what is not always possible, but some guidelines may help delineate the division of labor.

Responsibilities of Human Resources Specialists

This section is meant as a broad overview. Major areas will be examined in more detail in subsequent chapters.

Familiarization With the Details of a Job

Although human resources experts need not be as familiar with the technical aspects of a job as the manager directly involved with the position, there is still a great deal that they need to know in order to handle various matters effectively. These details include knowledge of a position's primary duties and responsibilities, the education and prior experience needed to perform it, the specific work environment, the job's reporting relationship, its degree and level of decision-making authority, the job's exemption status, its salary range, its union status, what growth opportunities it offers, any unique requirements, and any other relevant information such as the preferred work style of the manager in charge. This information will make it possible for a human resources representative to act responsibly in matters such as recruitment, interviewing, promotions, transfers, demotions, performance reviews, compensation considerations, grievances, disciplinary matters, and even terminations.

Recruitment

This human resources responsibility includes exploring various recruitment sources; comparing their advantages and disadvantages; and screening applicants by phone, via their resumés, and through preliminary interviews.

Interviewing

One of the most critical responsibilities of the human resources function is employment interviewing. Interviewers should understand various components of both preparing for and conducting a successful interview. These include:

- Allowing a sufficient block of time for the interview
- Planning an appropriate environment
- Planning basic questions based on the job requirements and the applicant's qualifications
- Being familiar with relevant EEO legislation
- Establishing rapport
- Understanding the importance of active listening
- Knowing how and when to take notes
- Understanding the role of body language (both the applicant's and the interviewer's)

- Being familiar with different types of interview questions
- Knowing how to encourage an applicant to continue talking
- Knowing how to deal with various problem applicants, such as extremely shy or overly talkative ones
- Knowing how and when to close an interview

The more familiar interviewers are with a specific department and its particular needs, the more successful they will be in conducting interviews and referring the most appropriate candidates for hiring consideration. Hence human resources staff responsible for interviewing should spend as much time as possible in various departments, becoming familiar with their operation and observing the workers.

EEO and Workplace Diversity

All human resources professionals should have an extensive knowledge and understanding of EEO laws and requirements. In addition to understanding how the laws work, they must know how the various requirements affect their own particular organization. Since there are new developments in the areas of EEO all the time, this is an ongoing learning process. Finally, human resources professionals are responsible for advising managers in matters of workplace diversity. This is part of HR's training and development responsibility.

Checking References

It is generally the responsibility of human resources to conduct the reference checks of candidates under serious consideration. The human resources staff contacts previous employers and, depending on the requirements of the job, may also verify educational credentials.

Employment references are commonly checked by mail or phone. Because written reference letters often take some time to arrive, telephone reference checks are more useful for obtaining prompt verification of an applicant's experience. They are also more likely to yield important information, such as reservations about intangible aspects of a candidate's performance that would not be conveyed in a letter.

Once an applicant provides written consent to contact the schools he or she has attended, they may be contacted to release relevant educational records. A small fee is usually required. It is important to note that educational references should be checked only when a position clearly calls for specific educational achievements.

Personal references should be avoided unless there is absolutely no other source of employment or educational information that may be checked. Of the three types of references, they are the least relevant to the candidate's job performance.

Employment Testing

The Uniform Guidelines on Employee Selection Procedures were adopted by the Equal Employment Opportunity Commission, Civil Service Commission, and Department of Labor in 1978 to provide a uniform set of principles for the use of tests and other selection procedures. In those instances when a test has been deemed an appropriate measure of job performance, it should be conducted by a skilled human resources representative in a controlled environment. Some tests require validation—that is, evidence that the test is a valid predictor of job success.

Orientation of New Employees

All organizations, regardless of size, should provide an orientation program for recently hired employees. Taking the time to familiarize new workers with their environment can help them form positive first impressions and develop more of a commitment to their work.

There are two equally important types of orientation programs: the departmental orientation, which is the responsibility of the manager in charge of a new hire, and a formal organizational orientation, which is the responsibility of human resources. An organizational orientation program should acquaint new employees with the organization as a whole, rather than the specific job or department.

For small and mid-sized companies, a half-day or full-day orientation session is generally adequate. (Large corporations frequently devote a week or more to orientation, as well as later follow-up sessions.)

Compensation Programs

Compensation—which includes performing position evaluations, conducting salary surveys, writing job descriptions, assigning grades, and establishing salary ranges—should be a human resources responsibility. Because it is a multifaceted area, companies with more than approximately 250 employees are advised to have a compensation expert in their human resources department. In addition to the tasks noted above, the person in charge of this function is also responsible for setting salary increase guidelines to help managers determine the most appropriate increases for their employees. Since increases are commonly linked to performance, whoever is in charge of compensation is usually also responsible for monitoring performance appraisals to see that recommended salary increases coincide with performance ratings.

Benefits Programs

Like compensation, benefits administration is a multifaceted area requiring the expertise of a specialist. Most organizations with more than approximately 250 employees hire someone to monitor and administrate such benefits as insurance plans, unemployment compensation, workers' compensation, compliance with OSHA regulations,* and health and medical services.

Records Maintenance

All employee records should be kept in the human resources department. Each employee's file should contain:

- His or her employment application and resumé
- All memos and correspondence about job performance
- Copies of all formal performance evaluations
- Salary change notices
- Any warning notices
- All correspondence regarding transfers, demotions, or promotions
- Requests for vacations, leaves of absence, and personal days
- Any other information about the employee's work or relationship with the company

Insurance claims and the like are generally kept in a separate file.
Human resources should also be responsible for maintaining EEO compliance records.

HR Policies and Procedures Manual

Any organization large enough to have a human resources function should have a policies and procedures manual. The contents of each company's manual will be determined by its own particular environment and

---

*OSHA is the Occupational Safety and Health Act of 1970.

needs, but in general, manuals should contain basic information that will enable managers to perform their jobs more effectively. Categories in a typical HR policies and procedures manual for a small or mid-sized company might include:

- The employment process
- Compensation
- Benefits administration
- Records maintenance
- Employee relations
- Training and development
- Employee activities

As the company grows and changes, additions or other modifications may be necessary. HR should be responsible for these changes and for making certain that every manager has an up-to-date manual.

Employee Handbook

An employee handbook may be viewed as the employee's version of the policies and procedures handbook. In addition to identifying management's objectives, it outlines company rules and regulations and identifies an organization's expectations. HR should be in charge of ensuring that each employee both receives and understands the contents of this important document.

Counseling, Grievances, and Disciplinary Procedures

HR representatives may be called on to participate in a counseling, grievance, or disciplinary session between an employee and his or her manager. Frequently the human resources representative lends the neutrality needed to resolve whatever issue is at hand.

Human Resources Planning

Human resources planning is critical to the growth and development of any organization. Human resources professionals must systematically review current and future job needs with consideration of all employees who may be qualified for new opportunities.

The development and maintenance of a human resources plan is clearly the responsibility of the human resources department. Of course, cooperation and assistance from the management is crucial to the success of any program.

Career planning should be developed along with human resources planning. For career planning purposes, human resources should take and regularly update an inventory of biographical data on each employee for use in future decision making. These data should include the interests and talents of each employee.

In relatively small companies, each employee's experience may be well known to everyone. However, as a company grows, it is dangerous to assume that top management still knows everything about all its employees, so it is important that the company develop a specific career plan for everyone.

Training and Development

Depending on how concerned a company is with long-term planning, a company's training and development function may consist of such aspects as skills training, management development, and tuition aid, in addition to career planning. The first two areas—skills training and management development—may be accomplished either in-house or at seminars and workshops outside the company. In-house programs are conducted by either human resources staff members or consultants who are brought into the company.

If training programs are conducted in-house by a human resources representative, it is absolutely crucial that he or she be knowledgeable about the subject matter and have excellent platform and interpersonal skills. In small companies, where a training specialist is unlikely to be part of a relatively small human resources department, it is more logical either to bring consultants into the company or to send employees out to workshops. Although this can become costly, the investment in future human resources development is a crucial and necessary aspect of any company's growth.

Even if the human resources representative is not doing the training, he or she is still responsible for either bringing in consultants or for processing requests to attend outside programs.

A tuition aid policy should be developed by top management, but it is HR's responsibility to monitor the tuition aid program and process whatever paperwork is necessary. Guidelines for the tuition aid program should be clearly outlined in the company's HR policies and procedures manual.

Employee Communication

Every company should have some system of employee communication. Some have bulletin boards where various company notices are posted, along with news of job openings and even personal ads. Others issue newsletters on a regular basis. And some companies have employee suggestion programs, which invite employees to offer ideas that may help the company improve.

Evaluation of Performance Appraisals and Salary Recommendations

One of the most critical responsibilities of human resources is to monitor and evaluate completed performance appraisals and accompanying salary recommendations. It is very important to adhere to established standards and to maintain consistency between the overall evaluation of an employee's performance and a recommended increase in pay. The HR representative should bring any inconsistencies to the attention of the evaluating manager so that changes can be made accordingly. Appropriate recommendations should be processed as expeditiously as possible.

The human resources representative is also responsible for reminding managers of the due dates for evaluating the employees in their departments. Managers should be reminded approximately six weeks prior to the date an employee is scheduled for a formal review, to allow ample time for preparation.

Exit Interviews

All terminating employees should be given exit interviews by human resources. At that time, they will have an opportunity to explain why they are leaving if it is a voluntary termination, to describe what aspects of their job they found satisfying and unsatisfying, and to make any comments they may have regarding the company's benefits, working conditions, compensation, and so on. This is an opportunity for the HR representative to learn what suggestions departing employees might have for improvements in the company overall and the specific department in which they worked.

Often, when several employees leave the same department within a relatively short period of time, a pattern of reasons for leaving begins to develop. Whenever this happens, the HR representative conducting the exit interviews should discuss matters with the appropriate department head so that a resolution may be reached.

Exit interviews require the same skills as those used during employment interviews; therefore they should be conducted by people skilled in interviewing.

Responsibilities of Non–Human Resources Practitioners

The role of non–human resources practitioners in the organization warrants a close look, because managers often fail to realize the scope of their human resources responsibilities in addition to their other duties.

Familiarity With the Job

Department heads and managers will certainly be more familiar with the jobs within their own units than will human resources representatives, but they should still familiarize themselves with the degree and level of responsibility required for every position before interviewing prospective employees. In addition, they should ask themselves three key questions:

1. Are the required tasks realistic?
2. Are the education and experience requirements relevant to the overall job function?
3. Do the responsibilities overlap with the tasks of other positions?

The department manager should review the details of a job every time a position becomes available. This process will ensure accurate, up-to-date job information and help the manager choose the best candidate available.

Job Requisitions

When departmental representatives know that they are going to have an opening in their department, they should prepare a written job requisition and submit it to human resources. The job requisition form is essentially a mini job description. The more job information the departmental representative can provide, the better able HR will be to find the most suitable candidate.

Ideally, human resources should not begin recruitment efforts until a completed, signed job requisition form has been received.

Interviewing

Departmental representatives with job openings should be prepared to conduct employment interviews of qualified candidates. In most instances, these candidates will have already been screened by HR and sent on to the department for further consideration. When this occurs, the departmental representative conducting the interview should feel safe in assuming that the candidate meets the basic requirements of the job. Therefore, it is his or her responsibility to conduct a more detailed and thorough interview, asking specific questions relating to the job's daily functions.

The same interviewing skills and techniques employed by HR representatives should be used by the manager during the department interview, so it is extremely important for departmental representatives to be trained in proper interviewing techniques.

EEO

Anyone having anything whatsoever to do with employer-employee relations must have a basic knowledge of EEO and its impact on the employment process. This includes a basic knowledge of key categories of discrimination defined by federal legislation, the impact of EEO on the employment process, legal and illegal preemployment inquiries, and guidelines for experience and education requirements.

All managers should receive training in these areas of EEO to ensure full compliance with the laws and to preclude, as much as possible, discrimination charges from being brought against their organizations. Such training may be provided within a company by skilled human resources professionals well versed in all facets of EEO, or by experts outside the organization who either conduct public seminars or provide in-house training or consulting services.

Making the Final Selection

Ideally, everyone who participated in the interviewing process should agree on the best candidate for an opening. Occasionally, however, the departmental representative will favor one person and the HR representative will favor another. If there are no EEO violations, and affirmative action goals have been taken into consideration, then the departmental representative should make the final selection.

Departmental Orientation

In addition to an overall organizational orientation conducted by the human resources department for new employees, each department should conduct an orientation session focusing on specific job-related areas. This departmental orientation should take place as soon after a new employee begins work as possible.

Creating a Motivating Environment

There is a direct link between employee motivation and productivity. Managers can help create an environment conducive to the maximum utilization of each employee's skills and interests by:

- Offering incentives and rewards, as appropriate
- Providing comfortable and safe working conditions (tools and equipment, space, facilities, light, heat, and ventilation)
- Providing a pleasant work environment
- Providing opportunities for employees to try new tasks
- Providing opportunities for growth and advancement
- Maintaining ongoing two-way communication
- Conducting fair and honest performance appraisals
- Offering fair and competitive salaries and increases

By creating a motivating environment, managers can make certain that the talent they have hired is put to the best possible use, both from the company's viewpoint and the employees'.

On-the-Job Training

On-the-job training is essential for all new employees, regardless of their existing skill levels. Understanding how a new organization functions overall—and, more specifically, how their department operates—is necessary before employees can be expected to perform effectively.

On-the-job training is an ongoing process that should continue for as long as an employee is working for a company. It may mean assigning a more experienced worker to teach a less experienced employee in certain techniques and methods. Or it may include attending workshops and seminars in the person's area of expertise, either to bring the employee up to date on the latest information in the field or to reinforce what he or she already knows. In addition to sharpening their skills, on-the-job training also helps employees maintain a high level of interest in their work.

Performance Appraisals

Managers are responsible for planning and conducting performance appraisal interviews with their employees. This includes completing the appraisal form, preparing the employee, and conducting the actual meeting. During the face-to-face meeting with an employee, the manager is responsible for maintaining open two-way communication.

Recommending Increases

In most organizations, managers make recommendations for salary increases and forward them to human resources. These recommendations follow guidelines established by the human resources department, and are usually linked with performance.

Recommending Changes in Employee Status

Changes in an employee's status may be requested by the employee or recommended by his or her manager. These changes are promotion, transfer, demotion, and discharge. In each of these instances, the manager involved should have sound documentation of why the requested change is in order. This becomes particularly important in areas of negative change—that is, demotion and discharge.

Coaching and Counseling

Coaching is the day-to-day interaction between an employee and his or her manager. Good coaching is crucial for making the best use of employees' potential and for keeping them satisfied with their work. It also improves the organization's overall productivity.

Counseling is the interaction between a manager and his or her employees that focuses on specific work-related issues. Effective counseling results in the ability of employees to function more productively on the job in accordance with specified policies and procedures.

All the areas of responsibility described above for human resources specialists and non–human resources practitioners will be discussed in greater detail in subsequent chapters.

Summary

Every organization, regardless of its size, must concern itself with basic human resources–related issues such as benefits administration, EEO, grievances and disciplinary procedures, position evaluations, performance appraisals, records maintenance, HR policies and procedures, recruitment and employment, and compensation.

There are, however, differences in how small and mid-sized companies, as opposed to large organizations, manage these areas. This chapter distinguished the human resources function in large companies from that of small and mid-sized organizations. It also discussed how a small or mid-sized company should determine when a separate human resources function is needed, who should be assigned responsibility for various human resources–related areas, and how a human resources function relates to other aspects of an organization.

3

Human Resources and the Law

EEO laws will be helpful only if employers can gauge their effect on the employment process.

The subjects of equal employment opportunity (EEO), affirmative action, and related legal issues are not for human resources people only. Anyone having anything whatsoever to do with any aspect of the employment process—including recruitment, interviewing, hiring, orientation, performance appraisals, promotions, transfers, demotions, salary changes, or terminations—is responsible for having a basic knowledge and understanding of relevant legislation and its impact on employer-employee relations. Stated another way, if your company gets involved in a discrimination suit, ignorance of the law is not a defense!

This chapter will focus on EEO/discrimination issues. Other HR-related laws and regulations will be discussed in Chapter 5 ("Pre-employment and Employment Testing") and Chapter 8 ("Benefits Administration").

The information in this book is current as of this writing. However, it is absolutely essential that whoever is in charge of EEO and affirmative action in your organization keep abreast of news in this ever-changing field. One way of doing this is by reading about recent EEO cases and other similar developments in professional journals and newsletters. *The HR Manager's Legal Reporter* may be helpful in this regard. This newsletter is written for human resources specialists and non-HR practitioners alike, and often describes the implications of recent court decisions. It is issued on a monthly basis by Ransom & Benjamin Publishers, which is located at P.O. Box 606, Old Greenwich, CT 06870. A yearly subscription costs $95. Major daily newspapers (such as the *New York Times* and the *Wall Street Journal*) also contain information on recent EEO and affirmative action lawsuit settlements and changes in legislation.

Contacting your local offices of the Equal Employment Opportunity Commission (EEOC) and the Department of Labor for recent literature can also yield valuable information. In addition, periodically consulting with legal counsel experienced in matters of EEO and affirmative action can add to your knowledge in this area. Also consult some of the numerous legal newspapers and periodicals—either borrow them from your lawyer or visit a local law library. While sometimes more difficult to read than publications not written in "legalese," they provide valuable summaries of recent court decisions.

You might also network with people responsible for EEO and affirmative action in other organizations, exchanging relevant information. Attending workshops and seminars designed to highlight recent developments will afford you the dual opportunity of acquiring information and having your specific questions answered as well. By making an active effort, anyone concerned with the areas of EEO and affirmative action should have no difficulty in keeping up to date and well informed.

Relevant Legislation and Categories of Discrimination

The following fair employment laws and categories of discrimination reflect federal statutes, rules, and regulations. State laws may differ and should also be considered. Failure to comply with these laws could result in costly litigation. Readers are urged to consult with in-house or outside counsel in the event their organization is charged with discrimination.

Civil Rights Act of 1866

EEO legislation in this country dates back over 120 years, to the Civil Rights Act of 1866. Section 1981, Title 42, of this early piece of legislation essentially made it illegal to discriminate against someone in making contracts—including employment contracts, written or implied. It referred primarily to cases of race discrimination; however, in 1982, in the case of *Ortiz* v. *Bank of America*, it was extended to include national origin discrimination. Private-sector businesses regardless of the number of employees are covered by this act.

Violations may result in punitive damages as well as compensatory damages, such as back pay. Although the awards for violation of this act can be substantial, the claimant must establish intent to discriminate on the part of the employer. That is, it is necessary to prove that the employer deliberately denied an individual an opportunity for employment or promotion on the basis of race or national origin. This is to be distinguished from establishing effect, which means that although one or more representatives of an organization did not intend to deny equal employment opportunity on the basis of race, the effect of a certain employment practice (such as exclusively using employee referrals as a recruitment source) was discriminatory. It is usually more difficult to establish intent to discriminate than to show effect.

Civil Rights Act of 1964

Title VII of this act prohibits discrimination on the basis of race, color, religion, sex, or national origin in all facets of the employment process. Any company doing business in the United States that has fifteen or more employees is covered. Title VII does *not* regulate the employment practices of U.S. companies employing American citizens outside the United States. Violations are monitored by the EEOC.

Plaintiffs in Title VII suits generally need not prove intent; rather, they may challenge apparently neutral employment policies that have a discriminatory effect.

Violators of Title VII are generally required to "make whole." This includes providing reinstatement, if relevant, and back pay.

The EEOC's 1980 guidelines on sexual harassment have become an important aspect of the Civil Rights Act of 1964. Defined as unwelcome sexual advances, requests for sexual favors, or other unwanted verbal or physical conduct of a sexual nature, sexual harassment is considered a violation of Title VII if submission to, or rejection of, such conduct is made a term or condition of employment; substantially interferes with a person's work performance; or creates an intimidating, hostile, or offensive working environment. Examples of such behavior include:

- Verbal abuse
- Sexist remarks
- Dirty or sexual jokes
- Sexually suggestive cartoons
- Suggestive or insulting sounds
- Constant talk of sexual experiences
- Repeatedly asking an employee for a date
- Patting, leaning over, or brushing up against someone
- Suggestive looks or gestures
- Leering

- Obscene gestures
- Pinching
- Physical assaults

Men as well as women may be victims of sexual harassment.

The EEOC guidelines state that employers are absolutely responsible for acts of sexual harassment if they are committed by a supervisor. If the acts are committed by rank-and-file employees or nonemployees, such as customers or vendors, employers are liable only if they knew or should have known of the situation and failed to take action.

Affirmative Action

Because Title VII did not immediately have the desired effect against discrimination, a series of executive orders (EOs) were issued by the federal government, first by President Kennedy in 1961 and later strengthened by President Johnson in 1965. The best known was EO 11246. Companies doing business with the federal government are obliged to make a series of commitments in accordance with an EEO clause as set forth by this executive order.

Three commitments with regard to employment are significant:

1. A commitment to nondiscrimination in its employment practices. Failure to meet this commitment could effectively be construed as a violation of its contract; the ramifications might include contract cancellation and even debarment, which means that the government would no longer do business with that company.

2. A commitment to obey the rules and regulations of the Department of Labor. In addition, the company must agree to allow the periodic checking of its business premises by representatives from the Department of Labor to ensure compliance with the other two commitments.

3. A commitment to *affirmative action*, which is essentially a commitment to ensuring equal employment opportunities for everyone by hiring, training, and promoting a certain percentage of qualified women and minorities. The actual percentage is based on the number of women and minorities in the particular geographic area, referred to as a Standard Metropolitan Statistical Area (SMSA). Employers should contact the Office of Federal Contract Compliance Programs (OFCCP) to determine the most recent requirements for separate affirmative action plans pertaining to different establishments. Ask, too, for the OFCCP's *Compliance Manual*, out-

lining the specific steps to be followed in reviewing and monitoring affirmative action plans.

It is strongly recommended that *all* employers develop a written plan, even if it is not required. Having a written plan and a proven commitment to achieving affirmative action goals may be viewed as a bona-fide effort toward precluding discriminatory practices. Of course, the plan must be practiced, not just written.

Equal Pay Act of 1963

This act requires equal pay for men and women performing substantially equal work in the same job classification. The work must be of comparable skill, effort, and responsibility, performed under similar working conditions. There must be at least two employees for this law to apply, and it protects women only; minorities who feel that they have been discriminated against may sue for violation of Title VII of the Civil Rights Act of 1964.

Unequal pay for equal work may be permitted in certain instances. For example, wage differences that are based on superior educational credentials, extensive prior experience, or a bona-fide seniority system may be allowed.

An important issue related to equal pay is *comparable worth*. Currently about half a dozen states have implemented programs for comparable-worth pay, whereby employers are required to compare completely different job categories. Those held predominantly by women, such as nursing and secretarial work, must be compared with those occupied predominantly by men, such as truck driving and warehouse work. Point systems then determine the level of skill involved in each job, as well as its economic value. If, to the employer, the female-dominated jobs are deemed comparable in terms of worth to the male-dominated jobs, pay adjustments must be made to reduce the differences in wages. (Such pay adjustments must increase the wages of the women, not decrease the wages of the men!)

The key distinction between comparable worth and equal pay under the Equal Pay Act of 1963 is that comparable worth allows comparisons between completely different job categories. Since there is now no federal law regarding comparable worth, related issues fall under Title VII of the Civil Rights Act of 1964.

While the controversy over comparable worth continues, companies are urged to assess their job classifications voluntarily and their hiring, promotion, and salary increase practices, with a view toward minimizing specifically female or male categories.

Age Discrimination in Employment Act of 1967

The federal Age Discrimination in Employment Act of 1967 (ADEA) protects workers ages 40 and up. Qualifying private sector and federal, state, and local government employees cannot be discriminated against in matters of pay, benefits, or continued employment, provided the employer has at least twenty employees (part-time employees are included). The law also pertains to employment agencies, labor organizations (with a minimum of twenty-five workers), and U.S. citizens working outside the United States.

The ADEA contains an exemption for bona-fide executives or high-level policymakers who may be retired as early as age 65, according to the following EEOC guidelines:

- Those who exercise discretionary powers on a regular basis
- Those who direct the work of at least two employees on a regular basis
- Those whose primary duty is the management of an entire organization, department, or subdivision
- Those who are authorized to hire, promote, and terminate employees
- Those who devote less than 20 percent of their time to activities other than those described above

Each of these conditions must be met for the two-year period prior to retirement in order for the exemption to be valid.

High-level policymakers are defined as those "who have little or no line authority, but whose position and responsibility are such that they play a significant role in the development of corporate policy and effectively recommend the implementation thereof."

Rehabilitation Act of 1973

This law protects qualified individuals with disabilities against discrimination in employment. The term *qualified* means capable of performing the essential functions of the job; the term *handicapped* refers to physical or mental impairments that substantially limit one or more major life activities. People with a record of such an impairment, or who are regarded as having such an impairment, may be defined as handicapped as well. Someone with a history of alcoholism or drug addiction may also be considered handicapped. However, this law does not apply to anyone whose current use of alcohol or drugs prevents the effective performance of job duties or who might constitute a threat to the property or safety of others. The Rehabilitation Act of 1973 applies to recipients of federal financial assistance and to contractors and subcontractors whose federal government contracts exceed $2,500.

Under affirmative action, an employee is obliged to make every effort to accommodate qualified applicants or employees with disabilities as long as this accommodation does not create an undue hardship. Undue hardship is determined after considering such factors as the size of the organization, the type of work involved, and the nature and cost of the accommodation.

In March 1987 the Supreme Court ruled that recipients of federal funds may not discriminate against individuals who are impaired by contagious diseases. While the decision did not directly involve acquired immune deficiency syndrome (AIDS), the ruling further broadens the meaning of *handicapped* to encompass those with AIDS.

At this time most experts are advising employers to treat people with AIDS like any other employees with a disabling illness. Essentially this means that the employer must show that reasonable accommodation would not make a difference in risk.

The Americans with Disabilities Act of 1990

The Americans with Disabilities Act of 1990 (ADA) affects an estimated 43 million Americans with some type of disability. It prohibits employers with fifteen or more employees, including privately owned businesses and local governments, from discriminating against employees or applicants with disabilities. The federal government, government-owned corporations, Indian tribes, and bona-fide tax-exempt private membership clubs are exempt. Religious organizations are permitted to give preference to the employment of their own members. The law also requires every kind of establishment to be accessible to and usable by people with disabilities.

The term *disability* is defined the same as in the Rehabilitation Act of 1973: a physical or mental impairment that substantially limits an individual's major life activities. The definition also encompasses the history of an impairment and the perception of having an impairment. All in all, over one thousand different impairments are covered by this act.

Current users of illegal drugs or alcohol are not protected by the ADA. Nor are people with contagious diseases or those posing a direct threat to the health or safety of others.

Employers are required to make a "reasonable accommodation" for those applicants or employees capable of performing the "essential" functions of the job with reasonable proficiency. Reasonable accommodation might include job restructuring, allowing part-time or modified work schedules, reassignment, hiring additional workers to aid disabled employees in the performance of their jobs, and installing new equipment or modifying existing equipment. An accommodation is considered unreasonable only if undue physical or financial hardship is placed on the employer. Such hardship is determined according to the overall size of an organization in relation to the size of its work force, its budget, and the nature and cost of the required accommodation. Generally large organizations are expected to make greater accommodations than are small or mid-sized companies.

Also relevant to the subject of people with disabilities is the issue of preemployment physicals. According to the ADA, employers cannot single out individuals with disabilities for medical exams. If they are shown to be job related and consistent with the requirements of the business, medical examinations are permitted after an offer of employment has been made to a job applicant, prior to the start of work. In this instance, an employer may condition an offer of employment on the results of the physical examination.

AIDS

Individuals with AIDS are protected by federal, state, and local legislation governing discrimination against employees with disabilities. In addition, in accordance with section 510 of the Employee Retirement Income Security Act of 1974 (ERISA), it is unlawful for any person to discipline, suspend, or discharge a plan participant for exercising his or her rights according to the provisions of any employee benefits plan. This includes employees with AIDS. Hence, ERISA prohibits employers from discharging AIDS employees for the purpose of denying them earned benefits. Also, the Comprehensive Omnibus Benefits and Retirement Act (COBRA) extends the eligibility of an employee with AIDS for continued medical benefits to eighteen months after termination. Furthermore, because it is generally accepted that AIDS is not transmitted by casual contact and thus does not constitute a risk in the workplace, the employment of a person with AIDS does not violate OSHA.

Accordingly, employers should treat employees infected with the AIDS virus the same as employees suffering from other serious illnesses. As with other disabilities, employers are required to make reasonable accommodations for employees with AIDS.

Information concerning educational programs designed specifically to help employers deal with the issue of AIDS in the workplace is available from the Professional Development Program of Rockefeller College, State University of New York (518/442-5731) or the San Francisco AIDS Foundation (415/864-4376).

Pregnancy Discrimination Act of 1978

This act states that pregnancy is a temporary disability and that pregnant women may not be treated differently from other employees with disabilities in matters of employment. If an organization is going to have special rules for pregnancy, it must be able to prove that they are related to issues of safety or health or dictated by business necessity. As long as pregnant women are able to perform the essential functions of their jobs, they must be permitted to work. Therefore, dates for beginning maternity leave may not be arbitrarily set, and each woman must be allowed to continue working as long as she is physically able.

In January 1987 the Supreme Court ruled that states may require employers to grant special job protection to employees who are physically unable to work because of pregnancy. In *California Federal Savings and Loan Association* v. *Guerra*, the court upheld a California law requiring employees to grant up to four months of unpaid leave to women disabled by pregnancy and childbirth. It added that California employers are free to grant comparable benefits to other employees with disabilities, thereby eliminating any accusations of preferential treatment. The court stressed that this decision does not violate the Pregnancy Discrimination Act of 1978, which prohibits preferential treatment of pregnant women, since it "allows women, as well as men, to have families without losing their jobs," thereby promoting EEO.

Religious Discrimination

Recent revisions to federal guidelines prohibit discrimination on the basis of religious convictions in any aspect of the employment process. The EEOC defines a religious practice as including "moral or ethical beliefs as to what is right and wrong which are sincerely held with the strength of traditional religious views." This means that claimants need not be affiliated with a large, popular, well-known religious sect in order to maintain that some aspect of employment practices interferes with their religious beliefs.

An organization must make a reasonable effort to accommodate an individual's religious practice as long as it does not create an undue hardship. As with accommodating people with disabilities, exactly what constitutes undue hardship depends on a number of factors, including prohibitive cost. Generally the larger the company is, the more it is expected to be able to spend on accommodation.

Sometimes employees are able to meet a job's work schedule when they are hired but subsequently become involved with a particular religious practice and are no longer able to do so. Good-faith attempts should be made by the employer to accommodate religious-based scheduling requests, for example, by adjusting work schedules, implementing flexible working hours, or responding to other employee suggestions that will integrate the employee's religious needs with the needs of the company.

Balancing an employee's religious beliefs with an organization's dress and grooming practices may also become an issue. When the safety of the employee or others is at stake, the employee may be required to conform to company policy in spite of any religious convictions. If, on the other hand, preference, and not safety, is a factor, the employer should make a reasonable effort to accommodate religious-based attire and grooming requests.

Finally, religion and work should be kept separate. This means that employers have the right to require "quiet and unobtrusive" observance.

National Origin Discrimination

The EEOC broadly defines national origin discrimination as including "denial of equal employment opportunity because of an individual's or his or her ancestors' place of origin; or because an individual has the physical, cultural, or linguistic characteristics of a national origin group."

Citizenship requirements for employment may not be valid when the purpose or effect is discrimination on the basis of national origin. Selection criteria that appear neutral on the surface, such as height and weight, may have an adverse impact on certain national origin groups. In addition, "speak English only" rules, when applied without exception, may be considered unreasonable and discriminatory. Similarly, permitting ethnic slurs in the workplace may be viewed as a form of national origin discrimination.

The question of whether it is legal to hire a U.S. citizen over an equally qualified authorized alien is frequently asked. The answer, according to the Immigration and Naturalization Service, is, "On an individual basis, the employer may prefer a United States citizen or national over an equally qualified alien." This is not to say, however, that bias against qualified aliens may be practiced with impunity or that charges of national origin discrimination may not result if a hiring decision is based on factors other than job qualifications. The U.S. Justice Department's Office of Special Counsel for Immigration Related Unfair Employment Practices handles charges of discrimination on the basis of national origin or citizenship status. The EEOC also has jurisdiction over some cases.

The Immigration Reform and Control Act of 1986

According to this act, effective November 6, 1986, employers must verify the citizenship status of all new employees—Americans and aliens—within three days after they are hired. Applicants without the necessary documentation will be given twenty-one days to obtain it, as long as they can present a receipt of application for the documented material within three days. A single document, for example, a U.S. passport or a certificate of U.S. citizenship or naturalization, may be submitted as both proof of identity and employment eligibility. Double documentation, for example, a driver's license with picture as proof of identity and a social security card as proof of employment eligibility, may also be submitted.

Employers must file Form I-9. Since this form could contain sensitive information, employers are advised to keep it separate from other personnel files.

The Immigration Act of 1990

The Immigration Act of 1990 went into effect in October 1991. Prior to its passage the annual number of legal immigrant entries into the United States was 455,000. The Immigration Act raised legal immigrant levels to 700,000 per year—a 35 percent increase over the maximum previously in effect.

Reverse Discrimination

Reverse discrimination occurs when nonminorities—usually white males—are denied equal employment opportunities because of favoritism shown to minorities or women. This occurs most often when affirmative action programs have the effect of limiting opportunities for employment, promotions, and training for nonminorities.

In 1986, the U.S. Supreme Court addressed the issue of reverse discrimination in affirmative action hiring. In *Wygant* v. *Jackson*, by a five-to-four vote, the Court held unconstitutional a negotiated labor contract that sought to preserve recent gains in the hiring of minority teachers in Michigan by requiring the layoff of white teachers with more seniority.

Employers are afforded a certain degree of protection against charges of reverse discrimination by the EEOC. According to 1979 guidelines, employers demonstrating that they have conducted a reasonable self-analysis and have, accordingly, developed a sound basis for concluding that affirmative action is appropriate may be immunized from reverse discrimination complaints filed with that agency.

The Civil Rights Act of 1991

The Civil Rights Act of 1991 went well beyond the Civil Rights Act of 1964's Title VII "make-whole" remedies of back pay, reinstatement, and some attorneys' fees:

- Coverage has been extended to U.S. citizens employed at a U.S. company's foreign site.
- Burden of proof is placed on employers to show lack of discrimination.
- Awards of compensatory and punitive damages are permitted in cases of intentional discrimination.
- Jury trials are permitted.
- Victims of intentional sex discrimination are permitted to seek compensatory and punitive damages up to $300,000.
- Victims of race discrimination are permitted to seek unlimited damages. (This has prompted some companies to require nonunion employees to submit discrimination claims to binding arbitration. Some companies also request that job applicants give up the right to sue as a condition of employment.)
- A "glass ceiling" commission has been established to develop policies for the removal of barriers to women and minorities seeking advancement.
- "Race norming," or the practice of adjusting test scores by race, is banned.

Overall, then, the Civil Rights Act of 1991 seems to favor employees over employers.

Family and Medical Leave Act of 1993

Covering private businesses with fifty or more employees, state and federal employees, public agencies, and private elementary and secondary schools, the Family and Medical Leave Act of 1993 (FMLA) affords employees time off from work to tend to certain family matters without being penalized. Specifically, employees may take twelve weeks of intermittent, unpaid leave during any twelve-month period for the birth of a child; placement of a child for adoption or foster care; or caring for a spouse, child, or parent with a serious health problem or for the worker's own serious health condition. To qualify, the employee must have worked for at least twelve months and not fewer than 1,250 hours in the past year, and must give thirty days' notice of the leave, when practical.

Employers may require a doctor's certification to substantiate the employee's request to tend to family medical problems (these forms are available from the Department of Labor). Employees may also be required to use up all of their accrued vacation or personal or sick leave before taking unpaid leave. Employers may deny leave to salaried employees within the highest-paid 10 percent of the workforce, if such leave would create undue hardship for the company.

Upon returning to work, employees are entitled to the same job or one that is equal in status and pay and continued health and other benefits.

FMLA may not interfere with collective bargaining agreements, more generous company policies, or less restrictive state or local laws.

The Impact of EEO on Employment

EEO laws will be helpful only if employers can gauge their effect on the employment process. Employers have the right to select the candidate deemed best qualified to perform the duties and responsibilities of a given job. This does not necessarily mean selecting the most qualified candidate as long as the front-runner meets the minimum requirements of the job. Other factors should also be considered, however.

First, employers must make certain not to deny anyone equal employment opportunity, either inadvertently or because of personal bias.

Second, employers should check employment practices for possible systemic discrimination, that is, some aspect of a company's recruiting or hiring system that may be inherently discriminatory. For example, businesses that do most of their recruiting by word of mouth might be charged with systemic discrimination if the word is being passed almost exclusively by a white male population to white male colleagues. In this instance, discrimination may not be intended, but women and minorities having no knowledge of the opening certainly cannot compete for it. Hence, there is a systemic denial of equal employment opportunities.

Third, employers should make certain that job requirements are related to the position and not arbitrarily set. With regard to education, this means ensuring that there is valid, objective documentation for job criteria. If high school is required, it must be relevant to the job. Subjective judgment should not be relied on. Is a high school diploma necessary for an employee to perform the essential duties and responsibilities of this job? If not, one should not be required. The same guideline applies to college degrees. However, since such degrees are usually required for higher-level positions with fewer tangible requirements, the guidelines are also less tangible. For example, degree requirements are permitted when the consequences of employing an unqualified person are grave, especially when public health or safety is involved. Positions demanding a great deal of judgment often have degree requirements, as well as those demanding knowledge of technical or professional subject matter. Also, when making a reliable assessment of an applicant's "absolute" qualifications is difficult, the degree requirements may provide an adequate substitute.

Although it may appear at first glance that requiring a college degree for a higher-level position is relatively safe, caution is urged. The burden of proof may be on employers to show job relatedness. The less tangible the reason is, the more difficult this will be. It is often wiser to state "degree preferred" or "degree highly desirable." Even better is to spell out very clearly exactly what knowledge and skill level you are seeking. That way, applicants who have additional years of experience or have attended college without receiving a degree will not be locked out of consideration. You are helping yourself as well as such candidates by not narrowing the field of choice.

Be certain, too, that education requirements are relevant to the actual position for which the person is applying. In situations where the degree is not necessary for the immediate job, but will be for future jobs to which the employee will be expected to progress, you may have the requirement, if the job is a true stepping-stone. To be on the safe side, however, it is better if your organization offers educational assistance, so that the employee may acquire the necessary supplementary education while working for you.

One other word about education requirements: Be careful about changing them. If you have an opening with specific requirements and find someone you want for the job who does not quite meet them, do not lower the requirements or hire the applicant. You are leaving yourself wide open to discrimination charges by other applicants. Also, if you have an opening with set education requirements and an applicant meets them, but you then decide in retrospect that the requirements are not stringent enough, you are asking for trouble. If you want to change them once they are set, you must reevaluate the entire job in relation to the specific duties. Only then can you properly determine whether the education requirements warrant adjustment.

As with education, requirements for previous work experience should be job related. The standards should never be arbitrary, artificial, or unnecessary.

The more complex the job is, the more reasonable it is to have experience requirements. However, if you have not required specific experience in the past, and the job has not changed substantially in its level of responsibility or specific duties, do not start now. The new requirements may have a greater negative impact on women and minorities than on white males. The greater this disparity is between past and current job requirements, the greater the burden will be on you to prove the necessity for the requirements.

Be careful, too, about asking for a specific number of years of experience. It is difficult to prove that four years' experience is not adequate and five years is. How did you determine this? It is not enough to say that one previous incumbent had five years' prior experience and did a fine job, or that another had only four years' experience and required a great deal of on-the-job training. Those were two specific individuals, and it is dangerous to use them as the basis for your reasoning. It is also difficult to justify preference for someone with a little more experience as opposed to just enough. As with degrees, it is best to say that five years' experience is preferred—not required. Remember, not only is it unwise from an EEO standpoint to ask for a specific number of years of experience, but you may be preventing yourself from hiring someone who strikes you as the best candidate for other reasons. You cannot select someone who does not meet your requirements over others who do.

Occasionally the requirements of a position may only seem to be discriminatory in nature, such as jobs stipulating that only male or female candidates need apply. However, closer investigation may disclose that the EEO concept of bona-fide occupational qualification (BFOQ) prevails. By definition, a BFOQ is a criterion that appears to be discriminatory but can be justified by business necessity. For example, an employer may have an opening for a model to demonstrate a designer's new line of dresses, so that being female would be a BFOQ. An example of an unacceptable BFOQ would be a position requiring heavy lifting where only male applicants are considered. The requirement of lifting may be tested; all applicants—male and female—could be asked to lift the amount of weight that would normally be required on the job. Those who were unable to perform this task need not be considered, including all those men, as well as all the women, not meeting that requirement. And women capable of lifting the weight would have to be given an equal opportunity for the job.

Bona-fide occupational qualifications may apply to religion, sex, age, and national origin but never to race. Furthermore, general company preference does not constitute a legitimate BFOQ. The most valid BFOQ or business-necessity defense is safety.

When there is doubt, the following business-necessity guidelines should be followed:

- Document the business necessity.
- Explore alternative practices.
- Ensure across-the-board administration of the practice.
- Be sure that the business necessity is not based on stereotypical thinking, arbitrary standards, or tradition.

Remember that there are very few instances in which BFOQ applies. Employers who believe that their requirements qualify are advised to consult an EEO specialist or attorney before proceeding.

Finally, employers need to focus on their organization's affirmative action goals when weighing the qualifications of women and minorities versus white males. Full compliance with a company's affirmative action goals should be the overall objective, and employers should make every effort to achieve this end whenever there is an opening to fill.

If after considering all of these factors and assessing both the tangible and intangible qualifications of all your candidates, it is determined that the most suitable person for the job happens to be a white male, you are free to make that person a job offer. However, if the credentials of two candidates—one a white male and the other a minority or a woman—are essentially the same, and your affirmative action goals have not been met, hiring the minority or the woman is urged.

Employment and Termination-at-Will

By definition, "employment and termination-at-will" is the right of an employer to terminate, at any time, for any reason, with or without cause, the employment of an individual who does not have a written contract defining the terms of employment. In exercising this employment and termination-at-will right, the employer, under previous case law, incurs no legal liability.

The employment and termination-at-will doctrine has been seriously eroded, however, by legislation such as Title VII of the Civil Rights Act of 1964, the Age Discrimination in Employment Act, the ADA, and the Civil Rights Act of 1991, as well as other laws described earlier in this chapter. Such legislation prohibits employers from denying equal employment opportunities to all individuals and further prevents them from discharging employees because of non-job-related factors. Employees now have additional rights protecting them from arbitrary acts of termination-at-will. The broadest form of protection, implied covenants of good faith and fair dealing, requires employers to prove "just cause" before terminating an employee. Public policy rights may also protect employees from being fired for exercising rights such as whistle-blowing—public disclosure of illegal actions taken by one's company—or for refusal to perform illegal acts on behalf of an employer. Moreover, the issue of implied contract rights may arise when the protection provided by statements on the employment application form, in HR manuals and employee handbooks, or in other company documents is interpreted as binding contracts.

With regard to the fact that HR manuals, employee handbooks, and other company documents are increasingly viewed as legally binding contracts, it is advisable for companies to develop at-will policies for inclusion in these documents. The ten guidelines that follow should be applied when developing a company's at-will policy:

1. *State the at-will principle.* It is important to declare that your company's handbook or manual is neither an employment contract nor a guarantee of employment. Consider the following sample from an employee handbook:

> This handbook has been designed to serve as a general summary of our current policies, procedures, and benefits for general information purposes. It provides guidance with regard to what you may expect from us and what we expect from you. We will make every effort to recognize the privileges described herein, unless doing so would impair the operation of business or expose the company to legal liability or financial loss. No provision of this handbook is to be construed as a guarantee of employment.

This simple disclaimer may not be enough, however, since courts have also examined actual practices. Make certain to consult with an attorney knowledgeable in these areas for the most appropriate language to use.

2. *Do not make statements regarding job security.* Avoid phrases such as "as long as your performance is satisfactory, you are guaranteed employment," or "as an employee of [company name], you can look forward to a long and rewarding future," or "we treat employees of [company name] like members of our family and look forward to having you with us for a long time."

3. *Preserve the right to alter policies.* Clearly state that, at the discretion of the employer, certain policies and procedures may be amended, deleted, or replaced as deemed appropriate.

4. *Avoid naming a prospective employee's salary in yearly numbers when extending a written job offer.* A statement of annual salary may imply a one-year employment contract. Instead, weekly, biweekly, or monthly numbers may be used.

5. *Avoid using the word* fair. The term is subject to interpretation. Instead, use the word *consistent*.

6. *Avoid attempting a list that is all-inclusive,* particularly with respect to acts considered cause for disciplinary action.

7. *Avoid using the term* probationary period. It implies that, once a given period of time is over, the employee is there to stay. Similarly, avoid the term *permanent employee;* instead, substitute *regular employee.*

8. *Include employment-at-will statements on tuition reimbursement forms.* This will help safeguard against possible claims that the granting of tuition reimbursement implies a certain degree of job security.

9. *Apply sound, consistent management practices and principles to termination decisions.* Avoid arbitrary, artificial, or non-job-related reasons for termination; apply equal employment opportunity guidelines; document reasons leading up to termination; and terminate for cause only.

10. *Ask employees to acknowledge having read and understood the contents of the company's at-will policy by signing a statement so indicating.* For example, "I understand that the handbook and all other written and oral material provided to me are intended for informational purposes only. Neither it, company practices, nor other communications create an employment contract."

Employers can also minimize the possibility of wrongful discharge allegations and can put the company in a better position to defend successfully against such action by following certain guidelines:

1. Prospective employees should be advised in writing at the beginning of the application process that, if hired, they will be at-will employees. This may best be accomplished by an at-will statement on the application form.
2. Application forms should be in full compliance with applicable EEO laws.
3. Managers and supervisors should be trained in effective and legal interviewing skills.
4. Applicants should clearly understand the position they are being considered for prior to being offered the job.
5. All employees should have a clear understanding of what their job entails, in terms of both content and scope of responsibility.
6. Job descriptions should be accurate and job standards consistent with what is actually required.
7. All employees should have an up-to-date copy of the company's employee handbook; it should be made clear that the handbook does not constitute an employment contract.
8. A consistent method of evaluating job performance should be established and followed.
9. Salary increases should be granted according to an individual's skills and knowledge as they relate to a specific job.
10. Managers and supervisors should be skilled at coaching and counseling.
11. Managers and supervisors should be familiar with pertinent EEO laws, rules, and regulations.
12. A progressive disciplinary system should be established and followed.
13. Grievance procedures for employees who are dissatisfied with working terms or conditions should be established and followed.
14. Managers and supervisors should understand and practice effective documentation principles and techniques.
15. All employees should be granted exit interviews.
16. All terminations should be handled such that employees are more likely to feel that they have been treated in a consistent manner and will therefore be less inclined to bring a wrongful dismissal suit against the company.

While employees may now more readily bring claims against employers who terminate employment for capricious or discriminatory reasons, violate public policy rights, or breach implied contracts, there may be restrictions on the damages awarded in such suits. An important example is the 1989 Supreme Court of California ruling in *Foley* v. *Interactive Data Corporation*. Briefly, the case involved an employee whose performance over his seven years of employment had been deemed, at the least, to be satisfactory. Problems developed when he began reporting to a new supervisor who was under investigation for embezzling from a former employer. The employee reported this information to his former supervisor, adding that he was uncomfortable working for someone who was under investigation for criminal activity. Within approximately two months, the employee was terminated. He sued, claiming three things:

1. The termination violated "public policy" because he had a duty to tell his employer about the criminal investigation of his supervisor.
2. The termination violated the terms of an oral/implied contract in which the employer had promised not to fire him without good cause.
3. The employer had violated its "duty" to act in "good faith" in its dealings with him as an employee.

The first two claims were actions in contract, whereby the object of a decision is to "enforce the intentions of the parties," such as pay them the money they would have earned in salary, benefits, and so on. The last claim was an action in tort, which may result in an award of punitive damages. While contract damages can be substantial, depending on the employee's salary, they are limited; there is no limit to the amount of an award for punitive damages in a tort action.

The court's decision was to limit the employee's damages to lost wages and other "contract" damages. This is a significant precedent, in that employees claiming bad faith in employment and termination-at-will cases are now less likely to be awarded tort damages unless they can prove a tort other than bad faith, such as libel, intentional infliction of emotional distress, or false arrest.

Although the court's decision applies to California employers only, legal experts maintain that *Foley* is a landmark case that may well set precedent for similar cases in other states.

Because the legal issues involving employment and termination-at-will are still evolving, including the Uniform Employment Termination Act, employers are advised to have employee handbooks, HR manuals, application forms, and all other written materials pertaining to the employment process reviewed by counsel annually.

Negligent Hiring and Retention

Negligent hiring and retention, a relatively new form of liability that has been sustained by court decisions since the mid-1980s, occurs when employers fail to exercise reasonable care in hiring or retaining employees. Increasingly, employers are being held liable for the acts of their employees both in the workplace and away from it. Named in such lawsuits are usually the employer, the employee who caused the injury, and the person directly responsible for hiring. Findings of personal liability are not uncommon. Negligent hiring actions have been brought by employees as well as by innocent third parties, such as customers, visitors, and clients who have been injured by the criminal, violent, or negligent acts of an employee.

Plaintiffs must prove that the employee who caused the injury was unfit for hiring or retention, that the employer's hiring or retention of the unfit employee was the cause of the plaintiff's injuries, and that the employer knew or should have known of the employee's unfit condition. The deciding factor is generally whether an employer can establish that he or she exercised reasonable care in ensuring the safety of others. Reasonable care may include conducting preemployment testing, checking references, investigating gaps in an applicant's employment history, verifying academic achievements, conducting a criminal investigation, checking an applicant's credit history, or verifying the individual's driving record. The type of position an employee is hired for often plays a role in how extensive the investigation should be. For example, unsupervised positions in which the employee has a great deal of contact with customers, clients, visitors, or other employees may require more in-depth preemployment investigation than will jobs that are highly supervised.

Employers are cautioned against being overly concerned with possible charges of negligent hiring by automatically disqualifying a candidate because of some aspect of his or her history. For example, if an investigation reveals that an individual has a conviction record, such information must be relevant to the job in question in order for it to constitute automatic grounds for disqualification.

Employers who end up in court because of negligent hiring or retention charges report that juries generally find for the plaintiff. The trial of such actions may involve the examination of a number of issues, including what the employer actually knew about the employee, as opposed to what it tried to learn; whether the potential risk to others could have been reasonably discovered through a reference or background check; and whether the risk to others was greater because of the nature of the job.

Consideration of these questions may implicate the employer in an act of negligent hiring or retention. Employers should note that such lawsuits may prove more costly than typical employee litigation because of potentially higher awards of punitive damages. For example, in one negligent hiring case the plaintiff rejected a settlement offer of $500,000; the jury verdict was $5 million.

From all that has been stated, it is apparent that preventive measures are an employer's best defense against charges of negligent hiring or retention. In this regard, employers are advised to:

- Conduct comprehensive employment interviews.
- Check for gaps in employment.
- Determine what kind of background check is needed for each position.
- Conduct preemployment tests as deemed appropriate.
- Conduct thorough professional and, if needed, personal reference checks.
- Keep written notes of information received when checking references.
- Decide whether a criminal investigation, credit check, or other form of investigation is warranted, based on the information received.
- Immediately investigate any allegations of employee misconduct.
- Consult with legal counsel when in doubt as to what course of action to take.

Summary

This chapter has offered an overview of legal issues affecting the employment process. Specific legislation and categories of discrimination have been described, as well as the impact of EEO on employment. The latter included a discussion of systemic discrimination, as well as the importance of establishing job-related educational and experiential job requirements. In addition, the issue of BFOQs in relation to certain job requirements was covered. Finally, two relatively new areas of employment and the law have been analyzed: employment and termination-at-will, and negligent hiring and retention.

EEO and affirmative action regulations are always changing, and small and mid-sized employers are reminded to keep abreast of those changes that are likely to affect their businesses. The importance of familiarity with these aspects of the employment process cannot be stressed enough.

4

The Employment Process

Being thoroughly prepared for an interview will help you learn key information about each candidate, avoid possible discrimination charges, and use your interview time efficiently.

Effective use of human resources requires the development and maintenance of a comprehensive and professional employment process. Small companies should have a system in place, ready to expand if and when they experience a period of rapid growth.

The employment process refers to a great deal more than just hiring people. It includes:

- Prerecruitment activities
- Recruitment sources
- Interviewing techniques
- Selection guidelines
- Orientation programs
- Promotions, transfers, and demotions
- Terminations and exit interviews

Depending on the size of a company, these areas may be the responsibility of human resources specialists or non-HR practitioners. In many instances, they are a shared responsibility.

Prerecruitment Activities

Three steps should be completed at the beginning of the employment process: writing a job description, preparing a job requisition, and developing an employee profile.

Job Descriptions

Job descriptions are valuable tools that may be used during every aspect of the employment process outlined above. In addition, they are helpful in matters of compensation, employer-employee relations, and training. Because they are so useful, writing or reviewing a job description should be the first step in the prerecruitment stage of the employment process.

There are two types of job descriptions: generic and specific. The number and nature of job classifications within an organization will determine which format should be used.

Generic job descriptions are written in broad, general terms and may be used for several similar positions in different departments of the same company. For example, there may be one generic job description for the position "secretary" as opposed to a separate secretarial job description for each department in a company. When preparing generic job descriptions, be careful to list only those duties that all positions of the same title have in common.

Specific job descriptions define the duties and tasks of one particular position, such as "director of human resources." They are written when a position has unique responsibilities that distinguish it from other jobs. Most small and many mid-sized companies manage quite effectively with generic job descriptions for most positions. As a company grows and adds more specialized jobs to its payroll, additional specific job descriptions are then written.

All job descriptions, whether generic or specific, should be concise and straightforward, using definitive, uncomplicated language. Each job description should include:

Job title
Division and/or department
Reporting relationship
Location of job
Work schedule
Exemption status
Grade and salary range
Brief summary of the job's primary duties and responsibilities
Detailed list of the primary duties and responsibilities
Education, prior work experience, and specialized skills and knowl-
    edge required
Name of the job analyst
Date prepared

Additional categories, as relevant, may include:

Physical environment and working conditions
Equipment and machinery used
Other (such as customer contact or access to confidential information)

Small organizations without human resources specialists skilled in writing job descriptions can delegate this task to managers familiar with positions in their respective departments. Anyone writing job descriptions should find the following guidelines helpful:

- Arrange duties and responsibilities in a logical, sequential order. Begin with the task requiring the greatest amount of time or carrying the greatest responsibility.
- State separate duties clearly and concisely so anyone can glance at the description and easily identify each duty.
- Try to avoid generalizations or ambiguous words. Use specific language and be exact in your meaning. To illustrate, "handles mail" might be better expressed as "sorts mail" or "distributes mail."
- Do not try to list every task. Use the phrase "primary duties and responsibilities" at the beginning of your job description and proceed from there. You should also close with a phrase such as "performs other related duties and assignments as required."
- Include specific examples of duties whenever possible.
- Use nontechnical language. A good job description explains the responsibilities of a job in terms that are understandable to everyone using it.
- Indicate the frequency of occurrence of each duty. One popular way of doing this is to have a column next to the list of tasks with corresponding percentages that represent the estimated amount of time devoted to each primary duty.
- List duties individually and concisely, rather than using narrative paragraph form. A job description is not an English composition.
- Do not refer to specific people. Instead, refer to titles and positions. Incumbents are likely to change positions long before the positions themselves are revamped or eliminated.
- Use the present tense; it reads more smoothly.
- Be objective and accurate in describing the job. Be careful not to describe the present incumbent, yourself when you held that particular job, someone who may have just been fired for poor performance, or someone who was recently promoted for outstanding job

performance. Describe the job as it should realistically be performed.

- Stress what the incumbent does instead of attempting to explain a procedure that must be used. For example, use "records appointments" rather than "a record of appointments must be kept."
- Be certain that all requirements are job related and are in accordance with EEO laws and regulations.
- Eliminate unnecessary articles, such as "a" and "the." Do not make the description too wordy. The length of a job description does not increase the importance of the job.
- Use action words. This means any word that describes a specific function, such as "organizes." Action words do not leave room for confusion. Within any sentence, a single word should stand out as the most descriptive: a word that can essentially stand alone, conveying to the reader a certain degree of responsibility. For example, compare "directs" to "under the direction of . . ." Since the first word used should introduce the function being described, try to begin each sentence with an action word.

Here is a list of action words that may be drawn from when writing job descriptions:

administers	edits	negotiates
advises	evaluates	notifies
analyzes	examines	observes
assigns	files	obtains
assists	follows up	operates
audits	formulates	organizes
balances	generates	performs
calculates	guides	plans
classifies	identifies	prepares
collects	informs	proposes
compiles	initiates	receives
constructs	interviews	recommends
coordinates	itemizes	records
creates	lists	reports
decides	locates	researches
delegates	maintains	reviews
designs	measures	revises
determines	modifies	schedules
develops	monitors	screens

selects	tabulates	types
studies	trains	utilizes
summarizes	transcribes	verifies
supervises	troubleshoots	writes

Once a job description is written, it should be reviewed on a semiannual or annual basis to make certain that the nature of the job has not changed substantially. This is particularly important with growing small and mid-sized organizations.

Chapter 6 contains additional information on job descriptions as they relate to compensation. A blank job description form appears in Appendix A, and a sample job description is shown in Appendix B.

Job Requisitions

Managers should notify their human resources department as soon as a job opening becomes available. The most efficient way of doing this is to use a job requisition form. The job requisition form should include nearly all the same information as the job description, with three distinctions. First, it should not include a detailed list of duties and responsibilities; a brief summary is adequate. Second, it should include the reason for the opening, such as the retirement or promotion of the former jobholder. And third, appropriate signatures to authorize filling the opening should be provided. The exemption status, grade, and salary range may be completed by the HR representative, but all other information should be provided by the manager in charge.

The job requisition form is relatively simple to complete and very important to the employment process. It supplements the content of the more detailed job description and gives the human resources representative official authorization to begin recruiting.

A sample job requisition form appears in Appendix C.

Employee Profiles

On receiving the completed and signed job requisition form, the human resources representative should arrange to meet with the requesting manager to discuss a profile of the ideal candidate for the job. In addition to discussing the concrete education and experience requirements of the job, the manager should describe some of the job-related intangible requirements being sought. Intangible factors might include management style; ability to get along with coworkers, management, and subordinates; initiative; creativity and imagination; self-confidence; personality; temperament; responsiveness; appearance; and maturity.

This profile of the ideal candidate will provide the HR representative who will be doing the recruiting with a clear picture of the type of individual best suited for the position. Intangible factors can be particularly helpful if there are two or more applicants with similar backgrounds. The interviewer must be careful, however, not to weigh intangibles too heavily. They are highly subjective, and selecting someone solely on the basis of these factors is not recommended. If used to make selection or rejection decisions, such factors must be job related.

Recruitment Sources

Once prerecruitment activities have been completed, the human resources representative can proceed to develop a recruiting strategy and consider the various recruitment sources available.

Primary Recruitment Sources

The recruitment sources most commonly used by small and mid-sized organizations are either cost free or of nominal cost, and/or can help fill positions quickly. This section will look at some of the most popular recruitment sources in detail.

Job Posting

In order to improve employee motivation and to assist employees in developing career paths, many organizations establish an internal job-posting system and use it as the first recruitment source whenever a position becomes available. Not only is job posting a morale booster, but it also helps the company save time and money by promoting or transferring an employee who is already familiar with the structure and procedures of the organization.

The success of a job-posting program depends largely on how well it is designed and monitored. The sample job-posting system described below, when modified to suit an organization's particular environment, should be useful.

1. The human resources department should prepare each job-posting notice based on the information contained in the job requisition

form prepared by the requesting manager. The job-posting notice should contain the title, location, primary duties and responsibilities, and eligibility requirements of the job. The application procedure should also be outlined.

2. Copies of the job-posting notice should be posted on department bulletin boards, as well as other locations accessible to all employees.

3. Employees who are interested in applying for the position should discuss it with their supervisor. Authorization from an employee's supervisor is generally required before HR will accept applications.

4. A period of from one to two weeks is usually allowed for employees to apply for a position once it has been posted. The manager is generally not permitted to interview outside applicants until this time period has elapsed.

5. When evaluating employees who have applied for a posted job, the HR representative should take into account their qualifications for the particular position, their performance in current and previous jobs, and their record of attendance.

6. Upon assessing basic job eligibility, human resources will interview and recommend for further consideration those employees who seem best suited for the available opening.

7. The manager with the opening will interview candidates referred by human resources.

8. The final decision is made jointly by HR and the manager having the opening. If there is a difference in opinion, the manager should make the ultimate decision.

It is recommended that employees be permitted to apply for as many positions as they choose and as frequently as they choose. However, certain conditions should be met before an employee may apply for a posted job:

- The employee must meet the basic job requirements.
- The employee must have a minimum period of service with the organization, generally from six to eighteen months.
- The employee's previous performance appraisal must be satisfactory or better.
- When an employee has applied and been accepted for a position via the job-posting system, he or she must wait a certain period of time before filing another application, generally from six to twelve months.

The manager with the opening is generally expected to wait two weeks for the transfer to take place so that the employee's current manager can look for a replacement. Unusual circumstances may permit either an earlier or a later transfer.

Managers and supervisors should encourage their employees to apply for internal positions consistent with their interests and skills. Employees who are held back will not feel motivated in their current jobs, and their productivity is certain to decline.

Rejection for one position should never be used in any way against an employee applying for future jobs.

A sample job-posting notice form appears in Appendix D, and a sample job-posting application form appears in Appendix E.

Word of Mouth

One of the most frequently used, cheapest, and quickest recruitment sources is word of mouth. As soon as it is known that an opening is to occur, the word spreads. A department head may tell other department heads; employees talk with one another; word is carried outside the organization to family, friends, and acquaintances. Sometimes, as an added incentive to help fill the job quickly, organizations offer a bonus to employees whose recommendations result in hiring. In small and mid-sized companies, these bonuses generally range from $25 to $100. Generally, the recommending person can collect the bonus only if the new employee remains with the company for at least one year and receives a satisfactory or higher performance rating.

On the surface, word of mouth may appear to be an ideal recruitment source. But although it is highly effective, be careful using it. As stated earlier, it has been shown statistically that like tends to refer like. For example, white males tend to refer other white males. The result of this kind of referral system could be the unintentional creation or perpetuation of systematic discrimination whereby women and minorities are not given equal opportunity to apply for certain positions. This is one important reason that word of mouth should be used only in conjunction with other recruitment sources.

HR Files

Well-maintained HR files of previous applicants often reveal qualified candidates when openings become available. Once the application is pulled, the applicant's skills and experience can readily be compared with the requirements of the existing position. Pay careful attention to the notes of the previous interviewer, but do not assume that because a candidate was rejected for a position in the past, it means that he or she is not qualified for current or future positions.

Whether you choose to maintain a manual file or a computerized record system will depend on the total number of employees in an organization as well as other factors. This will be discussed in greater detail in Chapter 11.

Walk-Ins, Call-Ins, and Write-Ins

From a public relations point of view, nothing could be better than being able to hire walk-ins, call-ins, and write-ins. Generally, nonexempt applicants (clerical workers and other nonprofessionals) walk in or call in, and exempt applicants (supervisors, managers, and other professionals) submit resumés.

Unfortunately, these are not usually treated as serious recruitment sources. In many companies, walk-ins are automatically told by the receptionist that there are no openings at the present time, and the application forms they complete are filed without being reviewed by an interviewer. Call-ins are generally asked to apply in person—only to be told that there are no openings once they arrive. (This is certainly not good public relations!) Similarly, unsolicited resumés are given a quick glance at best and then filed. Sometimes courteous letters of acknowledgment are sent, but often there is no communication whatsoever.

Setting up a procedure for handling this group of applicants can yield excellent results. Here is a simple system that can be modified for use in any organization.

• Provide the receptionist in the human resources department with an up-to-date list of job openings accompanied by a brief job description for each opening. This list should be referred to each time a walk-in applies for a position. If the applicant is interested in a position on the list, the receptionist should inform an interviewer, who can look over the completed application and determine whether an interview would be appropriate. If the interviewer is too busy to see the applicant right away, a later interview can be scheduled.

• When applicants call in, the receptionist should check the same list of openings and transfer callers to the interviewer responsible for filling a particular job. A brief telephone interview can usually be conducted on the spot to establish further interest, and an appointment can then be scheduled for a later date.

• Unsolicited resumés may also be reviewed against the same list of openings. Possible job matches can then be pursued by either telephone or mail.

Government Agencies

State and federal employment agencies can refer numerous job candidates because they have access to a large pool of applicants. Candidates referred by government agencies are usually unemployed at the time and thus are able to work right away—a definite advantage for employers who are anxious to fill openings as quickly as possible. An additional advantage to working with state and federal agencies is that they maintain careful EEO records and therefore can help an organization meet its affirmative action goals.

When working with a government agency, clearly stipulate the requirements for an available position. This is crucial, since government agencies may refer job applicants without screening them thoroughly for relevant qualifications.

Government agencies can be most helpful in filling entry-level or nonspecialized positions.

Advertising

Although it can be costly, advertising is one of the best ways to reach a large audience quickly. Identifying your company's name and address or telephone number will attract more applicants faster than running a blind ad using a post office box number.

Plan carefully the content, timing, location, and specific publications selected for your ad. Remember that certain publications are more widely read by exempt-level individuals. Business magazines, for example, will carry ads only for professional positions. Similarly, certain newspapers are more likely to attract nonexempt-level people. Your company's affirmative action goals should also be kept in mind when deciding which publication will carry your ad, since certain papers and magazines have a large female and/or minority readership.

The day of the week an ad appears in a newspaper can also make a difference in the number of responses received.

Here are some guidelines to help you develop successful recruitment ads.

• Clearly state the qualities and background you are seeking in a candidate for your opening.

• Highlight the duties and responsibilities to be performed.

• Briefly describe your company's primary product or service.

• If you are a growing company, stress this fact, and briefly summarize your growth to date, if possible.

• Describe the job in positive yet realistic terms. Do not misrepresent the job.

• Emphasize any outstanding benefits offered by your company.

• Use advertising space effectively. In other words, do not run a full-page ad when a half-page ad will suffice. On the other hand, do not try to squeeze your message into a small space in order to save money. The graphics, copy, and size of the ad should all work together and be in proportion to the level of the available position, the size of your organization, the number of applicants you are seeking, and the competitiveness of the marketplace.

• Research various publications and select those most compatible with the available position.

• In most instances, small and mid-sized organizations should be able to write their own ads, calling on experts for assistance in the areas of use of space and graphics, when needed.

Agencies and Search Firms

Employment agencies and search firms can readily scout the market for qualified candidates and can fill positions more quickly than companies generally can on their own, since they have access to a large labor pool. Search firms handle professional or exempt positions; employment agencies primarily recruit nonexempt people.

The primary disadvantage of using agencies and search firms is their cost. Agencies' fee structures differ, but they usually work on a contingency basis—that is, they collect their fees if and when referred applicants are hired.

Since working with agencies and search firms can be expensive, consider the following guidelines before agreeing to enter any contracts.

• Be sure that the agency will carefully screen and evaluate applicants, referring only those who meet the standards stipulated.

• Be firm about the job's requirements, and refuse to consider anyone who does not meet them.

• Ask for a written agreement describing the agency's fee arrangement, including the total cost, when it is to be paid, and any other related conditions. Be sure to ask about policies regarding refunds for a percentage of the fee if a referred employee is terminated within the first three to six months of work.

• Be selective in determining which agencies and search firms will receive your business. Interview representatives in advance to make certain that they clearly understand your objectives. Establish their degree of knowledge in the area for which they will be recruiting, and make sure you feel comfortable working with them. Ask for information regarding their work methods, experience, and track record. Do not hesitate to ask for references or to investigate their reputation in the field. Also be sure that the person you meet will actually be handling your company's account. Having a good rapport with the agency representative is important.

• Formally notify all agencies and search firms with which you will be working that you are an equal opportunity employer. Also share information about your organization's affirmative action plan.

• Once you have decided to work with a particular agency or search firm, allow agency representatives to learn as much as possible about both your organization and the specific job openings. The more information the agency has, the better able it will be to meet your needs quickly and effectively.

Secondary Recruitment Sources

Although the seven recruitment sources described above are the most commonly used by small and mid-sized organizations, you may want to consider several additional recruitment sources.

Campus Recruiting

Colleges are an excellent source of talent for organizations to tap. Recent graduates are highly desirable as potential employees, and companies may aggressively compete to hire, groom, and develop recruits from top schools. For small and mid-sized companies, however, there are two major drawbacks to campus recruiting: It can be extremely expensive, especially if primarily out-of-state colleges are approached; and smaller companies may find it difficult to compete with major corporations for top talent, since many graduates seek placement with Fortune 500 companies.

Job Fairs

Job fairs serve as meeting grounds for representatives from several organizations and potential employees. Numerous applicants are interviewed over a period of one or two days. These fairs often specialize in a particular field such as engineering, or in specific affirmative action categories such as women, minorities, or people with disabilities. The fairs are generally held during a weekend at a conference center; for a flat fee, recruiters may interview and hire as many people as they choose. In order to see as many people as possible, recruiters conduct only brief interviews during the fair and schedule promising candidates for more extensive interviews later.

Like campus recruiting, job fairs can be very costly with no guarantees of finding anyone suitable for your openings. Also, as with campus recruiting, small and mid-sized companies are competing with larger organizations that can probably offer more in the way of starting salaries and benefits. In the brief period of time allotted for each interview, it may be difficult for smaller companies to sell themselves successfully. It is therefore recommended that recruiters provide the interviewees with literature describing their companies' products or services, histories, recent growth, and future plans.

Open Houses

In preparing for an open house, companies place ads in newspapers in selected geographic locations, announcing a recruitment drive in those areas on specific dates. All available jobs are listed. A detailed description of the company's products, reputation, starting salaries, and benefits package is also included. On the date of the open house, company recruiters appear at the designated location to interview anyone expressing an interest in working for them. Recruiters sometimes reach decisions during the open house or, more commonly, arrange for selected applicants to return to the company later for additional interviews.

With the advertising costs and the expense required to host an open house, this form of recruitment can be costly and time-consuming. It is also risky because the size of the turnout is unpredictable. Large companies can generally afford to risk an open house more readily than small companies can. One way to reduce the amount of risk involved is to prescreen applicants by telephone or ask applicants to submit resumés in advance.

Direct Mail Recruitment

In a direct mail campaign, a company contacts certain individuals about a specific opening, hoping for a job match. Several mailing lists are usually necessary in order to determine whom to contact. List information as well as actual lists may be obtained through professional associations, business directories, trade groups, and magazine subscription services. You may also opt to hire direct mail specialists or consultants.

Even large organizations tend to shy away from direct mail recruitment. Despite the advantage of being highly personal, direct mail campaigns often fail because recipients either do not open the envelope or view the contents suspiciously and fail to follow through. This form of recruitment, then, is recommended only when other more reliable recruitment sources have failed.

Radio and Television

Radio and television advertising appeals to a very large audience in a very short period of time. In addition, you can reach and tempt prospects who are not actively looking for a job. These advantages are offset, however, by the cost. Even one radio or television spot can be very expensive, since success depends on certain particulars of your message being repeated frequently. Local radio stations charge less than network radio stations or television stations, so explore them first as a viable option.

Computerized Systems

A computerized recruitment system matches specific jobs with viable candidates. Some of these systems put candidates in direct contact with prospective employers; others act as a liaison, contacting companies as representatives of the applicants. Computerized systems can be very helpful in finding qualified applicants, often in much less time than any of the other means described above.

However, computerized methods of recruitment generally may not be deemed suitable for small and mid-sized companies for two reasons: They may be expensive, with charges for passwords, listing fees, and daily job display fees, and they may require that employers buy the appropriate computer and modem.

Professional Associations

Human resources specialists belonging to professional associations can exchange information about job applicants and share the resumés of candidates who applied, but were rejected for, positions within their company. These candidates may well be suited for positions in other organizations.

Work with a few other HR representatives from different companies belonging to the same professional association. Agree to prepare and exchange, on a regular basis, a file containing the applications and/or resumés for candidates whom you have either interviewed or whose qualifications you have reviewed but are not currently interested in hiring. In addition to the cost-effectiveness of these exchanges, you may benefit from someone else's impressions of a candidate and decide you want the person for some future opening.

Research Firms

Research firms are abbreviated full-service executive search firms, offering roughly half the services. They provide organizations with information about professional employees but do not conduct interviews or evaluate their qualifications. Research firms generally charge by the hour, although some offer flat-rate fees, and they may be a cost-effective way to recruit top-level professionals.

When evaluating the services of a research firm, consider whether the company serves a wide range of industries or specializes in one particular field. Also, try to determine its success rate and reputation.

Preemployment Training

Preemployment training provides individuals with the basic knowledge and skills needed to perform a given job without extending them an actual job offer. The emphasis, then, is on preparation, so that when jobs do become available, active recruitment will not be necessary; the individuals trained are given first consideration. If these pretrained individuals are hired, the amount of time needed for both job and organizational orientation will also be greatly reduced.

Preemployment training generally works best in plant or manufacturing environments where the operation of equipment or machinery is required.

Interviewing Techniques

Interviewing should be the joint responsibility of representatives from the human resources department and the department in which an opening exists. In most small and mid-sized organizations, the following interview procedure seems to work best:

1. The human resources representative conducts the initial interview, during which basic job suitability is established. In addition to establishing eligibility in terms of concrete requirements, the human resources representative also determines which applicants most closely meet the intangible requirements of the opening.
2. The department representative or manager meets with those candidates referred by human resources. At this time, a more in-depth, detailed interview should be conducted.
3. The department head conducts an interview with the one or two candidates most favored by the manager. These interviews are generally brief, focusing on the candidates' intangible qualifications.

Team Interviewing

One variation on this procedure is team interviewing, involving two or more interviewers. The team usually consists of a human resources representative, the department manager, and the department head. This type of interview may be conducted to save time or to compare impressions of an applicant.

Team interviews can be very effective if carefully planned. For example, each interviewer's role should be agreed on ahead of time. Generally the human resources representative begins by asking broad questions to determine overall job suitability; then the manager asks more detailed, technical questions; finally, the department head pursues the candidate's potential as well as other intangible factors.

Regardless of how the questions are divided, applicants should always be advised ahead of time that a team interview is going to take place. Otherwise it can be quite unnerving for the applicant to see more than one interviewer in the room. Seating should also be carefully arranged. Unlike a one-on-one interview, where the proximity of the interviewer's chair to the applicant's chair is inconsequential, a team interview situation can create an uncomfortable and intimidating environment for the applicant. The applicant's chair should not be surrounded, with one seat on either side and one seat directly in front. This can result in a "tennis match" sort of interview, with the candidate continually turning his or her head from one side to the other, trying to address everyone in the room. Instead, the interviewers' chairs should form a soft arc in front of the applicant. This setting is less structured and more conducive to a productive exchange.

Preinterview Guidelines

Being thoroughly prepared for an interview will help you learn key information about each candidate, avoid possible discrimination charges, and use your interview time efficiently.

Become Familiar With the Applicant's Background and Qualifications

Never conduct an interview without first reviewing the applicant's completed application form and/or resumé. Regardless of how pressed for time you may be, it is critical that you set aside time for this important step, because it will allow you to draw some preliminary conclusions about the person's job suitability and identify key areas about which you will require additional information.

Every organization should have an application form that reflects its own particular environment. However, certain categories are common to most organizations and appear on most application forms:

Statement regarding the organization's commitment to EEO
Date
Name
Address
Telephone number
Social security number
Position applied for
Date available to begin work
Referral source
Whether applicant ever applied to, or worked for, the company before
Whether above minimum working age
Eligibility to work in the United States

Conviction record

Physical, mental, or medical impairments that would interfere with performance of the job applied for

U.S. military service record

Job-related languages spoken, read, or written fluently

Membership in professional organizations related to position applied for

Employment experience

Education and training

Additional qualifications

References

Special notice to veterans and other individuals with disabilities (for organizations with government contracts)

Agreement statement

At-will statement

A sample application form appears in Appendix F.

Applications and resumés should be reviewed for the following key areas before the actual interview is conducted:

- *Overall appearance.* The application and resumé should be neat, legible, and easy to read. If communication skills are a relevant job factor, then grammar and spelling should be correct.
- *Blanks and omissions.* Follow up on any missing information during the interview.
- *Gaps in time.* Inquire about any gaps of more than one month.
- *Overlaps in time.* Pursue overlapping dates, such as working at two job simultaneously or attending school and working at the same time.
- *Inconsistencies.* Question any inconsistencies, such as a master's degree and a series of nonexempt jobs.
- *Frequency of job changes.* Investigate an excessive number of job changes in a short period of time, that is, an average of more than one job change per year.
- *Salary history.* Ask about radical changes in salary, either upward or downward.
- *Reasons for leaving previous positions.* Explore patterns of reasons for leaving previous employers, especially if job changes have been fairly frequent.
- *Job titles.* Many job titles are not functional or descriptive, so ask about actual responsibilities if this information is not included on the application form.

- *"Red-flag" areas.* Follow up on any information that does not seem to make sense or that leaves you with an uneasy feeling.

The purpose of reviewing completed applications and resumés in this way is to identify areas to probe during the interview, not to make judgments and decisions about job suitability.

Be Certain That All Inquiries Are Job Related

When reviewing your company's application form, make sure all categories are job related, or you could be accused of violating EEO laws. The same holds true for all verbal preemployment inquiries.

Most people have a general idea of what categories to steer clear of during an employment interview. They know that questions related to race, religion, sex, national origin, and age should be avoided. Some questions, however, have traditionally been considered acceptable during an interview, and the reader may not realize that they are discriminatory.

It is important to note that asking these questions is not, in and of itself, illegal. Rather, once you have ascertained the information, you may be charged with illegal usage. For example, asking a female applicant whether she has children is not an illegal question. If, however, you decide not to hire her because she answers affirmatively and you anticipate excessive absenteeism, this may constitute illegal discrimination. Even if you decide not to hire her for other reasons, she may charge you with discrimination, and you will have to show that her having children had no impact on your hiring decision.

Bear in mind, too, that just because you do not directly ask an applicant—either via the application form or verbally—for specific information, he or she may offer it. If this occurs, you are just as liable. Suppose, for instance, you inform an applicant that the position for which she is being considered involves travel. You then ask whether she foresees any problem in being able to leave for a business trip with very little advance notice. She responds by saying, "Oh, that will be no problem at all. My mother has been baby-sitting for my three kids ever since my divorce last year." The applicant has just volunteered information about two categories that are not job related: children and marital status. If she is rejected, she might conceivably claim discrimination on the basis of this information, even though you did not solicit it.

Should a candidate provide you with information you know you should not have, make certain of three things:

1. Do not, under any circumstances, write the information down.
2. Do not pursue the subject with the applicant.
3. Tell the applicant that the information is not job related and that you want to return to discussing his or her qualifications for the job opening.

Table 1 shows the most common categories and questions to avoid during the employment interview, both verbally and on the application form. Recommended inquiries are also listed, as well as the categories of applicants against whom the nonrecommended inquiries might discriminate. Note, however, that in instances where these inquiries can be shown to be bona-fide occupational qualifications (BFOQs)—that is, legitimate job requirements—then certain of these questions are acceptable.

After looking over the table, you may fear that there is very little you can ask an applicant. Although there are many categories interviewers must avoid, the categories of education and experience will provide most of the information needed to make an effective hiring decision, without violating any EEO laws.

Carefully Schedule Interviews

Professional or exempt interviews generally take from 45 to 60 minutes. They should never exceed 90 minutes. If your interviews take longer than this, it is probably because you are repeating certain questions, seeking unnecessary information, or letting the conversation wander off on tangents. If you cannot complete the interview in 90 minutes, arrange for a break, or schedule another appointment at a later date. You can absorb only so much information at one time, and lengthy interviews can be unnecessarily stressful for the candidate.

Nonexempt interviews generally last 30 to 45 minutes. More concrete areas are probed at this level, such as specific job duties and attendance records. These take less time to explore than the many intangible areas examined at the exempt level, such as management style, degree of creativity, and initiative.

Remember to allow an additional 5 to 10 minutes before the interview to review the application and/or resumé and to plan questions, as well as another 5 to 10 minutes afterward for writing up notes and arranging additional interviews if appropriate. (Extra time will be needed if you are conducting and evaluating any preemployment tests.) See Appendix G for an interview evaluation form that may prove helpful for writing up your interview notes.

(Text continues on page 99.)

Table 1. Preemployment inquiries.

Category of Inquiry	Inquiries Not Recommended	Inquiries Recommended	Possible Categories of Discrimination
Name	"What is your maiden name?" "Have you ever used any other name?" "Have you ever changed your name?"	"Have you ever worked for this company under any other name?" "Is there any information about a change of name that would help us in conducting a reference check?"	Women Minorities Applicants of foreign national origin
Address	"Do you rent or own your own home?"	"Where do you live? How long have you lived there?"	Women Minorities
Age	"How old are you?" "What is your date of birth?" "Are you between 18 and 24, 25 and 34, etc.?" "Please show proof of age."	"Are you over the age of [minimum working age]?" "Are you above the minimum working age?"	Older applicants
Physical appearance	"How tall are you?" "How much do you weigh?"	No inquiries pertaining to physical appearance, unless they are job related	Women Applicants of foreign national origin
Citizenship and national origin	"Of what country are you a citizen?" "Where were you born?" "Where were your parents born?" "Are you a naturalized or a native-born citizen?" "What is your nationality?"	"Are you legally permitted to work in the United States? If so, will you be prepared to produce proof at the time of hire in accordance with the Immigration Reform and Control Act of 1986?"	Applicants of foreign national origin

(continues)

Category of Inquiry	Inquiries Not Recommended	Inquiries Recommended	Possible Categories of Discrimination
Marital status	"What is your marital status?" "Do you wish to be addressed as Mrs., Miss, or Ms.?"	No inquiries pertaining to marital status	Women
Children	"Do you have any children?" "How many children do you have?" "What child care arrangements have you made?" "Do you intend to have children?"	No inquiries pertaining to children	Women
Police records	"Have you ever been arrested?"	"Have you ever been convicted of a crime? felony? crime greater than a misdemeanor?"	Minorities
Religion	"What is your religious background?" "Is there anything in your religious beliefs that would prevent you from working on a Saturday or a Sunday?"	No inquiries about religion. If information on Saturday or Sunday availability is needed, ask, "Is there any reason you would be unable to work on a Saturday or Sunday, as required of this job?"	Applicants practicing certain religious beliefs
Disabilities	"Do you have any disabilities?" "Have you ever been treated for any of the following diseases?"	"Are you able to perform the essential functions of the job for which you are applying with or without a reasonable accommodation?"	Applicants with disabilities

Category of Inquiry	Inquiries Not Recommended	Inquiries Recommended	Possible Categories of Discrimination
	"Do you have any physical, mental, or medical impediments that would interfere with your ability to perform the job for which you are applying?" "Are there any positions or duties for which you should not be considered because of existing medical, physical, or mental disabilities?"	without a reasonable accommodation?"	
Photographs	Any requirement that a photo be supplied before hiring	Statement that a photo may be required after hiring	Women Minorities
Languages (if job related)	"What is your native language?" "How did you learn a foreign language?"	"What languages do you speak, read, or write fluently? What is the degree of fluency?"	Applicants of foreign national origin
Relatives	"Whom should we notify in the event of an emergency?" Any inquiry calling for the names, addresses, ages, number, or other information regarding the applicant's relatives not employed by the company	"Do you have any relatives, other than a spouse, already employed by this company?"	Applicants of foreign national origin
Military experience	"Have you ever served in the armed forces of any country?" "What kind of discharge did you re-	"Have you ever served in any of the U.S. military services?" "Describe your du-	Women Minorities Applicants of foreign national origin

(continues)

Category of Inquiry	Inquiries Not Recommended	Inquiries Recommended	Possible Categories of Discrimination
	ceive from the service?"	ties while in the U.S. service."	
Organizations	"What clubs or organizations do you belong to?"	"What professional organizations or business activities are you involved with relevant to your ability to perform the job to which you are applying?"	Women Minorities Applicants of foreign national origin Applicants practicing certain religious beliefs
References	A requirement that a reference be supplied by a particular kind of person, such as a religious leader	Names of people willing to provide professional references	Women Minorities
Finances	"Do you have any overdue bills?"	No inquiries regarding an applicant's financial status	Women Minorities
Education	"Are you a high school/college graduate?"	"What is the highest grade you completed?" "What academic, vocational, or professional schools have you attended and when?"	Women Minorities
Experience	Any inquiry regarding work experience not related to the job	"Describe all your prior work experience, concentrating on how it relates to the position for which you are applying."	Women Minorities

Provide a Comfortable Environment for the Applicant

There should be no interruptions during an interview. The environment should also be private so that the applicant will be more likely to reveal important job-related information. Of course, a comfortable seating arrangement and an offer of refreshments also contribute to an ideal interview environment.

Review Your Goals and Objectives

Consider the goals of the overall organization, division, and department; the general atmosphere in your organization; the distribution of responsibilities in the department; and the personalities of coworkers and managers with whom the new employee will be working. This will help you form a clear picture of the type of applicant who will fit in best.

Prepare Key Questions

Planning basic questions prior to meeting an applicant will help you focus on key areas and elicit the information needed to make an effective hiring decision.

Be sure that most of your questions are open-ended and broad enough so that the applicant's response will trigger additional questions. (More detail about open-ended questions appears later in this chapter.) As discussed earlier, identify information on the completed application form and/or resumé requiring elaboration. You might also review the job description, identifying required skills and experience and developing questions to determine whether the applicant meets the established standards. No more than half a dozen questions need to be prepared in advance.

Here are some general questions about experience that may be planned in advance:

- "Please describe your activities during a typical day at your present (or most recent) job."
- "What do (did) you like most and least about your present (most recent) job? Why?"
- "Describe a situation in your present (most recent) job involving _____. How did you handle it?"
- "What are (were) some of the duties in your present (most recent) job that you find (found) difficult? Why?"

- "Why do (did) you want to leave your present (most recent) job?"
- "How do you generally approach tasks you dislike? Please give me a specific example related to your present (most recent) job."

And here are some general questions about education that may be planned in advance:

- "What were your favorite and least favorite subjects in school (high school, college, and so on)? Why?"
- "Why did you decide to major in _____?"
- "Describe your study habits."
- "How do you feel your studies in the area of _____ prepared you for this job?"

For basic entry-level positions that do not require prior experience or specific education, interviewers may prepare questions about hypothetical situations that are likely to occur on the job and ask the applicant how he or she would handle them.

Consider the Role of Perception During an Interview

We all develop opinions about others, often before having an opportunity to get to know them very well. During the interview process, this may occur in a variety of ways:

- We may form early opinions when reading an applicant's resumé or completed application form.
- We may be influenced by something we hear about a person, such as from a referral source.
- We may form first impressions based on a person's clothing, appearance, or grooming.
- We may make decisions based on an applicant's response to a single question.
- We may misinterpret nonverbal messages.
- We may interpret the behavior of others on the basis of our own personal values and standards.

Be aware of these perception traps, and instead objectively evaluate applicants on the basis of their job-related skills and experience.

Establish an Interview Format

Developing a system will lend structure and form to the interview. The format chosen should reflect your individual style and personality, but every format should include the following important ingredients:

- Asking questions
- Providing job-related information
- Describing the organization
- Describing the available position
- Allowing the applicant to ask questions
- Telling the applicant what will happen following the interview

Interview Guidelines

These pointers will help managers, department heads, and human resources representatives conduct effective interviews.

Establish Rapport

Taking a few moments at the beginning of an interview to put the applicant at ease will result in a more relaxed atmosphere and, consequently, a greater exchange of information. Neutral "icebreaker" statements or questions, such as those relating to the weather or traffic, are excellent rapport-building beginners to an employment interview.

Practice Active Listening Skills

Interviewers should concentrate closely on what the applicant is saying and should talk no more than 30 percent of the time. The interviewer's 30 percent of the talking should focus on asking questions, providing information, answering questions, encouraging the applicant to talk, periodically summarizing, and keeping the applicant on track.

Take Notes

Write down key words and ideas during the interview. Immediately following the interview, review, elaborate on, and clarify your notes as necessary.

Practice Using and Interpreting Body Language

Nonverbal communication, or body language, can easily be misinterpreted, so you should try to use gestures and movements that are likely to be interpreted positively. For example, smiling, nodding, and leaning forward usually indicate agreement, understanding, encouragement, or interest. Avoiding eye contact, yawning, excessive shifting about in your seat, and folding your arms may be interpreted negatively, so avoid these. Also strive for consistency between verbal statements and nonverbal expressions.

Be aware of the applicant's nonverbal pattern. Each of us has our own pattern of body language. Be patient, and allow the applicant's nonverbal pattern to emerge during an interview. Be especially careful not to interpret an applicant's body language according to your pattern.

Interviewers should also watch for sudden changes in an applicant's body language when a particular question is asked. This is a clue that additional probing is needed, even if the accompanying verbal response seems acceptable.

Encourage the Applicant to Talk

Some applicants have no trouble whatsoever talking about themselves. Others, however, need to be drawn out. Using positive body language yourself will encourage applicants to talk. Brief verbal statements such as "Really," "How interesting," and "Please tell me more" are also encouraging. In addition, periodically summarizing what the applicant has said or repeating part of his or her most recent statement often encourages an applicant to provide additional information.

Practice Effective Questioning Techniques

Hypothetical and open-ended questions will yield the most valuable information during an interview. Hypothetical questions present situations related to the available position to the applicant for solution. The questions are generally introduced with phrases such as, "What would you do if . . . ?" or "How would you handle . . . ?" Open-ended questions yield the most information and allow the applicant considerable latitude in responding. Even more important, they provide information on which additional questions may be built. It is significant to note that any question that can be answered yes or no can be converted into an open-ended question. For example, instead of asking, "Do you like your present job?" ask, "What do you like about your present job?" Or in lieu of "Would you describe your present work as hard?" say, "Describe those aspects of your present job that you find most difficult. Why do you feel that's so?"

Adjust Your Approach When Dealing With Difficult Applicants

For the most part, applicants strive to put their best foot forward during an employment interview. After all, if they hope to be selected for a job, it is logical to assume that they will do their best to make a good impression. However, you may occasionally find yourself face-to-face with a contrary, nervous, defensive, angry, shy, overly talkative, or distraught applicant. These applicants require some variation from your regular interviewing approach:

Contrary applicants. Actively listen to what is being said and try to uncover the underlying reason for the applicant's behavior. Do not become defensive or challenge the applicant. Periodically establish whether the applicant is still interested in the available position, and try to focus on job-related skills and qualifications.

Nervous applicants. Explain the purpose and outline the format of the interview. Begin by discussing areas with which the applicant is likely to feel most familiar and comfortable. Encourage the applicant to ask questions.

Defensive applicants. Repeatedly express an interest in the applicant's skills and qualifications. Explain that your goal is to determine job suitability and that you therefore wish to focus on specific job-related areas. To achieve this, ask a series of specific, closed-ended questions.

Angry applicants. Allow the applicant to blow off steam for a few moments, listening closely for any valid reasons for the anger. Assure the applicant that an expression of feelings will not be held against him or her, but that a continuation of such behavior will make it increasingly difficult for you to conduct an objective interview. If the situation becomes too emotionally charged, suggest that the applicant call you later to discuss the possibility of rescheduling the interview.

Shy applicants. Try asking a few closed-ended questions to put the applicant more at ease. Make your questions simple, relating to areas with which the applicant has experience. Use a softer tone of voice, and pay particular attention to using positive body language and words of encouragement.

Overly talkative applicants. Interrupt the applicant to bring him or her back on track or when you have received sufficient information in response to a particular question. Periodically remind the applicant that you have only a limited amount of time for the interview.

Distraught applicants. Extend empathy, as opposed to sympathy, to applicants who may weep or plead for jobs. Emotional involvement will cloud your objectivity. Allow such applicants a few moments to collect themselves before proceeding. Explain that they will be given equal consideration with all the other applicants for the job. Focus on job-related areas, and encourage the applicant to talk about specific skills and qualifications.

Pitfalls to Avoid

Here are some common pitfalls that interviewers should try to avoid:

- Avoid interrupting the applicant as long as what he or she is saying is relevant.
- Avoid expressing agreement or disagreement; express only interest or understanding.
- Avoid terminology or language the applicant is unlikely to understand.
- Do not allow the applicant to interview you or to control the interview.
- Avoid reading the application form or resumé back to the applicant.
- Avoid comparing the applicant with yourself when you had the job, the incumbent, or the last person in the job.
- Avoid asking more than one question at a time.
- Avoid asking questions that might be considered illegal, even in a roundabout way.
- Do not be insensitive to cultural or educational differences between yourself and the applicant.

Selection Guidelines

All those involved in the interviewing process should share their impression of the applicants under final consideration. This usually includes a representative from the human resources department and one or more representatives from the department in which the opening exists. In most cases, an analysis of all the data collected as they relate to the requirements of the position will point in the direction of one candidate, and everyone will agree that he or she should be the one hired. However, sometimes the human resources representative will favor one candidate and the departmental representative will prefer another. If this should occur, the departmental representative should be the one to make the final hiring decision. After all, he or she is the one who will be working with the new hire every day.

Here are some guidelines that may help you reach a final hiring decision:

- Review your goals and objectives.
- Review the duties and responsibilities of the available position, as well as required skills and knowledge.
- Consider the intangible requirements of the job.
- Review and compare the experience and education of all the candidates under final consideration.
- Review and compare the intangible qualities of all the candidates.
- Be wary of applicants who did not let you end the interview, bad-mouthed former employers, asked questions about areas you had already discussed, had difficulty with or refused to answer certain questions, seemed more interested in the photographs on your desk than in what you were saying, or arrived late and did not offer to explain why.
- Review and compare the applicants' reactions to key questions asked during the face-to-face interview.
- Consider the patterns of body language exhibited by each candidate during the interview.
- Consider the salary requirements of each candidate in relation to the salary range for the position.
- Review each applicant's reason for leaving previous employers.
- Conduct reference checks and compare the feedback received.
- Assess each applicant's potential.
- Consider your company's affirmative action goals.

Orientation Programs

A comprehensive orientation program for new employees consists of both a formal organizational orientation program managed by the human resources department and a departmental orientation program.

Organizational Orientation Programs

The organizational orientation program generally runs from half a day to a full day. It is meant to help new employees become accustomed to their surroundings, acquire a sense of belonging, and learn what the organization has to offer and what it expects of them—thus providing an overall perspective of their new employer. This broad perspective can benefit new employees in their present jobs, help them develop a sense of commitment to the organization, and help them plan a future with the company.

In some companies, new hires in all job classifications participate in the same program. In others, one presentation is offered to exempt employees, and another is provided for nonexempt employees. This is usually done when there is a substantial difference in the specific information offered, such as managerial benefits and policies pertaining to executives. In very small companies, everyone usually attends the same session, regardless of exemption status or title.

Although orientation programs are designed for new employees, some companies invite existing employees as well. A refresher on such matters as organizational goals and standards of performance can be very helpful. Attending an orientation program can also motivate existing employees by making them feel that they are still important to the company. Having them attend the same session as new hires may be effective since it allows for an exchange between the newcomers and the existing workers. In general, however, a separate session is scheduled to avoid unnecessary repetition of certain points.

Because discussion is an important element of an effective orientation program, the number of participants should be limited to a maximum of twenty. The ideal group size is from twelve to fifteen; this encourages an exchange among the new hires and still allows them to ask questions.

The site selected for your organizational orientation program should be centrally located and convenient for most employees to reach. It should easily accommodate the number of people scheduled to attend but not be too large. Tables should be provided, since literature is likely to be distributed; also, employees will probably want to jot down notes during the presentation. Tables and chairs should be arranged in a casual manner—perhaps round tables as opposed to classroom style.

There are six main topics that should be covered in the orientation program of a small or mid-sized company:

1. An overview of the organization's history, overall function, and present status

2. A description of the company's philosophy, goals, and objectives, and how important each employee is in helping to achieve them
3. General industry information and special terminology
4. An explanation of the organization's structure and unique features
5. An outline of company standards of performance, rules, expectations, policies, procedures, and safety and security practices
6. A description of benefits and employee services

Someone from human resources should be in charge of the overall program. This responsibility entails:

- Planning the specific content
- Scheduling the speakers
- Preparing the presentation media and supplemental material
- Reserving space
- Scheduling employees
- Making opening and closing remarks
- Introducing each speaker
- Conducting tours

Because of this wide range of responsibilities, the human resources representative selected should be knowledgeable about the organization and have presentation skills. The latter is important for generating enthusiasm and interest among the participants.

In mid-sized companies, experts in various human resources topics should also be involved. For example:

- A benefits expert might discuss insurance and OSHA regulations.
- A salary administrator might discuss the grading system, the performance appraisal process, and salary increase guidelines.
- A training and development specialist might discuss growth opportunities and tuition reimbursement.

Just like the human resources generalist, these topical experts should be knowledgeable and possess presentation skills. Particularly with dry subjects like insurance, it is critical for the presenters to be able to generate interest and facilitate retention.

Also, all employees, regardless of classification, should be familiar with key officers of the organization. Having representatives from senior management participate briefly in the orientation program will accomplish this end. In addition to welcoming the new hires to the organization, officers might briefly describe the primary functions of their departments and discuss how their units relate to the organization as a whole. This will add to the employees' holistic view of the company. Furthermore, female and minority representatives from senior management may serve to promote an organization's EEO and affirmative action policy and inspire future growth.

Orientation information can be imparted in a variety of ways:

- Lecture by one or more speakers
- Transparencies and charts
- Handout materials
- Films and slides
- Question-and-answer periods
- Tours

Straight lecture, even by representatives from several different departments, can be boring. Supplemental transparencies and/or charts highlighting key points will help the employees both understand and retain what is being presented. Handout materials are useful because employees can refer to them later. Professionally prepared films or slides can be very effective as well. Bear in mind that updating a film is far more difficult and costly than revising slides. In addition, questions raised during the course of the film have to wait until the end to be addressed.

Answering questions as soon as they occur is far preferable to having a formal question-and-answer period. Encouraging a free exchange between speakers and participants promotes a more relaxed, less intimidating atmosphere.

A tour of major company departments enables employees to understand more fully how their work relates to other units of the organization.

Employees should attend orientation as soon after beginning work as possible. (Some organizations even require new hires to attend before their first day on the job, but this is impractical because most people continue to work for another employer until beginning a new position.) The first or second day of work is the best time to begin orientation. Employees are not yet caught up in the details of their jobs, and there is little chance of their receiving inaccurate information from other sources.

Departmental Orientation Programs

Managers should be responsible for providing a separate orientation program for all new employees in their departments. This plays an important role in shaping a new employee's attitude toward the company and the specific job, since first impressions have been shown to greatly influence employee turnover, attendance, and performance. Thus managers should be careful to be as encouraging, supportive, and sincere as possible.

During the departmental orientation, managers should describe procedures and introduce new employees to their coworkers. Some of the topics that might be included in a departmental orientation are:

- The department's hierarchy
- Specific responsibilities of the department
- Relationships between departments
- Reporting relationships
- Specific job duties and responsibilities
- Work schedule
- Overtime requirements
- Scheduling of meals and breaks
- Department rules, such as those about personal telephone calls and visitors

New employees should be encouraged to ask questions and to come and see the manager as needed. Lines of communication should be kept open from the outset.

As soon as a prospective employee's starting date is confirmed, his or her manager should make a notation to keep that day as free from appointments as possible. This way, the manager can give full attention to meeting the needs of the new worker. If a clear calendar cannot be arranged, then at least some time during the day—preferably first thing in the morning—should be set aside to spend with the new employee. Arrangements should also be made for a sponsor to assist the new hire in getting settled throughout the day.

When the new employee reports to work for the first time, devote several minutes to putting him or her at ease and establishing rapport. Then take a few moments to describe the scheduled activities of the day. If a great deal has been planned, a typed agenda is appropriate. Otherwise, briefly describe what is to occur. To illustrate:

> Janet, after we finish talking, I'll take you around the department to meet everyone. Then I'm going to turn you over to Bruce Jenkins, our production manager. He'll show you your office, tell you where everything is, and essentially explain how to get around. I'll meet you back here at 11:45 so that we can go

to lunch. I've made reservations for us at the officers' dining room; the food there is quite good. Then, at 1:00, Bruce will take you over to the human resources department for the organizational orientation program. When that ends at 4:45, come back to my office so that we can talk. I'll answer any questions you may have formed throughout the day, and we can discuss what's been scheduled for tomorrow.

Now it is time to introduce the new worker to others with whom he or she will be working. Generally these people will all be in the same department, but introductions may extend to employees in other units if the new hire will be working with them regularly. If there are to be more than half a dozen introductions, it is a good idea to have a sheet typed up in advance with everyone's name, title, and office location, and telephone extension if applicable. This can help make the experience less overwhelming.

As you take the new hire around, be careful not to express your opinions about each person—for example, "Janet, the next person you're going to meet is Bob Johnson. Watch out for him during staff meetings; he's notorious for stealing ideas and submitting them as his own." Or, "When I introduce you to Fred Walters, don't take it personally if he acts as if he doesn't like you. He applied for your position through job posting but was rejected. He thinks you cheated him out of a promotion." Positive statements should be avoided as well: "Janet, I'd like you to meet Rod Perret. Rod can always be counted on to help you meet impossible deadlines."

New employees should be permitted to form their own opinions about their coworkers. Therefore, any statement that is subjective or judgmental should be avoided. Instead, focus on being descriptive. As you approach each worker, briefly describe his or her overall function. Limit yourself to one or two sentences per person so that the new employee can later remember what you said.

Once the introductions have been completed, it is time to show the employee exactly where he or she will be working and to explain where everything is located. Generally, the manager assigns a sponsor to the new hire for this purpose. Be certain that the person selected is thoroughly familiar with the layout of the area and can devote the necessary amount of time to explain everything.

Preparation for this stage of the new hire's departmental orientation should include a checklist of items to make certain no details are omitted. This list might include the following points:

1. *Show the new employee his or her office, desk, or work area.* This is probably the first time the employee will be seeing exactly where he or she will be working. If others work nearby, explain what they do in relation to the new worker's responsibilities. If the employee has a private office, describe any company policies about pictures on the walls and plants. (Some organizations are rather inflexible about such matters, and employees should be informed of this right away.)

2. *Show the employee where supplies are located, and explain how to order them.* The desks of new office employees, and the work areas of other new employees, should be stocked with all necessary supplies. Describe the department's procedure for obtaining additional supplies. There may be a central supply room where employees merely go and take whatever they need. If this is the case, take the employee there and briefly explain where everything is located. Or your organization may require employees to fill out supply requisition forms. If so, explain where to get the forms, whom to give them to when completed, and approximately how long it takes to receive the requested items. Also explain any exceptions to the regular policies. For example, ordering a new chair or desk will undoubtedly require more paperwork and signatures than requesting a pair of scissors.

3. *Provide the employee with a telephone directory, and explain how the phone system works.* All employees should know how they can reach others within the organization, so provide a directory of departments, key employees and their titles, and telephone extensions and/or intercom numbers. Many organizations have rather complex phone systems; rarely can one pick up a telephone and simply dial the desired number. Be certain to explain thoroughly such factors as dialing prefixes, special codes, the intercom system, reaching numbers outside the organization, how to put someone on hold, and conference calls. If your phone system is complicated, a typed sheet describing it will be handy for the employee to refer to later.

4. *Show the employee the location of rest rooms and water fountains.* It is amazing how many employees hesitate to ask about the location of these two items. It only takes a moment to show the new employee where the rest rooms and water fountains are. If there are several throughout the department, point them out.

5. *Show the employee how to operate the photocopy machine, fax machine, or any other equipment he or she will use.* In some companies, all duplicating and faxing is done by a clerk. If this is the case, indicate who is in charge of these tasks and where he or she is located. If all employees do their

own photocopying and faxing in your company, demonstrate how the machines operate and explain whom to contact if they malfunction.

If the new employee will be using any other machinery or equipment, show where it is and how it works.

6. *Show the employee where files are.* Show the new hire where the department's files are located, and explain how they are set up. Also describe any procedure for signing out a file.

7. *Introduce the employee to the company food service program.* If your company has a cafeteria, take the new employee on a brief tour. Describe what kind of food is offered, the price range, and the hours it is open. If the employee is entitled to eat in an executive dining room, include this in your tour as well. Be sure to provide information about its hours, whether reservations are required, the method of payment, and the policy on guests.

If your organization has a coffee cart that comes around to each department, tell the new hire approximately what time to expect it each day, and where it stops. You might also describe what is offered and give a sample of prices.

8. *Show the employee the lounge.* If your organization has an employee lounge, take the new employee on a brief tour. Describe what activities are permitted and prohibited, such as eating, smoking, watching television, playing the radio, and playing cards or other games.

9. *Show the employee exercise facilities.* More and more companies are providing their employees with an exercise facility. This may include a running track, gymnastic equipment, and even group exercise classes scheduled before and after working hours. If your organization has such a program, be certain to describe its hours, who is eligible to participate, how often, and what gear or clothing is required.

10. *Explain the procedure for medical care.* Explain where the new employee should go for nonemergency medical care, any procedures to be followed, and any forms that must be filled out.

11. *Show the employee the child care facilities.* If your organization has a child care program, take the new hire on a brief tour and explain how it operates. Be sure to include eligibility requirements, a description of who watches the children, how many children are assigned to each caretaker, and the cost. Tell the employee whom to contact for additional information.

It is a good idea to give the new employee a list highlighting the applicable categories described above, so that he or she can jot down notes as you talk. Some of the points mentioned above—such as the cafeteria, employee lounge, exercise facility, and child care facility—may also be included in a tour conducted as part of the organizational orientation. At this stage, repetition can only serve to reinforce what the employee is being told and shown.

By the time the lunch hour rolls around on an employee's first day, he or she is probably feeling somewhat overwhelmed. Therefore, arrangements should be made for someone to take the new person to lunch. This is generally done by the employee's immediate boss or the sponsor who has been in charge of showing him or her around. Sometimes a new hire's coworkers assume this responsibility. In any event, it should be someone who will be likely to eat with this person again in the near future.

If your company has a cafeteria, it is a good idea to go there so that the new employee can begin to become familiar with its offerings. In addition, you can informally introduce other employees who are in the cafeteria at that time. If the company has an executive dining room and the new employee is eligible to eat there, then plan on doing so the first day.

Remember that your purpose in taking a new employee to lunch is to make the person feel welcome and comfortable. Be careful not to get carried away, as did the vice president who insisted on taking a new clerk in his department to the executive dining room. The executive's intentions were good, but the gesture was inappropriate. The clerk enjoyed the experience immensely and, quite understandably, expected it to be repeated. Since it was his very first job, he did not realize that lunch in the executive dining room was a one-shot deal. He waited for the vice president to invite him again, and when the invitation was not forthcoming, he assumed that there was a problem with his job performance. His work began to be affected, and, as a result, his six-month review reflected satisfactory rather than outstanding performance.

New employees should ideally attend organizational orientation for at least part of the first or second day. If this cannot be arranged for the first day, then the balance of the time should be devoted to introducing the employee to the department's policies and procedures. If the new hire will be working in a supervisory or managerial capacity, the department manager should be certain to provide him or her with a copy of the organization's HR policies and procedures manual. The manager should take time to familiarize the person with the overall content, explain how and when the manual is to be used, and also mention the person to contact if clarification is needed.

If appropriate, the manager should also provide the new hire with a departmental table of organization and walk the employee through it, describing the primary functions of each position and individual. In addition, the employee should be provided with work manuals, instructions, or any other printed materials relevant to his or her specific job.

Regardless of how the day is spent, it should conclude the way it began: with a meeting between the employee and his or her supervisor or manager. A period of approximately half an hour should be set aside to discuss what took place during the day, as well as to answer any questions the employee may have. In addition, the following day's agenda should be reviewed.

Promotions, Transfers, and Demotions

A *promotion* is the movement of an employee into a position in a higher salary grade involving greater responsibility or skill. There should be a salary increase at the time of promotion. Performance appraisal dates should be adjusted according to the date of promotion and salary increase. Under no circumstances should the salary of an employee fall below the minimum for the salary range of the new position.

It is cost-effective, efficient, and motivating to fill newly created or vacated positions through promotions from within an organization whenever possible. This way, an organization can fulfill its needs and make the best use of the talents and abilities of existing staff members.

A job-posting system monitored by the human resources department is the most popular means by which employees may be promoted. Under this system, promotions are awarded on the basis of an employee's current job performance and specific job-related qualifications.

Managers may also recommend employees for promotion. In fact, a good manager should be on the alert for employees who are qualified to move up.

The most successful promotion-from-within programs exist in organizations that promote ongoing training programs to help employees develop beyond their present skill levels. These organizations also have systems for recognizing and rewarding individual achievement.

If a position cannot be filled from within via promotion and someone from the outside is brought into the organization instead, it is advisable to post or distribute a brief description of the person's credentials. This should help alleviate any hard feelings on the part of employees who applied for and were denied a promotion to the available position.

A *transfer* is the movement of an employee into a position in the same salary grade involving comparable responsibilities or skills. Transfers may take place for a number of different reasons:

- An employee may not be appropriately suited to his or her present job.
- An employee's present job may be eliminated.
- There might be a work-related conflict between an employee and his or her coworkers or manager.
- A reorganization might necessitate the redistribution of labor.
- An employee might wish to work closer to home.
- An employee may need training in several different departments before achieving a certain job status.
- The expansion of a business may necessitate the transfer of in-house talent.

When an employee is transferred, his or her performance review date generally remains the same. The existing manager will review the employee at the time of transfer; the new manager will then evaluate the employee on his or her next regularly scheduled review date. If there has not been a sufficient period of time—at least three months—for the new manager to assess the employee's performance, the review date may be postponed for a period of up to three months, with any increase made retroactive to the original review date.

A *demotion* is the movement of an employee into a position in a lower salary grade involving less responsibility or skill. Demotions generally occur when an employee is unable to meet the performance requirements of his or her present assignment. Demotions should never be used punitively. When coaching, counseling, or training cannot help bring about an improvement in work behavior, demotion to a lower position may help place employees into more appropriate jobs, thereby allowing them to function more effectively. This also holds true for employees who were mismatched from the outset.

Most organizations are reluctant to reduce the earnings of demoted workers. If an employee's present earnings do not exceed the maximum of the salary range for the lower job category, the move generally takes place without a reduction in pay. Of course, future increases should be based on the new job classification.

All instances of demotion should be thoroughly discussed between the employee's manager and a human resources representative before any action is taken. The actual demotion should be handled with tact and diplomacy in order to make the transition as smooth as possible.

Terminations and Exit Interviews

When employees voluntarily terminate their employment with an organization, two to four weeks' notice is generally expected, depending on their level. Similarly, employees being terminated by an employer are often given two to four weeks' notice or pay in lieu of notice. Severance pay policies vary, often depending upon an employee's length of service with the company. Of course, severance pay is not required, and a formal severance pay policy is not necessary. In most cases, severance pay is provided when employees lose their jobs because of relocation of the company, a cutback in production, or an acquisition or merger.

Employees who terminate their employment for any reason are generally paid for any unused vacation time accrued under the company's vacation policy. Compensation for unused sick days may also be offered.

Deciding on whether to have a severance pay policy may well be one of the least complex issues surrounding termination. Far more complicated are the conditions under which an employer may terminate an employee. Generally, unless there is a written contract defining the terms of employment, an employer has the right to terminate an employee at any time without liability.

Employees terminating their employment with an organization for any reason should be given an *exit interview*. Ideally, there should be two exit interviews: one conducted by the employee's manager, and one conducted by a human resources representative. If only one exit interview can be arranged, then it should be with the human resources representative.

Exit interviews are vital in helping an organization continue to improve employer-employee relations. Management must have a clear understanding of why employees wish to leave their organization and seek employment elsewhere. Even if an employee is being terminated, it is important to determine how he or she felt about working conditions while employed.

Terminating employees should be reassured that the information requested during an exit interview will not be used against them in any way.

Questionnaires are often used as a guide during exit interviews to ensure that important areas are not overlooked. The questions should be asked verbally, and any notes taken by the interviewer should be verified for accuracy by the employee.

Here are some questions that might appear on an exit-interview questionnaire:

- "What is your reason for leaving?"
- "Was your job accurately represented and described at the time of hire?"
- "What did you enjoy most about working for this organization?"
- "What would you have changed about your employment if you could have?"
- "Do you feel that the benefits you received were comprehensive? Please explain."
- "Do you feel that you were fairly compensated for the work you did? Please explain."
- "How would you describe the environment in which you worked? Include interrelations with managers, coworkers, and subordinates."
- "How would you describe the working conditions?"
- "What, if anything, could have been done to dissuade you from terminating your employment with this organization?"

In addition to responding to the questions on the questionnaire, departing employees should be encouraged to add any additional comments. The completed exit interview questionnaire should be placed in the terminating employee's personnel folder.

It is the responsibility of human resources to investigate any departmental patterns that may become clear from a series of exit interviews. Several departing employees might report that they are leaving because the job was misrepresented at the time of hire, or because the working conditions are unsatisfactory, or because there is too much work and not enough staff. Such patterns should be brought to the attention of the department head so that the problem can be resolved and future voluntary terminations may be avoided.

Summary

Because the employment process encompasses so much, it serves as a foundation for the smooth and productive operation of an organization. This chapter examined the various components of the employment process, including recruitment activities; recruitment sources; interviewing techniques; selection guidelines; orientation programs; promotions, transfers, and demotions; and terminations and exit interviews. The respective responsibilities of human resources specialists and non-HR practitioners were identified for each of these areas.

5

Preemployment and Employment Testing

Approaching the subject of workplace testing with an open mind is the first step to developing a testing policy that is not only valid and reliable but also practical and realistic in terms of meeting your company's needs, expectations, and goals.

Most employers today, large and small alike, rely on preemployment and employment tests in one form or another. Typically, employers use preemployment tests to accomplish two objectives: eliciting a candidate's undesirable traits and identifying those characteristics of the candidate that most closely match the qualities required in the available job. Specifically, tests given to prospective employees may help to:

- Predict acceptable or unacceptable on-the-job behavior
- Minimize or eliminate bias in the interview and selection process
- Allow employers to identify potentially unfit workers
- Identify responsible individuals, capable of working under minimum supervision
- Reduce the cost of recruiting, hiring, and training
- Identify future "superstars"
- Identify additional job factors that should be taken into account
- Safeguard against so-called professional applicants, who pride themselves on being able to mislead interviewers
- Identify workers who will need extra assistance or training
- Flush out factors that could prove to be detrimental on the job

This chapter was adapted from Diane Arthur, *Workplace Testing* (New York: AMACOM, 1994).

Advocates of preemployment testing believe that employers can acquire this information through the use of a wide range of tests, including skills and aptitude, integrity, personality, psychological, physical, and drug use tests. The exams may be conducted at any point in the selection process, depending on the extent of an employer's commitment to test scores. Firm believers in testing generally require applicants to complete one or more tests as the first step. If the applicants achieve a predetermined minimum score, they will be interviewed and given further consideration. Otherwise, they are rejected.

Employers who place a greater value on the face-to-face meeting usually require tests only after the interview process is completed. These employers place little weight on test performance unless it conflicts with information ascertained during the interview or through reference checks.

Employers who place an equal emphasis on each main aspect of the selection process—interviewing, testing, and references—usually first discuss various aspects of the job with the candidate, then conduct tests, talk further with the applicant, and, finally, conduct reference checks. At this point, the results of each phase are studied and a hiring decision is made.

Employment tests are commonly used to evaluate existing employees' promotability or to identify hidden skills and talents for purposes of career pathing. Additionally, they may be used to ferret out certain suspected traits, such as drug use or a propensity toward theft. Specifically, these tests may:

- Improve employee/job matches
- Indicate potentialities for greater efficiency
- Determine promotability on a fair, impartial, and equitable basis
- Improve employer-employee understanding of job requirements
- Help replacement planning
- Reduce training and development costs
- Reduce performance errors
- Create a motivating environment by helping the employer to promote from within as much as possible
- Validate training and development programs
- Reduce selection on the basis of favoritism
- Improve employees' sense of confidence
- Help formulate new standards of performance

As with preemployment testing, employers tend to place varying degrees of emphasis on the testing of existing staff members. They may regard scores on tests for evaluating promotability as the first step in the evaluation process, ruling out anyone who fails to achieve a given level. On the other hand, scores may play a lesser role, being used with a current manager's evaluation, the employee's past performance appraisals, and a survey of the employee interests. When used for career planning, test results are often evaluated along with questionnaires that target employee on-the-job accomplishments and demonstrate job-related skills and knowledge, as well as short- and long-term aspirations. Management must also take into account organizational and departmental goals and managerial recommendations.

Employment tests to confirm suspicions about undesirable activities, such as on-the-job drug or alcohol use, are often controversial. Although some see these tests as an invasion of privacy, others argue that they are a way to protect the health and safety of other employees, customers, and the general public. When such testing is done randomly, it becomes even more controversial.

Advantages and Disadvantages of Testing

In order to use preemployment and employment tests most effectively, proponents must acknowledge that testing has certain disadvantages, and opponents should concede that testing offers several benefits. Approaching the subject of workplace testing with an open mind, then, is the first step to developing a testing policy and program that is not only valid and reliable but also practical and realistic in terms of meeting company needs, expectations, and goals.

Testing Advantages

Perhaps the primary and most appropriate reason for testing prospective and current employees is to seek out the best possible candidate for an available opening. This means matching, as closely as possible, an individual's abilities and potential with the requirements of a given job. Employers may also conduct tests to identify certain desirable and undesirable traits. Among the positive traits are honesty, reliability, competence, emotional stability, integrity, and motivation. Negative characteristics to be screened out include substance dependency and a propensity to steal. In sensitive jobs, where company and product security are of primary concern, ferreting out such traits becomes particularly important.

Another popular reason for workplace testing is to protect against charges of negligent hiring, the charge sometimes faced by employers who fail to exercise reasonable care in hiring or retaining employees. Increasingly, employers are being held responsible for the criminal, violent, or negligent acts of their employees, both in and away from the workplace. Generally the deciding factor is whether an employer can establish the exercise of reasonable care in ensuring the safety of others. One way of accomplishing this is through preemployment and employment testing.

Proponents also support workplace testing as a substitute for reference checks. Fear of being charged with invasion of privacy and defamation of character has led employers to refuse to divulge all but the most basic of information about former employees, such as dates of employment and job titles. This degree of caution is really not necessary, because defamation occurs only when one person makes a statement about another that is false or harms the person's reputation, and truth is an absolute defense against a charge of defamation even if the statements are negative (assuming the truth is not communicated with the intent to do harm). Nevertheless, many employers are hesitant to talk about a former employee's work. This is unfortunate; more information than is commonly given could, in fact, be shared, not only because truth is a complete defense but since the common law doctrine of qualified privilege states that an exchange of job-related information is in the best interest of both employers and the general public. Still, the fact remains that the sharing of reference-related information is limited, and consequently, employers are turning to other ways to determine job eligibility.

Another advantage of workplace testing is its overall objective nature. Assuming it has been validated, a test can help employers make unbiased job-related decisions. When tests are fair representations of the skills and knowledge needed to perform a given job, employers are likely to be portrayed as impartial; this, in turn, may serve to enhance the overall image of the organization.

Finally, tests may help distinguish between otherwise similarly qualified candidates. Although no two applicants may ever be perceived as identical in terms of skills, abilities, and potential, it is sometimes difficult to choose the one person likely to be the "best." Tests may help with the final decision.

Although there are valid arguments for the use of preemployment and employment testing, certain factors must be in place for testing to accomplish its purpose:

- A thorough job analysis, identifying the primary duties and responsibilities as well as educational and prior work experience requirements, must be completed before you seek an appropriate evaluative measure.

- Your organization should have a sound testing policy, known to and understood by everyone who might be involved in any phase of the testing process. A training program consisting of instruction and simulation is the best way to ensure comprehension.
- Care in the creation or selection of the most suitable test, in terms of validity and reliability, is crucial. When purchasing an exam from an outside vendor, you should conduct a thorough investigation of the vendor's credentials, history, and track record.
- The qualifications of those conducting the tests must be suitable. Testing conditions must be examined and determined to be fair and equitable to all test takers.
- Methods of scoring and interpreting the test results must be unbiased.

Testing Disadvantages

One of the greatest concerns expressed by testing opponents is a tendency to rely too heavily on tests. Certainly this is true when employers conduct tests prior to interviewing applicants, immediately dismissing those who do not score at a minimum level. This occurs frequently when the interviewers are not confident in their ability to ask questions and interpret answers, because of a lack of proper training or experience. Also, it is often seen in organizations that have been "burned," that is, involved in some sort of legal action that may have been avoided by a more thorough selection process.

This inclination to place too great an emphasis on tests can be avoided if they are administered after all other stages of screening are completed. Of course, this also means that the employee conducting the face-to-face interview must be equipped with the proper skills and interpretive abilities so that reliance may be placed on the interview outcome for later integration with test results.

Another common complaint about preemployment and employment testing grows out of the tendency to believe that tests can point to people who *will* do well, as opposed to those who are *likely* to do well in a given job or work environment. The predictive abilities of any exam are limited; results can only indicate which individuals are most likely to succeed. This is true even if a test is well designed, validated, and properly used.

Opponents to testing point out that many people react negatively to the mere idea of a test. There are individuals who may in fact be qualified but do not do well on tests, resulting in a distorted or incomplete picture of their abilities if test scores are overemphasized. Rejecting such a candidate is a disservice to the person and possibly to your organization.

Concern that preemployment and employment tests may be misused is also on the negative side of the testing ledger. Test misuse may occur when employers are interested in seeing what abilities a candidate possesses beyond those called for in a given job. This is usually done to help evaluate potential and future growth; after all, what employer doesn't want its employees to stay for a long period of time? This motivation cannot be faulted, but the method is inappropriate; tests should be given only to evaluate specific skills, abilities, and traits as called for in the available job.

Testing may also be inappropriate when the qualities being sought may be acquired through a minimal amount of on-the-job training or education. In such instances, testing is an unnecessary expenditure of time, money, and energy.

Another objection to workplace testing has to do with the all-too-common view that it is the solution to virtually every employment problem, for example, high turnover. High turnover may be the result of numerous factors, including poor management, job misrepresentation, poor working conditions, and noncompetitive wages. Efforts to correct these problems would result in greater company commitment than any battery of tests.

Test Validation

In August 1978 the Uniform Guidelines on Employee Selection Procedures were adopted by the U.S. Equal Employment Opportunity Commission, the U.S. Civil Service Commission (renamed the Office of Personnel Management), the Office of Federal Contract Compliance of the U.S. Department of Labor, the U.S. Department of the Treasury, and the U.S. Department of Justice. The primary purpose of the Uniform Guidelines is to provide a framework for determining the proper use of tests and other selection procedures when they are to be the basis for any employment decision. The term *test* covers all formal, scored, quantified, or standardized techniques of assessing job suitability. *Other selection procedures* refers to application forms, interviews covering education and work experience, reference checks, performance evaluations, training programs, and trial periods of employment, as well as any other means for determining job suitability. The guidelines are also intended to preclude the use of any selection procedure that has an adverse impact on the hiring, promotion, or other employment opportunities of members of either sex of any race or ethnic group. When two or more substantially equal selection procedures are available, employers are expected to use the procedure that has been shown to have the lesser adverse impact on members of any protected group. These guidelines apply to private employers with fifteen or more employees, to state and local governments, and to most employment agencies, labor organizations, and contractors and subcontractors of the federal government.

Validation studies are required as a means of "proving" that a certain test or other selection procedure really works and does not unfairly discriminate against groups of protected individuals. The keys to proving validity are job relatedness and evidence that the test is a proven indicator of job success.

Consider administering a test that measures an individual's ability to understand and interpret instructions. Candidates who score high on the test are hired. Six months later, you return to measure the actual on-the-job performance of these employees, in terms of their ability to comprehend and follow instructions. If the test was valid, a high score on the test would translate into a high level of performance on the job. The test will have predicted a person's ability to understand and interpret instructions.

Types of Validity Studies

In broad terms, validation begins with a thorough job analysis to identify the requirements of the job. The next step entails identifying selection devices and standards that will isolate applicants or employees who meet the job requirements. Employers should then prepare a detailed validation report that outlines and documents the steps taken. The last part of the study is a summary explaining the study's conclusions and stating that the study found the selection procedure used to be valid and nondiscriminatory. Validity studies should be carried out under conditions ensuring the adequacy and accuracy of the research and the report.

The Uniform Guidelines recognize three specific methods of determining validity:

1. *Criterion-related validity,* a statistical relationship between scores on a test or some other selection procedure and the actual job performance of a sample of workers. There must be evidence that the selection procedure is predictive of job performance. For example, a study proving that college graduates perform a particular job better than high school graduates would be criterion related.

2. *Content validity,* which pertains to selection procedures that test a sample of significant parts of a particular job—that is, a demonstration that the content of a selection procedure is representative of important aspects of job performance. For example, the analysis of typing or shorthand for a secretary's position would constitute a content validity study.

3. *Construct validity,* which describes a relationship between something believed to be an underlying human trait or characteristic and successful job performance. Honesty, for example, might be such a characteristic, the presence and measure of which might be measures by a given selection procedure.

For all three methods, the guidelines specify that cutoff scores must be "set so as to be reasonable and consistent with normal expectations of acceptable proficiency within the work force."

Although the Uniform Guidelines do not state a preference of one validity method over the others, it is generally agreed that the criterion-related process, though effective, can be a long and expensive procedure. Construct validity has been the source of much debate and is considered to be the most difficult of the three to establish. Consequently, most employers rely on content validation, believing that it most accurately predicts job success.

The guidelines do not specify how frequently or under what conditions validity studies should be reviewed for currency. They do, however, urge employers to keep abreast of changes in the labor market, relating such changes to the validation strategy originally used, and revising their validation studies accordingly.

Employers may use tests and other selection procedures that have not been validated provided a legitimate validation study is under way. Until it is completed, however, employers are discouraged from making hiring decisions based on invalidated test results. In addition, alternative selection procedures should be explored. If, when the study is concluded, validity is not demonstrated, the employer will be responsible for any obligations and penalties under federal law, including possible back pay awards, claimants' attorney fees, and the loss of government contracts.

Conducting Validity Studies

Many large organizations conduct their own validity studies, targeting a representative number of applicants from their presumably extensive labor pool for testing. Small and mid-sized businesses are better advised to turn to outside sources for assistance, including: faculty in the psychology, education, or business administration departments of colleges and universities; independent consultants; members of consulting organizations; members of the American Psychological Association; members of state psychological associations; and individuals certified in an appropriate field of psychology by a state certification board or the American Board of Professional Psychology. Credentials, reputation, and publication records of any outside source should be checked carefully.

Employers are permitted to use tests and other selection procedures supported by validity studies conducted by other employers or test publishers, assuming two key conditions are met:

1. Applicants or employees in the employer's job and those in the other job for which the validity study was conducted must perform substantially equal work.
2. There must be sufficient evidence concerning test fairness.

Under no circumstances may the general reputation of a test or other selection procedure, its author or its publisher, or casual reference to its validity be accepted as a substitute for documented evidence of validity.

Regardless of who conducts the validity study, the standards set forth in the Uniform Guidelines must be followed. Purchasing or using a test that does not have a sound base can only increase potential liability and do little to ensure that you have hired those candidates with the best chance for success on the job.

Test Administration

Test Takers

The first consideration of test administration is who should be tested. At first thought, it might seem most equitable to require testing across the board, that is, a test for every job. Each job applicant walking through your door would be given a test, as would each internal candidate under consideration for transfer or promotion. Across-the-board testing precludes claims that certain individuals have been singled out for testing.

This method may seem fair on the surface, but it is actually laden with bias. Not all positions require tests. Since some job classifications, including some that do not warrant testing, have traditionally been filled by women and minorities, the result of such a "uniform" procedure would most likely be challenged. This being the case, it is important to consider carefully the factors leading to a determination of who should take tests.

To begin, identify the specific skills required to perform a particular job in a written-out job description. Next, ask yourself a simple but crucial question: "What do I hope to accomplish by conducting a test?" The answer—"I hope to identify those individuals who possess specific skills and knowledge deemed essential for the successful performance of a given job"—should help determine who should take tests.

Identifying the nature of the job and focusing on the purpose of testing should help employers think in terms of specific characteristics of a job instead of individual characteristics. For example, consider a job for which heavy lifting—more specifically, lifting cartons weighing an average of 50 pounds—is a primary duty. Now consider three candidates applying for the position: a man who looks as if he is well over 6 feet tall, weighing around 200 pounds; a man in a wheelchair; and a woman standing approximately 5 feet 2 inches tall, weighing about 110 pounds.

All three claim to be able to lift 50 pounds without difficulty. If you were to think in terms of individual characteristics as opposed to job characteristics, it is likely that you would assume the first candidate could easily manage the lifting requirement and not bother to test his ability. On the other hand, some employers would feel it necessary to test the lifting abilities of the other two candidates because of their particular physical traits and the gender—female—of one. If you think in terms of the specific skills needed to perform the duties of this job successfully, you are likely to draw two conclusions: a physical ability test is suitable, and all job candidates should be tested.

Test Administrators

The next aspect of test administration to be considered is who should conduct preemployment and employment tests. To ensure that tests are both effective and legal, it is crucial that all testing be carried out by competent individuals who possess expertise in employment testing. According to the American Psychological Association's (APA) Standard 6.6: "Responsibility for test use should be assumed by or delegated only to those individuals who have the training and expertise necessary to handle this responsibility in a professional and technically adequate manner."

The level and type of expertise of the tester should be commensurate with the complexity and level of the job in question and with the type of test involved. Testers must understand the importance of issuing a test in exactly the same way each time the test is given, but tests vary in the degree of training required of their administrators. For example, multiple choice tests can generally be conducted by individuals with a minimal degree of training and test administration knowledge, but assessment of personality or mental ability tests usually requires extensive training. Test publishers generally indicate the degree of psychological training required to administer and interpret their tests. A third type of testing, work sample tests, may be conducted and rated by individuals who are knowledgeable about the details of the job. This may include line supervisors as long as they are also familiar with basic testing procedures, including how to set up for the test, give instructions, and score.

Depending on the type of test in question, employers may select a professional already on staff to manage their testing programs, send someone on staff for professional training, or hire outside professionals. Regardless of who is selected, all testers must comply with the APA's Standard 15.1:

> In typical situations, test administrators should follow carefully the standardized procedures for administration and scoring specified by the test publisher. Specifications regarding instructions to test takers, time limits, the form of item presentation or response, and test materials or equipment should be strictly observed. Exceptions should be made only on the basis of carefully considered professional judgment, primarily in clinical situations.

Employers should carefully evaluate the credentials of outside vendors and/or test developers and should check their reputation in the field. In addition, it is prudent to review the test's underlying research and its relevance for meeting your goals.

Test Standardization

One of the most important elements of test administration is standardization. Each time a test is administered, it must be given in exactly the same way, in the same environment, and under the same conditions (that is, the same duration, instructions, materials, physical factors, and any other aspect that might affect testing outcome). Only when precise standards are adopted and all candidates are allowed to react to the same set of stimuli may legitimate conclusion be drawn about test scores and job suitability.

Every effort should also be made to eliminate or minimize distorting influences. This includes test administrators who mumble or speak with a pronounced accent, using tools that are in poor repair, excessive noise, interruptions during the test, uncomfortable seating, or poor lighting or ventilation. In this regard, the APA's Standard 15.2 states that "the testing environment should be one of reasonable comfort and with minimal distractions." Of course, if a particular job is routinely performed in a noisy atmosphere, then simulating that environment as part of the test would be appropriate.

Security

Another factor relevant to testing conditions is security. The APA's Standard 15.3 calls for "reasonable efforts to be made to assure the validity of test scores by eliminating opportunities for test takers to attain scores by fraudulent means." Such efforts may include the following:

- Keeping separate those individuals who have taken a test from those who have not yet been tested
- Limiting the number of people who have access to copies of the tests and answer sheets
- Keeping all exams locked away in a safe location
- Assigning seats randomly so that people who know one another are unable to sit together.
- Varying the order in which questions are asked for those sitting in even-numbered and odd-numbered rows

Although such measures may create negative feelings on the part of some test takers, they are often necessary for fair and meaningful test results.

Language Consistency

Maintaining consistency of language helps ensure equitable testing conditions. Linguistic factors may adversely affect the test performance of speakers of dialects or those who are unfamiliar with certain terms or situations. Unfamiliar words or word usage may prove to be a distraction or may create negative attitudes toward the test and testers, having a negative impact on test results. Employers therefore must make every effort to make certain there is no bias in the language of their tests.

Testing Policy

An analysis of appropriate testing conditions, the qualifications of testers, and a description of who should take tests should all be part of a written testing policy. This policy may be part of the policies and procedures manual, or it may be a separate document. Everyone concerned with conducting or interpreting tests, in addition to all those involved in any stage of the employment process, should become familiar with the policy through training workshops in which the organization's testing program is fully discussed and explained. Such familiarity should result from training workshops in which the organization's testing program is fully discussed and explained.

Regardless of its form, certain key information should appear in every organization's testing policy:

• *The primary objective of testing.* A general statement will usually suffice: "As part of _____ company's commitment to hire qualified individuals to fill positions as they become available, selected preemployment or employment tests may be conducted. Resulting test scores will contribute to making the final selection."

• *The organization's commitment to compliance with EEO laws.* A clear and concise statement will express the company's position: "It is _____ company's policy to employ qualified individuals regardless of race, creed, religion, national origin, sex, age or disability status. When an equally valid means of assessing candidates is known to be available, it will be used if it has less of an adverse impact on groups that are subject to discrimination."

• *Information pertaining to which job candidates will be tested.* First, a statement regarding the testing of similarly situated applicants or employees should appear: "All job candidates and employees applying for a position identified as suitable for testing will be given the same test. Such tests will be job related and relevant to the selection process. Reasonable accommodations will be made for disabled individuals." This statement should then be followed by a list of the positions that require tests.

• *Who will conduct and interpret the tests.* A general remark concerning the competency of test administrators should begin this section: "All testing will be carried out by those individuals having the training and expertise necessary to assume this responsibility in a professional and technically competent fashion. The actual degree and type of expertise will be commensurate with the complexity and level of a given job."

• *A description of testing conditions.* Begin by addressing the issue of standardization: "Each time a test is administered, it must be given in exactly the same way, in the same environment, and under the same conditions. This includes identical duration, instructions, materials and physical factors." Next, provide a detailed description of where tests are administered or, if tests are not always conducted in the same place, describe the ideal testing environment. Include such factors as type of seating, lighting, ventilation, tools, and materials. In addition, this section should address the issue of security to ensure fair test results, as well as the importance of eliminating any linguistic factors that may adversely affect test performance.

• *A description of all tests currently used by the company.* Begin with an introductory comment concerning the validation status of tests in the organization: "All tests used by this organization have been found to be valid and nondiscriminatory, both in content and practice." Then identify all of the tests currently being used, noting that these tests are reviewed on a regular basis for currency.

• *Modifications to normal testing procedures.* A statement dealing with exceptions to the company's testing policy should appear: "Modifications to normal testing procedures may be made under certain circumstances, such as tests for applicants and employees with disabilities. These modifications may include audio versions for the hearing impaired or braille or large-print editions for the visually impaired."

In addition to these factors, organizations may wish to have a separate policy statement pertaining to drug and alcohol testing. This is particularly relevant when random drug testing is conducted, either in matters of reasonable suspicion or routinely for certain positions, such as those involving public safety.

Types of Tests

Small and mid-sized businesses interested in implementing preemployment and/or employment testing will certainly have no trouble finding a vast array of tests from which to choose. There are numerous aptitude tests designed to measure a person's potential ability to perform a given task, achievement tests intended to measure current skills and existing abilities, and physical tests that may ensure a workforce of individuals who are physically able to perform the essential functions of their jobs without threatening the health or safety of others. Within each of these broad testing categories are several specific types of exams, including drug and alcohol, psychological, personality, and honesty. These subcategories are broken down further into hundreds of specific tests that claim to provide employers with a workforce that is free of substance abuse, psychologically well adjusted, and honest.

Drug and Alcohol Testing

Drug and alcohol testing is one of the most controversial and troublesome workplace issues employers face today. Substance/drug and alcohol abuse among American employees has become increasingly common and costly for all work environments, but especially troublesome for small businesses, which can scarcely afford the decline in overall productivity, higher insurance rates, and the increased incidence of theft or damage to company property that frequently occurs with addicted employees.

Detection is often difficult since individuals may be affected differently by the same drug or amount of alcohol. Also, certain legitimate prescribed medications mimic the effects of harmful drugs and alcohol. However, if at any time there is a reasonable cause for suspicion, particularly when the health or safety of others is concerned, the matter should be referred to a drug or alcohol treatment program. Disciplinary steps may also be taken, if performance and/or the welfare of others become factors.

The Controversy Over Testing

The controversy over whether to test applicants and employees for drug and alcohol use remains unresolved. Sound arguments may be made for both testing and not testing. Proponents point to the risks linked to substance and chemical abuse and maintain that testing will ferret out offenders, thereby ridding the workplace of numerous ills.

Those who oppose drug and alcohol testing are quick to point out that substance and chemical abuse cannot possibly be responsible for all that ails a company. An ineffective system of recruiting, interviewing, and selecting; inequitable salary and benefits programs; lack of growth opportunities; an unsatisfactory performance appraisal system; inadequate training and development programs; faulty equipment, and poor employer-employee relations may all contribute to less-than-ideal organizational outcomes.

There are other objections to drug and alcohol testing as well. Across-the-board substance abuse testing as part of a "zero tolerance" policy designed to deter drug use off the job as well as on the job has been criticized by some courts as an unwarranted invasion of privacy. Some methods used for detection, such as urine testing, are also considered invasive, thereby violating an individual's privacy.

Opponents object to drug testing as well because they fear it will subject companies to potential legal liability. Applicants or employees who have been accused of drug use may allege that positive test results do not prove any act of wrongdoing. For example, urine can retain traces of drugs for anywhere from a few days, in the case of cocaine and amphetamines, to a month, as with the drugs classified as cannabinoids. Consequently, although a urine test may indicate use of an illegal drug, it cannot establish with certainty that the drug was used during working hours, impaired the employee's ability to perform his or her work, interfered with the work of others, or endangered the safety of others.

Lawsuits may stem from false-positive test results caused by the use of legitimate, over-the-counter drugs. This is most likely to occur when urine screening tests are used, since they frequently report "drug detected" without distinguishing the drug that is involved. To reduce this possibility, it is advisable to ask test takers to identify all drug products used in the weeks prior to the test.

No matter how sophisticated a test may be, it does not always correctly identify all individuals who use drugs. Abstinence, faked samples, and false negatives are all obstacles to accurately identifying drug abusers. Additionally, few tests are able to differentiate users from abusers—an important distinction. Hence, the relationship between testing positive for substance abuse and job performance is debatable.

An adverse effect on employee morale is another concern expressed by opponents of drug and alcohol testing. They argue that an organization that implements such a program does not trust its employees to behave responsibly at work. It further implies that employees do not consider safety and productivity to be important issues or their responsibility. The resulting low morale can lead to such adverse consequences as carelessness, sloppy work, excessive error, high absenteeism, and low productivity.

Determining Whether to Test

To help you determine whether testing is appropriate for your company, consider these questions:

- Are there safety- or security-sensitive jobs where substance abuse or chemical dependency might endanger lives or property?
- Would the confidentiality of privileged information be jeopardized?
- Are other companies in the field conducting drug and alcohol testing?

- Is the industry one that is more heavily affected by substance abuse or chemical dependency than others?
- How successful have other companies with drug and alcohol testing programs been?
- How receptive are members of management and of the workforce to testing?
- If the organization decides to implement a substance and alcohol abuse testing program, will it be part of an overall workplace anti-drug and alcohol program?

Testing Job Applicants

Employers who decide to test applicants for drug use generally make a job offer conditional on passing a drug test, screening out applicants who either fail or refuse to submit to the test. Of course, employers must realize that word of their preemployment drug testing program will quickly spread; therefore, applicants will have ample opportunity to "test clean" by refraining from drug use for a period of time before the test.

Types of Testing Programs

The least controversial form of employee drug and alcohol testing is "reasonable suspicion" or "for-cause" testing, that is, giving a test when there is reason to believe that an employee's job performance is impaired because of the influence of illegal drugs or excessive consumption of alcohol. It is significant to note that "reasonableness" is difficult to define, and may vary among industries and circumstances. In many instances, the reasonable cause issue is closely related to safety. Hence in postaccident situations or when employers are acting out of concern for the health, safety, or welfare of the public, testing programs are less likely to be challenged. Testing in conjunction with a scheduled physical exam and during or after an employee's participation in a drug abuse or alcoholism treatment program is also generally considered "safe."

More complex is the issue of random testing. The primary benefit of random testing is obvious: it takes away an individual's ability to manage his or her drug or alcohol intake without getting caught. A random testing program can have a substantial deterrent effect, particularly if the company has a strict disciplinary policy with respect to those who test positive. However, random testing is clearly the most intrusive form of testing. It can easily generate employee resentment, seriously lowering morale and productivity. If a company does decide to do random testing, it is important to include representatives from every job classification, including senior management, every race, religion, and national origin, and both sexes, to rule out allegations of bias.

Many employers find that using different kinds of testing programs for different employees works best. For example, all job applicants may be routinely tested for drug use as a condition of employment; employees in sensitive positions may be required to undergo mandatory, random testing; some employees may be tested on the basis of reasonable cause; and still others may not be tested at all. The objective in each instance is to consider the purpose to be achieved and then select the most appropriate form of testing.

Obtaining Consent

Virtually all employers who conduct drug and alcohol tests require applicants and employees to sign a consent form. By signing, the individual agrees to submit to the terms and conditions of a specific test, including releasing the results to appropriate company personnel. These forms are not a complete defense to later legal challenges but do provide some protection for the employer.

Refusal to sign a consent form often means refusal to take a test. Should this occur, what recourse does an employer have? Generally if the test is requested as part of a random or periodic testing program, if there is no evidence that the employee is abusing drugs or alcohol, and if the employee had no notice of the consequences of refusal to submit to the test, there is little support for disciplinary action. Even if there is cause to test but the test entails a particularly intrusive invasion of an employee's privacy, the employee may be justified in refusing to submit.

Selecting the Testing Methods

Once it has been determined that drug and alcohol testing is appropriate for your organization, it is time to consider the various methods available and choose those most likely to meet your needs. When making your selection, take into account:

- The nature of the work performed by those to be tested
- What the test is designed to accomplish
- The test's record of effectiveness, reliability, and legal defensibility
- The specific means of collecting the specimen to be tested

- The degree of intrusiveness
- The test's cost

Urine sampling is the method chosen by most employers when it comes to testing for drugs. To reduce error, a screening test is conducted first, followed by a confirmatory test, but only if drug use is indicated. Confirmatory tests are highly technical in nature, making misidentification unlikely. Accordingly, the cost is significantly higher than that of a screening test. There are other options as well:

- *Blood tests,* which reveal that the person has used the drug very recently, usually within a matter of hours
- *Hair analysis,* based on the theory that chemicals in the bloodstream, both legal and illegal, are left in hair follicles and subsequently trapped as the hair grows, providing a record of past drug use
- *The critical tracking test,* which assesses on-the-spot employee fitness by measuring fine hand-eye coordination and quick reaction time
- *Pupillary-reaction tests,* which are based on the premise that the pupils of subjects under the influence of drugs or alcohol will react differently to light

Testing for Alcohol Abuse

The majority of employers concerned with testing for impairment focus on drugs. In fact, alcohol is the main substance of abuse in the workplace.

It is not always easy to draw the line between alcohol use and abuse. For our purposes, consider the alcohol abuser as someone who uses alcohol in excess and at times that are inappropriate, such as during work hours. Indeed, alcohol testing programs should not be designed to police social drinking; rather their function is to help an organization enforce its in-house policy regarding on-the-job intoxication.

Many people believe that intoxication can be detected by observation alone. It follows that a test to determine the actual level of intoxication is unnecessary. The truth of the matter is that intoxication cannot always be visibly determined, even by professionals. The symptoms of intoxication are not generally evident until the blood alcohol concentration reaches 0.15 percent or higher. That is nearly 50 percent more than the legal definition of intoxication (legal limits for intoxication vary from state to state). Accordingly, workers who have low levels (0.02 percent to 0.05 percent), impaired levels (0.05 percent to 0.10 percent), or even legally intoxicated levels of blood alcohol concentration (above 0.08 percent) may remain undetected without testing.

Unlike many of the tests for detecting drug abuse, tests for excessive alcohol consumption are simple, unintrusive, and relatively inexpensive. Breathalyzers should be used as a preliminary test for alcohol intoxication. That is, they should act as a screener. If alcohol is found to be present, blood or urine confirmations should follow. Because Breathalyzers can determine to what degree, if any, a worker's behavior is impaired, and since they are so easy and inexpensive to administer, some employers conduct these tests routinely on employees performing jobs where safety is a prevailing factor.

Organizational Policy on Testing

Employers electing to implement drug and alcohol testing should have a written policy. Indeed, some states mandate that employers establish a written policy delineating when and how drug testing will take place and how employees' privacy will be protected. Even if a statutory requirement does not exist, employers are urged to establish a written testing policy and to take appropriate steps to ensure that all managers and employees are aware of its terms and conditions. Establishing a policy also sends a clear message throughout the organization that drug and alcohol abuse will not be tolerated.

Each organization's drug and alcohol testing policy will differ by virtue of its individual philosophy and objectives, but all policies should have certain factors in common. Statements covering the following issues should appear in every company's policy:

- Organizational views, responsibilities, expectations of its workers, and objectives
- Validity of the company's testing procedures
- Relevant laws
- Types of tests to be conducted
- Who is to be tested
- Circumstances under which testing will be conducted
- Who will conduct the tests
- Grounds for retesting
- Security measures to ensure samples are not substituted or tampered with
- Meaning of test results
- Ramifications for refusal to take a test

- Possible disciplinary action if test results are positive
- Employee assistance programs
- Efforts to ensure confidentiality
- Definitions of key terms (e.g., "reasonable suspicion" and "random testing")
- Commitment to education of management and staff regarding such matters as how to detect problems and what is actionable
- A description of prohibited conduct

The policy should be reviewed semiannually or annually and revised as needed.

Psychological Testing

Psychological tests, defined here as measures of general intelligence or mental ability, are seen by proponents as tools for identifying and predicting behaviors that are relevant to a given position. For example, many industrial psychologists believe that an individual's propensity to leave an organization prematurely may be anticipated through testing. Similarly, in evaluating candidates for sales positions, a psychological test instrument might be used first to identify the characteristics judged most valuable in a sales representative and then to assess the likelihood that each applicant will exhibit those traits.

Psychological tests are also increasingly being used to evaluate specific traits, such as managerial effectiveness, business ethics, company loyalty, stability, cooperation, and independence. Can these tests really identify traits and predict behavior? Are they effective measures of intelligence or ability? Most important, can employers rely on their projections?

Objectors and Supporters

Consider the most commonly voiced objections to psychological testing in the workplace:

- The tests are intimidating.
- They invade the privacy of individuals.
- They set a negative tone for the workplace.
- They cannot accurately measure intelligence because intelligence defies definition.
- They promote labeling (e.g., referring to someone as "bright" or "slow").

- They may contain questions on topics with which test takers are uncomfortable.
- Their results may be misused.
- Their results may be misleading.
- They promote reliance on testing, to the exclusion of other selection factors.

On the other hand, employers who are fearful of charges of negligent hiring, who are unsuccessful at obtaining comprehensive references, or who are uncomfortable with the subjective nature of interviews are turning to psychological tests as a means of "knowing" a person before making a hiring decision. They argue that responsibly administered psychological tests designed to select employees whose abilities match the requirements of a job can:

- Be more objective than other selection procedures
- Be more cost-efficient than other screening devices
- Have a deterrent effect on deviant conduct among those hired
- Produce a more productive workforce
- Produce a workforce that is easier to supervise
- Reduce turnover
- Provide employers with peace of mind
- Provide employers with a competitive edge
- Make applicants and employees feel that they are being treated fairly and equally

Test Standards

The APA recommends using only tests that meet "high standards." Without a background in psychological testing, it is easy to become convinced of a test's general suitability for your testing needs. This is especially true when salespeople throw around key terms like *valid* and *reliable*. Thus, legal experts suggest that employers ask test publishers three key questions to protect against the risk of liability for usage:

1. Is the test now, or has it ever been, involved in litigation?
2. Is the test validated?
3. Is there any evidence that the test might adversely impact minorities and other protected classes?

In addition, employers are urged to follow these guidelines:

- Check the credentials and reputation of the test vendor; psychologists who wish to be viewed as true experts in their field will seek diplomat status through the APA's American Board of Professional Psychology.
- Do not assume that memberships in psychological associations are true indicators of how involved psychologists are in their profession's affairs and activities.
- Check the test author's publication record in legitimate psychological journals.
- Check the vendor's reputation in the field.
- Review the test's underlying research, and beware of tests for which little or no validation research exists.
- Beware of tests that use small numbers of participants to predict important job performance outcomes.
- Have the test takers sign consent forms.
- Make certain you understand exactly what the testing is designed to reveal.
- Find out whether the test really does what its promoters say it will.
- Do not rely exclusively on test results for making hiring decisions.
- Use the test in strict conformity with the publisher's directions.
- Obtain a legal opinion on use of a particular test before proceeding.

To be useful, psychological tests must be deemed reliable and valid. A test is considered *reliable* if the results are consistent under varying conditions. *Validation* means that a certain test has been shown to have job relatedness and is a proven indicator of job success. A test can be reliable without being valid, but the opposite is not true. A necessary prerequisite for validity is that a test must first have achieved an adequate level of reliability. A valid test, consequently, is one accurately measuring the variable it is intended to assess.

Any psychological test should include a comprehensive validation study, as well as a summary, explaining the study's conclusions. The validation study should document the test's ability to predict the future behavior of employees. The summary should conclude that the test was found to be valid and nondiscriminatory in nature and practice.

Test Types

Employers may choose from numerous types of psychological tests, including:

- *General intelligence tests,* which measure a wide range of traits
- *Aptitude tests,* which predict what a person can accomplish on the basis of what he or she knows
- *Achievement tests,* which measure current skills, knowledge, and accomplishments
- *Job knowledge* or *trade tests,* which require applicants to demonstrate their degree of existing knowledge on how a given job is performed by answering written or oral questions
- *Work sample tests,* which require test takers to demonstrate their existing level of skills using actual or simulated job-related equipment

Employers should make certain to accommodate applicants with disabilities with regard to all of these tests, enabling them to compete equally with unimpaired candidates. The extent and form of the modification will vary with the nature of the disability. In some instances, it may be appropriate to waive the test and substitute an alternative means for assessing job suitability.

Meeting Ethical Standards

Employers must make certain that the tests selected for administration comply not only with federal and state laws but meet with appropriate ethical principles as well. The ethical use of tests can be controlled to some extent by a code of ethics to which professional testers and publishers subscribe. Both the APA and the American Personnel and Guidance Association (APGA) are bound by ethical codes pertaining to test administration and other psychological services. These codes cover such issues as test validity, reliability, standardization, and administration. Test publishers must also control the release of tests to qualified persons only—those trained to use tests for their intended purposes alone. Publishers and distributors of psychological tests must make certain that the tests they market are designed properly and are of potential value to a particular organization and society as a whole. Of course, the mere existence of a set of standards or principles for test publishers does not guarantee that tests will be administered and interpreted properly. The responsibility for correct usage lies ultimately in the hands of the test administrators and interpreters.

It is imperative that employers obtaining test results understand exactly what is being measured by the tests given to prospective and current employees, as well as what is not being measured. Test scores are not fixed measures of an individual's mental status; rather, tests of general intelligence and special aptitudes reveal only the probability that a test taker will succeed in a particular job or field. In addition, test scores are susceptible to errors of measurement and to changes in abilities and achievements.

Personality Testing

Should personality, defined as that combination of qualities and characteristics distinguishing one individual from another, be a consideration when making a hiring decision? The answer to this question will vary with each job.

Clearly, some tasks will be carried out more effectively if the incumbent possesses certain intangible traits. For example, a friendly receptionist is certainly more desirable than one who is abrasive or abrupt, because a receptionist is generally the first contact a client or visitor has with a company, and a positive first impression could be a significant bridge to future dealings. Similarly, an interviewer who appears disinterested or judgmental could make an applicant feel uneasy and hesitant about revealing important background information. In these instances, certain aspects of an applicant's personality may be job related. On the other hand, for a programmer who has little interaction with any of his or her coworkers, or for a person hired to conduct research, personality has little, if any, relevance.

Consequently, job relatedness is the key to whether personality should be a consideration when making a hiring decision. But how can the job relatedness of an intangible be determined? One way is to ask yourself if one applicant without certain traits can perform a given job as effectively as another possessing those traits. If the answer is no, and you can go on to document why, then the personality requirements are probably valid. If the answer is yes, but an applicant with certain characteristics could probably do a better job, then the answer is less clear. If the answer is yes, but you would prefer to hire a particular personality, then the requirement is probably invalid.

Even when personality traits are job related, employers are cautioned that judgments about personality are subjective, and as such, susceptible to challenge. Care must be taken to avoid weighing personality too heavily or to use it as the sole basis for selection or rejection. Intangibles are most useful when there are two candidates with similar tangible skills or when there are no concrete requirements at all.

Advocates and Opponents

As with all other forms of testing, personality testing in the workplace is controversial. However, given the fact that personality tests are designed to assess factors that, unlike abilities, cannot be described in tangible, measurable, concrete, or observable terms, the controversy is that much greater.

Advocates of personality testing make these arguments:

- It is a valid indicator of job success; a workforce comprising individuals who have been selected in part because of their responses to personality test questions will work harder and more efficiently, improving productivity.
- Having been properly "matched" with their jobs, members of such a workforce are more inclined to stay with one employer for a longer period of time.
- This testing provides employers with a more complete picture of a candidate than do other selection criteria, such as application forms, resumés, face-to-face interviews or reference checks.
- Information may be gathered in such a way that applicants are unaware of exactly what is being revealed. Hence, there is little potential for allegations of discrimination and resulting lawsuits.
- Personality tests reduce recruitment costs because the tests can accurately identify those workers best suited for specific jobs, virtually eliminating "waste" in time, effort, or money.

Opponents of personality tests strongly disagree with these claims and make these arguments:

- Personality is extremely difficult to measure, and typing or labeling personalities is an imprecise process, focusing on one or more traits to the exclusion of all others.
- Even if it is shown that a particular quality prevails over others, this may be the result of unusual circumstances—perhaps a significant event in the applicant's life that, after a certain period of time, ceases being influential.
- The assumption that personalities do not change over time may be wrong.
- Matches deemed appropriate or otherwise at one time may not necessarily remain so.
- Employers that conduct personality tests might erroneously assume that a given job can be successfully performed by only one specific personality type. This kind of thinking discriminates against qualified applicants and may hurt the company.

Testing Caveats

Employers who decide to use personality tests to help make better hiring decisions; provide assistance in making decisions concerning the transfer and promotion of employees; improve communication between managers and employees during performance appraisals, counseling, and disciplinary sessions; identify what motivates an individual; or aid in identifying employees who will benefit most from specific forms of training and development should make certain the tests are developed in keeping with the APA's Standards for Educational and Psychological Testing. They must also be in full compliance with the Uniform Guidelines on Employee Selection Procedures and be validated and administered by individuals skilled and knowledgeable in matters of psychological testing. Compliance with other legislation, such as the Americans with Disabilities Act, is also required if employers wish to reduce the risk of liability.

Test questions should be constructed so as to minimize the potential for violating an individual's privacy and an individual's protection against self-incrimination. As an added precaution, it is always a good idea to have a labor attorney review the tests and testing procedures.

Types of Tests

There are numerous types of personality tests from which to choose. One of the most popular is the *projective test*. Most of these tests offer very little in the way of instructions, allowing examinees freedom to interpret and perceive the material in any variety of ways. Then their responses are projected into the workplace, and conclusions are drawn as to how they would handle specific situations. Among the most popular examples of projective tests are the following:

- The *Rorschach inkblot test*, whereby examinees are shown ten cards, each with a different inkblot, and asked to describe what they believe is represented
- The *Thematic Apperception Test* (TAT), which requires test takers to tell a story about a series of black-and-white picture cards showing people in various situations
- *Word associations*, which call for a series of 100 or so words to be read aloud to the test taker, who is instructed to answer with the very first word that comes to mind
- *Sentence completions*, which entail asking a person to complete a se-

ries of sentences, designed to reflect specific areas of emotion, such
as desires, fears, attitudes, and conflict
- *Projective drawings*, which require test takers to draw pictures of
people in various situations

Objective tests, also known as *personality inventories*, are another popular form of personality testing. These tests seek to uncover personal characteristics, thoughts, feelings, attitudes, and behavior. Respondents mark
those items on the test that they believe most closely describe themselves.
Among the frequently used objective tests are the Minnesota Multiphasic
Personality Inventory, the Myers-Briggs Type Indicator, the Employee Reliability Inventory, the Jenkins Activity Survey, and the Edward Personal
Preference Schedule.

Overall, objectives tests have greater merit as assessors of personality
than do projective tests and are considered more valid and reliable.

Integrity Testing

Experts tell us that it is difficult to determine absolutely if someone is
lying. This inability to identify truthfulness and dishonesty unerringly
creates an obvious dilemma for all employers. Is there some method of
separating truth from lies? Some employers believe the answer lies in integrity testing.

The Polygraph

The most popular form of integrity or lie detector test historically has
been the polygraph. However, the Employee Polygraph Protection Act of
1988 all but banned from use by private sector employers this mechanical
device, which monitors changes in a person's rate of respiration, blood
pressure, and perspiration as they sit with pneumatic straps or tubes
stretched around their chest and stomach and respond to questions. Exceptions include using the polygraph to screen applicants for security-
sensitive jobs and for pharmaceutical work, as well as for positions in
the manufacturing, distributing, or dispensing of controlled substances.
Moreover, businesses with access to highly classified information may
continue to use polygraph tests, as may federal agencies, state or local
governments, and companies that hold national defense or national security contracts. Use of polygraph testing is also permitted in the investigation of employees who are reasonably suspected of committing acts
resulting in economic loss or injury to the employer's business, such as

sabotage or theft. Access to stolen property alone, however, is not considered a reasonable basis for suspicion.

An employee who is believed to have committed an infraction justifying a polygraph test must first receive a written notice that identifies the loss being investigated, states the employer's basis for suspicion, and explains the employee's statutory rights under the federal polygraph act. Employees mut also be advised of their right to consult with counsel before and during the examination. Employers who are allowed by these exceptions to test employees must utilize the services of a licensed, bonded examiner.

Employees and applicants may refuse to take the polygraph test altogether or may choose to take it but terminate at any time. No test is allowed to last longer than ninety minutes. In addition, after the test results have been determined, employees and applicants may request a second test and hire an independent examiner for a second opinion. Test takers must not be asked degrading or intrusive questions or about sexual behavior, union activities, or religious, racial, or political beliefs. They must be given advance notice as to the testing conditions and, before the test begins, must be permitted to review all questions. Afterward, a written copy of the test questions must be provided, along with their responses, and any opinions based on the test results. In addition, test takers have the right to privacy; therefore, the examiners may disclose the test results only to the subject, any person the subject designates in writing, and the employer that ordered the test. Employers may reveal test results only to the test takers, persons the test taker designates in writing, and government agencies if there is an admission of criminal conduct.

Written Honesty Tests

With all the limitations placed on polygraphs, more and more employers are turning to written honesty tests, designed to accomplish three primary objectives:

1. To determine whether a person has committed certain dishonest or illegal acts in the past
2. To identify a person's attitudes toward questionable activities
3. To measure whether a person has a predisposition to lie or steal

There are two basic types of honesty tests from which to choose: overt and veiled purpose, or personality based. *Overt* tests pose questions that target an applicant's attitudes about specific aspects of dishonesty and probe any past involvement in such activities. *Veiled-purpose questions,* on the other hand, do not refer directly to theft or other dishonest activities. Instead, they pose seemingly irrelevant questions, the answers to which provide meaningful information to test administrators concerning the test taker's potential for counterproductive behavior.

Both the overt and the veiled-purpose test questions are considered to be equally effective, success being measured by the actual reduction of theft and/or other counterproductive behaviors in the workplace. However, a 1990 report by the Office of Technology Assessment (OTA) of the U.S. Congress on the use of integrity tests concludes that "the research on integrity tests has not yet produced data that clearly supports or dismisses the assertion that these tests can predict dishonest behavior."*

Test publishers, on the other hand, have pointed to their own research on theft and other counterproductive behaviors, which indicates an association between integrity test scores and forms of counterproductive behavior.

Written honesty tests are steeped in controversy. Many retailers, financial services businesses, supermarkets, fast food restaurants, and hotel chains swear by them; researchers are divided over them; applicants are suspicious of them. Statistics abound supporting their use, as do data recommending avoidance. What is the received wisdom regarding their use? Unfortunately, since the jury is still out, a definitive recommendation cannot be made. Each employer must be left to decide, legal restrictions withstanding, whether written honesty tests are appropriate selection tools. To help employers resolve their quandary, here is a summary of the pros and cons of honesty testing.

Advantages of Written Honesty Tests

- They can have an impact on "shrinkage," or inventory losses. For example, after honesty tests were adopted at two major California retailers, employee theft decreased by 30 to 35 percent within one year.
- They can contribute to a more harmonious work environment, because individuals inclined toward theft may have been screened out.
- They are generally considered less intrusive or intimidating than polygraphs.
- They are affordable, even for small employers. When compared

---

*Office of Technology Assessment, *The Use of Integrity Tests for Pre-Employment Screening,* OTA-SET-442 (Washington, D.C.: U.S. Government Printing Office, 1990).

with polygraphs, they are especially cost-effective: $5 to $20 per exam, as opposed to $100 or more per hour for the services of a licensed polygraph examiner.

- They take less than an hour to administer and under two minutes to score.
- They can help to fill in the gaps left by the employment interview. This become particularly important since it is increasingly difficult to ascertain information about an applicant's prior work history through references.
- Employers who issue written honesty tests, especially for positions involving cash or merchandise, send a message to applicants and employees that they will not tolerate dishonest behavior.
- The tests are legal in most states.
- Because honesty tests are purported to identify a person's propensity to steal and commit other forms of counterproductive behavior, employers administering these tests can help protect themselves against charges of negligent hiring, a situation that may occur when employers fail to exercise reasonable care in hiring employees.

Disadvantages of Written Honesty Testing

- The research base has not proven conclusively that written honesty tests succeed in identifying applicants likely to steal or commit other counterproductive acts in the workplace. At best, these tests carry a probability of accuracy.
- Many test takers end up being misclassified and possibly eliminated from the running for a job. Even though they receive low marks on honesty tests, they may never steal or behave in any of the unacceptable ways projected by their scores. This can be particularly damaging if, as test publishers claim, integrity test scores do not vary significantly over time. Individuals will then be repeatedly misclassified and systematically denied employment without cause.
- Although test publishers maintain that honesty tests should not be the sole determinant of whether a person is rejected, it is unusual for an employer to hire someone who tests negatively.
- Poor test scores can affect the morale and subsequent behavior of the subjects. Even if test results are revealed only to employers and not the test takers, they can influence the employer's perception of the individual, damaging employer-employee relations and ultimately affecting productivity.

- Written honesty tests are largely marketed to companies with staff lacking the psychological and statistical training needed to interpret sophisticated scores accurately. Hence, results are usually reported as, "recommend/not acceptable" or "low risk/marginal risk/high risk." These terms do not provide much insight into the subject's character.
- An individual who takes a written honesty test, "legitimately" scores poorly (that is, does in fact have a tendency to be dishonest), and then changes his or her behavior for the better has no way to demonstrate this change on subsequent tests. The answer to a typical question such as, "Did you ever steal?" would be the same despite this person's subsequent "transformation."
- Written honesty tests require applicants to disclose information of a personal nature that may not be job related and that they may not choose to reveal.
- Written honesty tests are not regulated. Standards issued by the APA and the American Test Publishers Association serve only as guidelines.
- The data relating to adverse impact are inconclusive. In some studies, there were no statistically significant differences in the average test scores of various protected groups; in other cases, there was a favorable bias toward protected groups; in still others, minority groups scored less favorably than whites.

The arguments for and against the use of written honesty tests are compelling. In addition to weighing these arguments, employers should consider one additional factor as suggested by the OTA before proceeding: Are the potentially harmful effects of the use of written honesty tests justified by the promise of gains in business efficiency and productivity growth? If the answer is yes, proceed—with care.

Physical Testing

Today there are more physical tests than ever before from which employers may choose. Typically, some employers eagerly implement a complete physical testing program to ensure—to the extent possible—a healthy workforce. Other will stand back, feeling uneasy about requiring any more than a basic preemployment physical exam. Most employers are advised to proceed cautiously and to study the necessity, job relatedness, validity, and legality of each physical test under consideration.

Preemployment Exams

Preemployment physical examinations are the most prevalent type of physical test required by companies and are used primarily to determine an applicant's current physical ability to perform the essential functions of a given job in a safe and effective manner. They can also be used for predictive screening purposes to assess an applicant's susceptibility to future injury because of a particular physical condition. In addition, they provide a record of the applicant's health at the time of employment. This documentation may prove decisive in helping an employer avoid future liability in the event an employee later claims that on-the-job conditions caused the development of a medical condition. Preemployment medical screening also identifies health conditions, such as the presence of any communicable disease.

Employers are cautioned, nevertheless, not to expose candidates to excessive testing and to keep in mind that these exams are not foolproof. They are limited in their capacity to predict future health risks and in the accuracy of their diagnosis. Additionally, erroneous test findings may result in an unfair denial of employment, or the company may hire an applicant incorrectly labeled as having a particular physical condition.

Employers who choose to conduct preemployment physical testing should follow these fifteen guidelines:

1. Prepare a detailed job analysis, identifying the specific duties and responsibilities to be performed by the incumbent.
2. Develop sound medical criteria, describing the physical requirements needed to perform the essential functions of the job.
3. Familiarize the physician administering the preemployment physicals with the essential tasks of the job.
4. Issue a policy statement, describing why the company is administering preemployment physical exams.
5. Inform job applicants as to what the exam will consist of, how long it is expected to last, and who will be present during it.
6. Advise applicants that no physician-patient relationship exists that requires physicians to keep confidential medical information relevant to employment.
7. Ask applicants to sign a consent form that describes the purpose and scope of the testing process.
8. Accommodate any reasonable objections—for example, those based on religious beliefs—to specific medical procedures.

9. Inform applicants that medical test results will contribute to the final hiring decision.
10. Ensure that the physician conducting the examination follows a particular format.
11. Have the physician evaluate the information obtained and compare it with the requirements of the job.
12. Have the physician identify any physical problems that may inhibit the individual from performing the essential functions of the job. If the applicant is disabled, the physician should recommend treatments that can reduce risk factors to an acceptable level or modifications to the workplace.
13. Discuss the results of the physical with the applicant (failure to do so could increase an employer's potential for liability should medical problems fail to be disclosed).
14. Incorporate medical findings into your employment decisions, but never rely on them alone.
15. Keep medical records separate from other records and treat them confidentially. State regulations covering retention of medical records and employee access vary.

In addition to preemployment physical exams, employers may conduct tests of physical ability, also known as strength and endurance, for positions requiring physical performance and psychomotor tests, used primarily for measuring abilities such as hand-eye coordination, motor ability, and manual dexterity.

Legal Considerations

Employers who feel justified in conducting any type of workplace testing should check with legal counsel to make certain they are not in violation of any federal statute. For example, employers who choose to bypass professional developed tests and use instead tests developed in-house may find themselves facing charges of violating Title VII of the Civil Rights Act of 1964, because homemade tests are more difficult to validate than professionally researched tests. Also, in accordance with the Rehabilitation Act of 1973 and the Americans with Disabilities Act of 1990, applicants with disabilities who are unable to take a required test must be allowed to demonstrate the ability to perform the essential functions of the job through alternative means. And the Civil Rights Act of 1991 clearly states that employers may be liable for damages if their selections result in adverse impact—that is, if their hiring or promotion practices have a disproportionately greater negative impact on any one protected group.

The issue of negligent hiring and retention is a relatively new form of liability that has been sustained by court decisions since the mid-1980s. Negligent hiring charges may be brought against employers that seemingly fail to exercise reasonable care in hiring or retaining employees who subsequently commit a crime or do harm to others, both in the workplace and away from it. While testing can help employers protect themselves against such charges, conducting tests—such as preemployment physical examinations, and psychological, integrity, and personality tests—for the express purpose of precluding charges of negligent hiring and retention is not appropriate.

The most effective method for avoiding test-related legal problems is to make certain that all tests and other selection procedures are administered in accordance with testing guidelines. Although adhering to the following points will not guarantee a litigation-free workplace, this should help to reduce the number of legitimate charges of unfair employment practices:

- Every job should have a formal, written job description.
- All tests must be in full compliance with the Uniform Guidelines on Employee Selection Procedures.
- All tests and other selection procedures must be job related.
- Tests must not have an adverse impact on members of any protected group.
- Tests must not violate any federal and/or state statute.
- Tests must not serve as the sole basis for determining job suitability.
- Except under specific circumstances in which an employer can demonstrate that an available position is a stepping-stone to other positions in the same job family, tests must be conducted and results evaluated only as they pertain to the job opening.
- Applicants and employees should be fully advised of the purpose of any test, how it will be conducted, the conditions under which it will be administered, the role it will play in the selection process, and who will have access to the results.
- Applicants and employees should be asked to provide their written consent to all tests.
- Legal counsel experienced in matters of workplace testing should be consulted to ensure the legal application of all tests.

Summary

Most employers rely on preemployment and employment testing in one form or another. Choices of tests include drug and alcohol, psychological, personality, integrity, and physical. Among the reasons for testing are identifying appropriate job skills, predicting acceptable workplace behavior, and flushing out factors that could prove detrimental on the job.

Advantages of testing include protection against charges of negligent hiring and the overall objective nature of validated tests. A tendency for employers to rely too heavily on test scores and the possible misuse of these results are among the disadvantages of testing.

Before testing, employers should carefully determine who should be tested, identify qualifications for test administrators, and ensure standardization of all testing factors.

6

Compensation

Written job descriptions form the foundation for an organization's compensation program, highlighting the primary duties and responsibilities of a job, as well as identifying the required skills and knowledge, so that the overall meaning of a job is clearly and accurately communicated.

Every company, regardless of size, needs a formal compensation program. Compensation is defined here as the actual salaries paid employees, excluding benefits and perquisites such as vacations and personal days. Even the smallest business needs a structured pay system that reflects the duties and responsibilities performed by its employees. This is not to say that there is no room for flexibility; indeed, some popular pay-for-performance compensation programs cluster many different jobs into just a few broad categories. Still, there is structure.

In contrast, consider what happens when managers pay individual employees whatever they deem appropriate, based on irrelevant factors such as personality, marital status, number of dependents, or financial need, regardless of the jobs performed. Upon learning what their coworkers are earning (and rest assured, salary information can and does leak out), employees making less money but performing similar tasks will most certainly feel unmotivated and unappreciated. Probably they end up quitting, leaving employers with productivity and morale problems that may well have been avoided. In addition, companies may be challenged for violation of various EEO laws, including the Equal Pay Act of 1963, which requires equal pay for men and women performing substantially equal work of comparable skill, effort, and responsibility, performed under similar working conditions. Virtually all small businesses are obliged to abide by this statute since the criterion for coverage is only two employees.

Characteristics of an Effective Compensation Program

The primary goal of any compensation program should be to attract, retain, and motivate maximally productive employees, usually with limited payroll dollars, to make the organization more effective and efficient. In order to accomplish this objective, a company's compensation system should strive to achieve the following:

- It should offer competitive rates for comparable jobs, with salary levels and practices prevailing in the labor market in which a company competes.
- It should be internally equitable.
- It should take into account the level of talent needed or wanted by the company.
- The time, cost, and energy devoted to the development and maintenance of it should be reasonable and in proportion to the other priorities and time demands of a company's resources.
- It must be supported by senior management, with this support clearly communicated to employees.
- Employees must understand the basis for the company's salary policies and believe that they are being impartially administered.
- It should contribute toward motivating employees to perform their responsibilities as effectively as possible and in a manner that supports organizational goals.
- It should allow for the growth and development of employees.
- It should be easy to administer and flexible enough to change over time without requiring a major overhaul.
- It should be defensible against legal challenges.
- The ranges should be broad enough to recognize varying levels of performance.
- It should instill a sense of confidence that salaries are not established at the whim of management.

Although these goals may be shared by all organizations, each company should examine its own objectives before establishing a compensation plan. Such objectives will act as specific guidelines for developing a pay system that facilitates day-to-day, salary-related decision making.

In addition to having its own specific set of goals, each organization is unique in terms of its products, hierarchy, management style, economics, and operating characteristics. And although no one compensation plan is appropriate to every environment, small and mid-sized organizations have no need for complex compensation programs calling for excessive amounts of time, money, and energy to design, implement, and maintain.

A small or mid-sized company should focus on developing comprehensive job descriptions and position evaluations so that realistic and applicable salary survey information may be ascertained. It can then design and implement a customized compensation plan reflecting its growth objectives. Employees' performance evaluations and recommended pay increases will then relate to the compensation system.

Because of the expertise required to perform these responsibilities effectively, any organization large enough to warrant more than one human resources expert should hire a specialist in the area of compensation. In addition, all managers should become familiar with both the goals and operation of their company's compensation program.

Job Descriptions

Written job descriptions are the foundation for an organization's compensation program, highlighting the primary duties and responsibilities of a job, as well as identifying the required skills and knowledge, so that the overall meaning of a job is clearly and accurately communicated. Accordingly, every position in an organization should have a written job description (The categories recommended for inclusion in all job descriptions were outlined in Chapter 4.)

Before attempting to write a job description, employers are advised to ask the following questions:

- Will the jobholder supervise the work of others? If so, provide job titles and a brief description of the responsibilities of those supervised.
- What duties will the jobholder perform regularly, periodically, and infrequently? List these in order of importance.
- What degree of supervision will be exercised over the jobholder?
- To what extent will instructions be necessary in assigning work to the jobholder?
- How much decision-making authority or judgment is to be allowed the jobholder in the performance of required duties?
- What are the working conditions?
- What skills are necessary for the successful performance of the job?

- What authority will the jobholder have in such matters as training other people or directing the work of others?
- At what stage of its completion will the jobholder's work be reviewed by the manager in charge?
- What machinery or equipment will the jobholder be responsible for operating? Describe the equipment's complexity.
- What would be the cost to management of serious errors that the jobholder might make in the regular performance of required duties?
- What employees within the organization, and customers or clients outside the organization, will the jobholder interact with on a regular basis?

In addition to asking these questions, it is also important to determine whether a generic or specific job description is called for. As you remember from Chapter 4, generic job descriptions are written in broad, general terms and may be used for several similar positions in different departments of the same organization. Specific job descriptions define the duties and tasks of one particular position. Companies should use generic job descriptions whenever possible, reserving specific job descriptions for single-incumbent positions.

Finally, before preparing a job description, consider the guidelines for effective writing described in Chapter 4. Appendix B shows a sample job description incorporating these guidelines; the position described is that of assistant to the director of human resources in a mid-sized organization.

Position Evaluations

Position evaluation is the systematic measurement of a job's duties against a predetermined yardstick so that its relative worth may be determined. Most evaluation programs consist of a combination of internal measures of job worth and the outside market value of similar jobs.

In order to be effective, an organization's position evaluation system must be applicable to a wide range of jobs. Both management and employees must perceive the rates of pay as reasonable and equitable. These rates should also reflect pay scales for comparable jobs in similar organizations, so that the organization's rates of pay stay in reasonable alignment with the labor market.

The four position evaluation systems most appropriate for small and mid-sized companies are the point evaluation system, the ranking system, the classification system, and the factor comparison system. Skilled human resources representatives or outside consultants can evaluate and review these systems and choose the most suitable one for your organization.

The Point Evaluation System

In this system, various factors for each job are selected and defined. Next, points are assigned to the varying degrees of each factor, and the point values for all the individual factors are added up to derive the total point value for each job. This total point value serves as the basis for conversion to the corresponding salary rate.

To illustrate this system, consider the factor "extent of related experience required." The first degree represents zero to three months and is worth 20 points; the second degree represents three months to one year and is worth 40 points; the third degree represents one to three years and is worth 60 points; the fourth degree represents three to five years and is worth 80 points; the fifth and final degree represents over five years and is worth 100 points. This process of assigning degrees and points will be repeated for the remaining factors of the job, and the resulting total will then be slotted into the appropriate salary range.

Many people consider the point evaluation method to be advantageous over other systems, primarily because its use of fixed, predetermined factors forces the evaluator to consider the same elements when rating every job. In addition, the assignment of point values indicates not only which job is worth more than another, but how much more it is worth.

Opponents of the system, however, maintain that it is extremely difficult to select relevant factors and assign appropriate point values to them. Furthermore, it is difficult to define each degree clearly so that it will serve as a meaningful guide to evaluators and also provide employees with an understandable explanation of the results.

The Ranking System

This method is best suited to small organizations with a limited number of jobs. It ranks one position against another without assigning point values. The evaluator simply compares two jobs and judges which is more difficult or complex. Once this determination has been made, a third job is compared with the first two and a similar decision is made. The process is repeated until all jobs have been ranked, ranging from the most difficult to the least difficult.

This system is one of the most accurate methods of evaluation because it is based on a job-against-job comparison—that is, a judgment of which of two jobs is more difficult, as opposed to a judgment of the absolute difficulty of either. It is also the simplest of all methods to implement.

On the negative side, the ranking system can indicate only that one job is more difficult than another, not how much more difficult. It is also very hard to explain or justify the result to employees or management since there is no quantitative record of the judgments of the evaluators.

An organization with more than a dozen or so positions wishing to use the ranking system might consider the *paired-comparison ranking system*, in which evaluators are given a list that pairs every job with another job. They are then asked to select which job in each pair ranks as the more difficult. The rankings are then analyzed statistically to produce a master list.

A second variation of the ranking system is the *factor-guided ranking system*. Using this method, evaluators rank jobs not just in terms of overall difficulty, but in terms of specific factors such as knowledge and physical effort required. When the evaluation is completed, a separate ranking is established for each factor. The jobs are then grouped according to similar levels of difficulty under each factor.

The Classification System

The classification, or rating, system measures jobs against a predetermined yardstick whose various categories define overall job value or difficulty. The evaluator compares each job against this yardstick and fits the job into the grade that best describes its characteristics and difficulties.

Most job evaluators agree that this system has shortcomings similar to those of the ranking system. In addition, they find it difficult to define levels of overall job worth in any meaningful way.

This system is most appropriate in organizations with a large number of employees working in relatively few kinds of jobs.

The Factors Comparison System

In this method, a handful of key jobs is selected for evaluation. These jobs are then compared to others in terms of factors common to all jobs. The factors most commonly used are knowledge, skill, authority, physical requirements, and level and degree of responsibility. The evaluator analyzes and ranks all jobs in terms of one factor, then ranks all in relation to a second factor, and so forth, until point rankings have been established for each of the factors used. The evaluator then totals the points assigned to a job under each of the factors to arrive at the job's overall relative worth.

This method is effective because it relies on a job-against-job comparison. However, the more factors there are, the more complicated the process becomes.

Salary Surveys

One way to determine whether an organization's salaries are competitive with comparable positions in other companies is to participate in salary surveys. Salary surveys may be conducted by one organization or sponsored by associations to which an organization belongs, by an industry of which a company is a member, or by a group of firms that are willing to share and compare data. Survey reports may also be obtained from the Bureau of Labor Statistics (BLS) as well as other government agencies. To obtain survey information from the BLS, call its information office at 202/606-7828.

Salary surveys cover benchmark jobs—that is, key jobs, or those easily defined and found within most organizations. Positions such as computer operator, typist, switchboard operator, and machinist might be considered benchmarks.

When collecting and compiling salary information, be sure that the data (1) refer to jobs with similar content and (2) are essentially comparable for each job. Similar job titles are not enough of an indicator; the specific content of the job—including duties, responsibilities, and prior experience required—must be examined before you can determine that the two jobs are comparable.

If you conduct your own salary survey, follow these five steps:

1. Carefully select the industry and organizations to be included in the survey. The greater the similarities are, the more likely it is that an accurate comparison can be made.
2. List key jobs and positions common to most firms. Include brief job descriptions so that comparisons will be valid.
3. Prepare a schedule of information to be obtained. This might include base salary, hours worked, shift premiums, other salary supplements, and methods of payment.
4. Proceed to collect accurate salary data on essentially similar jobs, by either questionnaire or interview.

5. Compile the salary gathered for each job, showing the range of rates paid and supplementary salary data.

Knowing which companies to include in a survey can be difficult. No two companies are alike, not even two companies of comparable size in the same business. In addition, many businesses operate in more than one labor market. Consider asking certain questions before deciding whether a particular company should be included in your survey:

- Does this organization compare with ours in the backgrounds and skills of its employees?
- Have any of our employees left to work for this company?
- Are this company's operations similar to ours?
- Do we have enough jobs in common to make the survey valid?
- Is this company reasonably competitive in terms of economic and operating characteristics?
- Can the company be counted on to supply accurate and reliable data?

Once suitable companies have been chosen, the surveying firm must select key jobs for comparison. They should represent a good cross section of the company's pay structure, including at least one job from each pay grade. These jobs should represent the various operating and functional units within the company.

Studies have shown that when pay surveys are properly conducted, they are accurate within 5 percent for operations positions and 10 percent for management positions.

Compensation Programs

Having identified the characteristics of an effective compensation program, written the job descriptions, developed a position evaluation system, and conducted salary surveys, an organization is ready to design a compensation program suitable for its specific needs.

Traditional Compensation Programs

The majority of employers today continue to choose between one of two basic types of traditional systems for determining salary increases: merit or single rate. A third traditional method, referred to as informal, is rarely, if ever, used anymore. It relies exclusively on managers to make individual increase decisions without any guidelines or controls. The varying standards of each manager can easily lead to personal favoritism, inequities between departments, and confusion on the part of employees regarding what is expected of them and what compensation they can anticipate. A lack of company-wide standards can result in serious ramifications for an organization, including charges of EEO violations.

Merit Increase System

In a merit increase system, the manager's evaluation of each employee's performance determines what increases will be granted. Merit increase systems are designed so that the salary ranges for all positions have a spread wide enough to accommodate the annual growth of an average to above-average employee. The human resources department should regularly review the ranges to make sure that they are still appropriate; this generally means a percentage increase in the minimum and maximum either annually or every other year. These adjustments will allow an employee to remain in a given salary grade for many years without having to be frozen at the maximum for that range. Some organizations assign increase percentages according to an employee's position within the applicable range (lower third, middle third, or upper third).

A merit pay system utilizes three factors: the frequency of merit reviews, the number of employees receiving increases, and the amounts of merit increases.

The frequency of merit reviews is usually based on the level of an employee's job, since it takes longer to observe and evaluate performance in higher-level jobs than in lower-level jobs. Therefore, employees in higher pay grades are generally reviewed less frequently than employees in lower pay grades. The more often an employee is reviewed, the lower the maximum percentage of salary increase should be.

The length of time on the job is also an important factor, since performance progress generally follows a curve: Employees learn most rapidly during the first several months on the job, with their rate of improvement then slowing down considerably. Hence, employees usually receive more frequent reviews when they are new to a job.

Most organizations using a merit increase program grant increases to between 80 and 90 percent of their employees. The remaining 10 percent to 20 percent not receiving increases are either above the maximum for their range, and are thus frozen, or are ineligible for an increase because of below-standard performance.

The actual pay increases granted to employees under a merit increase system will depend on a number of factors:

- Economic changes in the marketplace
- Departmental and organizational budgets
- Salaries paid by competing organizations for comparable positions
- Ability to attract and retain qualified employees
- Short- and long-term goals of the department and organization
- The prevailing cost-of-living index

Single Rates

The single-rate system of pay is customarily used in conjunction with step rates. For example, employees are given a starting rate while they are learning a job. Their pay then progresses by steps as performance increases to meet specified job standards.

Increases in the form of single rates of pay may be issued when many employees perform jobs of similar difficulty, employees work at approximately the same pace to reach preestablished goals and standards, or routines are very specific or schedules are so set that there is little opportunity for individual effort to affect output.

Single rates are frequently used in factory positions, where there are well-prescribed standards for quantity and quality of performance. Additionally, organizations are applying this practice to office operations, since many operations positions have characteristics similar to factory jobs: They require a relatively short learning time and standards of performance that are well prescribed.

The primary drawback to the single-rate system is that individual performance is not credited. This can have an adverse impact on employee motivation and incentive to remain with a company.

The single-rate system of pay increase should not be applied to jobs in which employee output can vary significantly.

Pay-for-Performance Compensation Programs

With current merit increases holding around 4 percent, representing just a bit more than a cost-of-living increase, many employers fear that traditional merit increase programs offer little motivation to employees. What is worse, since not much distinguishes the increases granted to superior workers from those given to borderline workers, the morale and productivity of a company's outstanding employees is bound to be affected. Simply stated, the old ways of paying people no longer work as effectively as they once did.

Increasingly, then, companies are turning to alternative methods of compensating employees. The rationale for these pay-for-performance programs is that employees are encouraged to view themselves as partners in their employer's business, sharing in both the financial risks and rewards. Many of these systems call for the transfer of certain pay decisions and responsibilities from human resources specialists to managers. Managers, it is reasoned, are better able to evaluate an employee's performance and to determine that employee's worth to the organization. This system puts compensation experts in more of an advisory role, creating guidelines rather than policy. In turn, managers must be made aware of and kept up to date on all aspects of the organization's compensation system.

Variable Pay

Variable pay links the amount of an employee's salary and subsequent increases with certain measurable accomplishments. A percentage of an employee's pay is risked: If certain goals are not met, salary does not rise above a certain rate. When companies do well financially, so do the employees. Conversely, employees failing to apply themselves will see that lackluster performance reflected in their paychecks.

Consider a customer service representative earning a base salary of $40,000. If the representative succeeds in reducing the number of customer complaints by 10 percent at the end of the calendar year, an additional $8,000 bonus would be paid. The base pay of $40,000 would start the next year with new objectives, designed to lead to an additional year-end bonus.

Variable pay has been a common practice applied to members of senior management for some time and is now becoming increasingly common for employees at all levels. Generally executives risk a higher percentage of their pay, usually up to 35 percent, in contrast to a rate of about 5 percent for lower-ranking positions. A portion of this percentage is based on the performance of an employee's department or division; the balance is based on individual performance. Typically, this split is sixty-forty, with 60 percent allocated for departmental achievements and 40 percent left for individual accomplishments. Some companies put more of an employee's pay at risk. At Taco Bell, for instance, managers receive a bonus worth about 30 percent of their base pay, on average, and payments that double the base amount are not uncommon.

According to a 1990 survey by the Conference Board in New York City, about 75 percent of companies that have variable-pay programs considered them a success at that time. Described as the most successful are variable-pay programs that put a significant amount of an employee's pay at risk. Asks Hoyt Doyel, principal of Effective Compensation Inc. in Lakewood, Colorado, "How much harder are you going to be willing to work for a 3 percent increase? Furthermore, the closer you can relate results to what an individual can truly influence, the greater the motivational impact."*

Variable-pay programs are not without problems, however. Emphasizing team awards can alienate individual achievers, and high individual incentives may conflict with team objectives. Also, longtime employees accustomed to a traditional merit increase system may find adjusting to variable pay difficult.

On the plus side, with variable-pay programs companies can weather business slowdowns without terminating workers. Most significantly, variable pay communicates to employees that their work is valued and that when the company does well they will share in the rewards.

Skill-Based Pay

Skill-based pay plans, also referred to as knowledge-based pay systems, compensate employees for the level and proficiency of their skills rather than for the specific job performed at any given time. Pay increases are given when the employees add to or improve their existing set of skills, as opposed to when a certain level of responsibility is achieved. Skill-based pay plans contrast with traditional approaches to pay that are job based and preclude employees from progressing in areas of responsibility or salary until there is a specific job opening available. With skill-based pay, employees who have learned a new skill and have demonstrated that they can perform it are eligible for another pay increase.

Skill-based pay programs are most typically found in manufacturing environments that utilize high-performance work teams where employees are required to learn and perform many different jobs. The system is prevalent at the nonexempt level because it is easier to identify skills utilized by hands-on workers than it is to identify knowledge required at a managerial level.

Various methods are used to determine the worth of a certain skill. While most companies assign prices to skills based on their relative worth

*Shari Caudron, "Master the Compensation Maze," *Personnel Journal* (June 1993), p. 64D.

to the company, others price each skill equally. Still others allow the employees themselves to determine the relative worth of each skill: the employer tells the workers what skills are needed to perform particular tasks and then allows the employees to select the jobs they want to perform. For example, the first three skills that an employee acquires might be worth $1.00 per hour per skill, the next three skills would be worth $.85 more an hour per skill, and so on. It does not matter which skills are learned first.

When employees have an active voice in the selection of skills to be learned and performed, training becomes a top priority. In fact, Peter LeBlanc, national practice director for work and reward system redesign for Chicago's Sibson and Company, said, "The number-one cause of failure is a lack of commitment to training, because from the employees' viewpoint, the only thing standing between them and their next pay raise is training availability. If training isn't available, the pay-for-skills system can become a demotivator."*

Other problems with skill-based pay systems include the difficulty in making the transition from a traditional system and what to do with employees who develop many new skills in a short period of time and then "max out" on the pay scale. According to the American Compensation Association, it takes an average of just three years for an employee to maximize in a skill-based pay system. Ways of motivating after that include instituting a variable-pay program that provides bonuses for exceptional individuals or teamwork.

In spite of these drawbacks, skill-based pay is one of the fastest growing new pay-for-performance plans in the United States. Employers implementing the plan report improved employee involvement, workforce flexibility, employee versatility, teamwork, and innovative use of technology.

Broadbanding

Broadbanding is a base-pay system that clusters many different jobs and salary ranges into a few broad categories with no job titles. This is accomplished by identifying the major skills and behaviors that are needed by employees and grouping those characteristics into a broad job-family structure. Employers then look at how the market prices those skills; managers use that information, coupled with an individual's level of performance, examine their budget, and make pay decisions accord-

*Ibid., pp. 64b–64o.

ingly. Contrast this system with traditional compensation systems that consist of many different job titles and numerous salary grades with accompanying ranges consisting of minimum to maximum salaries.

The primary objective of broadbanding is to pay individuals for what they actually contribute instead of relying on a narrow salary grade to determine an individual's worth. The system is also used for purposes of managing employee career growth and increasing the likelihood of cross-departmental transfers. With traditional compensation programs, employees rarely make lateral moves, much less move into a job that is classified in a lower grade, even if it represents an area of interest or relates to their field. Broad bands eliminate the "stigma" of grades and job classifications, thereby encouraging workers to move into a variety of jobs within the company. With fewer promotional levels, the primary means for an employee to advance is a bonus based on improved performance.

Additional Pay-for-Performance Plans

Other pay-for-performance plans are beginning to appear in the workplace as alternatives to traditional compensation programs. One such system is called *competency-based pay,* which focuses predominantly on blue-collar positions. Competency is defined as an important job trait or characteristic that an incumbent is expected to perform well. In a competency-based pay program, employers examine the characteristics of their top performers for any given position. Once the traits that contribute to the successful job performance have been isolated, employers proceed to label those elements as "competencies." From that point on, all employees performing that job will be compensated based on how well they meet the established competencies.

Gainsharing is another form of pay-for-performance compensation. A company's entire workforce is offered a bonus as an incentive to improve organizational performance. A goal is set in dollars that compares what employees cost in total versus the value of what is sold or produced. If employees can contain costs below the targeted amount, the company shares the cost improvement. If costs are not contained, there will be nothing to share.

To make gainsharing successful, productivity must be improved. Many employers believe that employees can be the most valuable source of suggestions and solutions to productivity problems. Not only do those performing the work often have the best ideas about how it should be done, but workers tend to be more receptive to their own ideas as well as those generated by their peers.

Program Administration

Whether you decide to implement a traditional compensation plan or adopt a pay-for-performance system, the success of your program depends largely on one key factor: communication with employees. Robert M. James, vice-president of Hay Management Consultants, reports that when it comes to communication with employees about compensation, "a lot is rarely enough. . . . It is abysmal how little is typically spent on communicating an organization's philosophy, competitiveness, salary opportunities, and the advantages and equity provided by salary administration procedures. Most organizations should shy away from communicating individual salaries. . . . Everything else should be communicated as often and as well as possible if maximum value is to be received from a salary program."*

John A. Rubino, senior manager in compensation consulting at Ernst & Young, offers the following guidelines for maximally effective communication between management and employees regarding a company's compensation program:

1. *Define the objectives.* Be clear about what aspects of your compensation program you want to communicate to employees. This should include a description of all components of the compensation system, how pay is determined, and what role individual performance plays. "You want not only to tell them, but to sell them."

2. *Find out how employees currently feel about your company's compensation program.* This may be done via a written survey or in small employee focus groups. Asking employees what they know and do not know and what their perceptions are will help management determine the information to disseminate.

3. *Develop a communication strategy.* Usually this means beginning with a letter from the chief executive officer to all employees, providing an overview of the compensation program. Managers then need to meet to discuss the details of the plan as well as the scope of their responsibilities.

4. *Select the most effective medium.* Determine which medium will best convey the message about your compensation program. Choose between audiovisuals such as videos or slides, print such as brochures or letters,

---

*Robert M. James, *AMA Handbook for Employee Recruitment and Retention* (New York: AMACOM, 1992).

electronics such as interactive computer programs, personal meetings, or some combination of these. Although they are time-consuming, face-to-face meetings are the ideal. They are personal and allow employees to ask questions.

5. *Communicate with employees.* Include a description of how the plan relates to business overall, and concentrate on explaining all the components fully. Be sure managers understand fully how the plan works, since employees will be going to them with questions later on.

6. *Evaluate the program.* Four to six months after the compensation plan has gone into effect, survey the employees to compare their initial responses with how they feel now. Do this regularly; employee feedback will help you improve and strengthen your compensation plan.[*]

Summary

This chapter has explained four primary compensation-related areas: characteristics of an effective compensation plan, job descriptions, position evaluations, and salary surveys. In addition, several types of traditional and pay-for-performance compensation programs have been examined. Small and mid-sized organizations should design programs that reflect their specific goals and objectives. In addition, programs should be flexible enough to expand as the company grows.

[*]As reported in Stephanie Overman, "Selling Your Compensation Plan," *HR* magazine (July 1994), p. 49.

7

Performance Appraisals

An effective performance appraisal system requires the cooperation and input of both human resources specialists and managers.

Compensation programs are closely tied to performance evaluation.
Therefore, any organization that has a formal compensation program
should also have a structured performance appraisal system. Even small
organizations with fifty or so employees should have some sort of formal
system for evaluating employee performance.

The key to a successful performance appraisal system is to structure
it in such a way that both the appraiser and the employee view the process
as problem solving rather than fault finding. A poorly planned or subjec-
tively implemented system, or the absence of an appraisal system altogether, can greatly weaken an organization and ultimately its ability to
perform.

Objectives and Uses

The primary objective of a performance appraisal system is to ensure the
maximum utilization of every employee's skills, knowledge, and interests.
Additional objectives include:

- Developing a mutual understanding between managers and employees with regard to performance expectations, goals, and measurement criteria
- Strengthening the working relationship between managers and employees
- Advising the employee as to job performance as it relates to agreed-
  upon expectations

- Helping the employee improve job performance in the future by clarifying what is expected
- Planning developmental and promotional opportunities by identifying employee strengths and areas requiring improvement
- Allowing employees to express themselves openly with regard to performance-related issues
- Identifying the organization's high-potential employees for future human resources planning purposes

Performance appraisals may also be used to:

- Provide feedback on past performance according to established standards of performance and specific job responsibilities
- Clarify job requirements and expectations
- Help to evaluate an individual's potential
- Identify strengths and areas requiring improvement
- Identify ways to improve performance
- Allow for open two-way communication
- Identify mismatches in hiring
- Allow managers to examine their own strengths and shortcomings
- Motivate
- Allow for more productive uses of human resources

If used properly, performance appraisal systems will prove beneficial to the organization overall, as well as to its managers and employees. The organization will also generate data useful in the establishment of an equitable compensation program, the identification of training and development needs, and the decision-making process relating to transfers, promotions, and other employee-related activities. Managers will be able to utilize staff more productively, gain greater awareness of unusual performance, both positive and negative, and develop a keener understanding of levels of responsibility and work distribution in their departments. Employees benefit too, through a clearer understanding of their duties and responsibilities, greater knowledge of how well these are being performed, and increased opportunity to express their opinions and concerns openly with regard to work-related matters.

Components of an Effective System

In order to ensure that a performance appraisal system is developed fairly, applied consistently, and evaluated objectively, make sure it meets seven key criteria.

1. *It should be job related.* An evaluation program should be founded on criteria that are directly related to the primary duties and responsibilities of a particular job. The criteria should be specific, observable, and measurable. The nature and responsibility level of each position should determine the amount of weight assigned to each factor measured.

2. *It should be reliable and valid.* To be reliable, an appraisal system should yield consistent data regardless of who does the appraising or when it is done. For the system to be valid, there must be a direct correlation between the factors being measured and the critical elements of a particular job. It is important to note that elements critical to one job may not be relevant at all in another job.

3. *It should be standardized and consistently applied.* A performance appraisal system should be standardized in its design and consistent in its administration. All managers and human resources specialists using the system should be given written guidelines and training in their implementation. Organizations should develop effective techniques for monitoring the degree of consistency in implementation.

4. *It should be practical and workable.* To be effective, a performance evaluation system should be practical, workable, and viewed by all concerned as a helpful tool. It should not be so complex or time-consuming to administer that managers view it as a burden. This can easily occur when forms are very lengthy to complete, multiple approval steps are required, or the system requires a forced distribution of results (such as 20 percent unsatisfactory, 60 percent average, and 20 percent outstanding).

5. *It should be acceptable to human resources specialists, managers, and employees.* A performance appraisal system should be deemed acceptable by the appraisers and the appraised. Ideally, everyone concerned should have some role in developing the system; many organizations now involve employees in the development of criteria for measuring their own performance.

6. *Managerial style should be conducive to employee growth.* In order to create the right climate for a successful performance appraisal system, managers must be encouraging and supportive of their employees' efforts. In addition, they should display confidence in their employees' ability to progress. Managers should ask themselves three key questions about how their style relates to performance appraisals:

- Do I know how my employees view me?
- Do I have sufficient confidence in my own skills to encourage the growth and development of others?

- Do I show interest in my employees and exhibit encouragement for greater accomplishment?

If these three questions can be answered affirmatively, the managerial style may be considered conducive to employee growth.

7. *Employees should be receptive to suggestions for improving performance.* There is a strong proven correlation between the overall manager-employee relationship and an employee's receptiveness during the performance appraisal interview. If this relationship is poor, the employee is not likely to be receptive to even the most well-intentioned suggestions for performance improvement.

Coaching and Counseling

Two important elements to a successful performance appraisal system are coaching and counseling. *Coaching* may be defined as the day-to-day interaction between an employee and his or her manager. In order to be an effective coach, a manager should make certain that his or her employees:

- Know what is expected of them at all times
- Have the opportunity to make the best use of their skills, knowledge, and interests
- Know what the manager thinks of their performance
- Know where to go for assistance
- Receive assistance as needed
- Are rewarded on the basis of their job performance

To succeed at this, managers should strive to:

- Set realistic goals and objectives
- Delegate tasks according to the knowledge, abilities, and interests of employees
- Provide ongoing feedback on performance
- Provide assistance and support
- Provide a motivating environment
- Create a supportive working relationship
- Emphasize the importance of continued growth and development
- Provide opportunities for future growth and advancement

These coaching guidelines will enable managers to help employees improve the performance of their current assignments and increase their opportunities for growth and advancement, and will improve overall job satisfaction for everyone.

Counseling may be defined as interaction between an employee and his or her manager focusing on a specific work-related issue. When attempts to alter an employee's performance through coaching fail, managers must shift their role to that of counselor. Effective counseling enables employees to examine their behavior, explore alternative ways of behaving, and review the possible consequences of each alternative. The counseling process enables managers to help employees bring about changes themselves.

Counseling may be preventive or corrective in nature. In either instance, the ultimate goal is for employees to function more effectively on the job and to pursue their career goals successfully.

Managers may utilize both directive and nondirective approaches to counseling meetings. With the *directive* approach, the manager determines in advance the specific items to be discussed during the meeting and further controls the course of the conversation with the employee. The *nondirective* approach encourages greater input by the employee. It does not preclude the use of specific or directive input by the manager but instead permits the employee a greater freedom of expression. The more the employee is permitted to participate in a counseling interview, the more likely is a positive outcome.

Nondirective counseling interviews generally follow three stages: the presentation of facts by the manager, a discussion with the employee, and problem solving. By the time the third stage is reached, the employee should be ready to examine various alternatives, and the manager and employee together can select the alternative most likely to result in improved behavior. It is important for managers to note that the employee must agree to and ultimately bring about the change.

The counseling process may run more smoothly if managers follow these eight steps:

1. Prepare for the discussion.
2. Advise the employee of the purpose of the meeting in advance.
3. Begin the meeting by stating the purpose of the discussion.
4. Define the problem.
5. Listen to the employee's side.
6. Clarify the problem.
7. Help the employee develop a solution.
8. Follow up.

How Performance Appraisal Responsibilities Are Divided

An effective performance appraisal system requires the cooperation and input of both human resources specialists and managers. Each has a specific set of responsibilities, and some responsibilities are shared. For example, understanding and applying applicable EEO laws must be accomplished by everyone concerned; no one is exempt from this.

Human resources specialists are generally responsible for establishing the most appropriate method of evaluating employee performance and for designing the form to be used during the face-to-face interview.

The planning and preparation stage is an important responsibility of the manager conducting the review. This includes completing the form and preparing the employee for the actual meeting (perhaps by having the employee conduct a self-evaluation that will be compared with the manager's evaluation during the performance appraisal session). The emphasis during the face-to-face meeting should be on the employee's success in meeting agreed-on goals and objectives, areas requiring improvement, how these improvements can be achieved, and goals for the upcoming review period.

Human resources will then review and process the completed performance appraisal form. Furthermore, the human resources department is responsible for formally monitoring the performance appraisal system to make sure that employees are reviewed on time and that all recommended salary increases are consistent with the overall evaluation. Any inconsistencies should be discussed with the evaluating manager.

Here is a summary of the components of an effective performance appraisal system, showing who is responsible for what:

Task	*Responsibility of*
Understanding EEO laws	Managers and human resources specialists
Establishing an appropriate method for evaluating performance	Human resources specialists
Designing appropriate performance appraisal forms	Human resources specialists
Reminding managers when their employees are due for appraisals	Human resources specialists

Task	*Responsibility of*
Planning for the interview and filling out the performance appraisal form	Managers
Preparing the employee for the interview	Managers
Conducting the face-to-face interview	Managers
Recommending salary increases	Managers
Reviewing and processing completed performance appraisal forms	Human resources specialists
Approving recommended salary increases	Human resources specialists
Formally monitoring the performance appraisal system	Human resources specialists

Performance Appraisal Methods

There are numerous ways to evaluate employee performance, ranging from extremely simple to highly complex. With all the different methods to choose from, it is important to understand the components of each, what it has to offer, and its drawbacks. The most commonly used methods for evaluating standards of performance are:

- Management by objectives
- Essay evaluation
- Graphic rating scale
- Weighted checklist
- Behaviorally anchored rating scale
- Forced choice
- Critical incident
- Ranking
- Paired comparison
- Forced distribution

Management by Objectives (MBO)

MBO entails managers and employees working together to set performance objectives. It calls for establishing specific standards by which to measure performance, and appraising each employee according to his or her ability to achieve set objectives. The objectives are stated in quantitative terms whenever possible. For example, one goal might be for an employee to increase sales by a certain percentage within the next year.

The MBO process focuses attention on the position rather than the individual, so that the performance appraisal evaluates progress made toward goals as opposed to individual behavior. Stated another way, MBO concentrates on what the person does as opposed to who he or she is.

MBO programs have both advantages and disadvantages. On the one hand, they often work well, and various MBO formats are considered highly useful in making promotion and salary decisions and/or highly relevant to counseling and employee development. On the other hand, in rapidly growing companies, organizational changes may occur too frequently for the objectives to be of any real value. The reliance on quantifiable results can also present difficulties in evaluating performance in certain jobs.

Essay Evaluation

The essay evaluation format of performance appraisal requires the evaluator to highlight in paragraph form both the employee's strengths and areas requiring improvement. This system depends heavily on the evaluator's ability to write clearly. The typical essay evaluation lists a series of open-ended questions about the employee's behavior and performance, projected training needs for the future, and potential for advancement.

The essay evaluation format is favored by many small and mid-sized organizations since it is virtually cost free, easy for employees to comprehend, and very useful in making decisions about promotions, salary increases, and employee development.

Graphic Rating Scale

The graphic rating scale is one of the most popular forms of performance appraisal. It lists various work factors, such as quantity of work, attendance, job knowledge, quality of work, problem solving, and decision making. Accompanying this list of factors is a series of boxes that the evaluator is asked to check off, each with a descriptive word generally ranging from "outstanding" to "unsatisfactory." Sometimes a point value is assigned to each of these words; for example, outstanding might receive 4 points, while unsatisfactory might receive 0 points. Finally, there is an overall summary rating at the end, either in descriptive terms (such as "outstanding") or in point form.

Common problems associated with the graphic rating scale system include:

- The same work factors do not necessarily have the same importance or meaning in all jobs throughout an organization.
- Some managers tend to play it safe and merely check off "satisfactory" right down the line regardless of a particular employee's performance level.
- In spite of the fact that many forms using the graphic rating scale call for comments, many evaluators simple check off the boxes and do not add specific comments.
- This system is conducive to the "halo or horns" effect, in which a manager's overall impression of an employee leads him or her to check off all the boxes at either the high or low end of the scale, rather than judging each individual factor objectively. One way to counteract this is to reverse the direction of the rating scale on some questions, so that "outstanding" is sometimes on the left and sometimes on the right. This slows down evaluators and encourages them to think about one question at a time.

The graphic rating scale system is highly useful in making promotion and salary decisions but only moderately relevant to counseling and employee development.

Weighted Checklist

The weighted-checklist system relies on a list of descriptive statements defining effective and ineffective behavior in a particular job. These items are then rated anywhere from poor to outstanding. Number values are also assigned to each item; however, in order to ensure maximum objectivity, managers receive the checklist without knowing the point values or weighted scores assigned to each statement. The total evaluation is the sum of the scores.

The weighted-checklist system is closely related to the graphic rating scale. It is not difficult for managers to implement, and employees can understand it easily. It is moderately useful in making promotion and salary decisions.

Behaviorally Anchored Rating Scale (BARS)

This evaluation technique is based on the characteristics of a specific job or job family. The primary duties and responsibilities of a job are identified on a form, as well as the most and least effective ways for accomplishing these functions. The manager then matches the employee's behavior to the most accurate descriptions. Well-written job descriptions are essential for this method to work effectively.

One of the major benefits of the BARS performance evaluation system is that it enables appraising managers to evaluate employees on the basis of specific work factors. For example, a secretary may be criticized for allowing the phone to ring too long, as opposed to being told to pay more attention to his or her work. Hence this method encourages specific comments, which are much more helpful to the employee than general ones.

The BARS performance evaluation system is highly useful in making promotion and salary decisions as well as highly relevant to counseling and employee development.

Forced Choice

The forced-choice method of performance evaluation was originally designed to reduce the chance of bias by setting up a system of four possible statements from which the evaluator must choose. The statements are grouped in such a way that the evaluating manager cannot easily determine which statements describe the most effective behavior. For example, four items in one group might be:

1. Hard worker
2. Effective group leader
3. Works well under stress
4. Focuses on details

Sometimes evaluators are asked to check which of the statements is most relevant and which is least relevant to the person being evaluated. Human resources specialists then determine which statements describe effective or ineffective behavior for a particular job. The number of statements in each category are then added up to develop what is called an "effectiveness index."

In order to work effectively, the forced-choice method must be based on a custom-tailored position description for each individual job. It is difficult to use for the purpose of counseling an employee in specific problem areas and is only somewhat useful in making promotion and salary decisions.

Critical Incident

This method of performance appraisal requires the evaluating manager to keep a log of all the positive and negative behavior of each employee. At the employee's scheduled performance appraisal, this log is used to develop a detailed picture of the employee's performance. This technique helps managers avoid the "recency bias," in which greater weight is assigned to more recent incidents. In order to be effective, this technique requires a specific list of job requirements and responsibilities for each position.

The critical incident technique is generally used when evaluating higher-level positions. Although highly relevant to counseling and employee development, it is only somewhat useful in making promotion and salary decisions. In addition, it is extremely time-consuming and difficult for managers to implement.

Ranking

This technique evaluates employees in comparison with one another. The evaluating manager is asked to rank his or her employees from highest to lowest, based on some overall criteria. Ranking is most effective when evaluating fewer than twenty employees. Managers who utilize this system report that it is far easier to rank the most effective and least effective workers than it is to rank the average workers.

This is not a difficult system for managers to implement, but it is not very useful for making promotion and salary decisions. It is also irrelevant to counseling and employee development.

Paired Comparison

This method is similar to the ranking system in that it evaluates employees in comparison with one another. In this system the names of employees who perform similar responsibilities are placed on separate sheets of paper. Then each employee is compared with the other employees one at a time, on the basis of ability to perform specific duties. The number of times a person is preferred is then added up. The results are similar to those of the ranking system: One employee is deemed the best performer, one employee is deemed the worst, and so on. Like the ranking system, the paired-comparison system is not very useful for promotion and salary decisions, and irrelevant to counseling and employee development.

Forced Distribution

This technique for evaluating employees in comparison with one another is similar to grading on a curve. Managers are asked to rate employees on the basis of percentage categories: for example, the top 10 percent of the group, the next 20 percent, the middle 40 percent, the next 20 percent, and the bottom 10 percent.

Managers frequently complain that forced distribution compels them to distribute the performance ratings for their department according to a predetermined pattern. This is awkward when nearly all the workers in a particular department are working at a superior or outstanding level; some will end up with a rating considerably lower. This system is particularly unfair when the performance evaluation is linked directly to salary increases.

Once again, this system is not useful for promotion and salary decisions, counseling, or employee development.

Choosing the Most Appropriate Performance Appraisal System

Before considering which system is most effective for your company's needs, it is critical to keep in mind that even the best performance evaluation system is likely to fail if it is not effectively implemented and monitored. Well-trained evaluators are essential to any performance appraisal system.

When selecting the most appropriate appraisal system for your company, take the following factors into account.

Specific purpose of the appraisal. If the primary purpose of your performance appraisal program is to evaluate employee growth and development, then the BARS system might be most appropriate.

Cost considerations. If money is a major concern, then an essay or BARS system might be selected.

Level of employees being evaluated. MBO is generally reserved for management positions. A graphic rating scale might be more appropriate for clerical positions.

Management climate. The performance appraisal system selected must be compatible with your organization's overall management style. For example, MBO will work best in a progressive environment that emphasizes

employee participation and a high degree of mutual trust. In more traditional climates, a weighted-checklist or forced-choice system might be
more appropriate.

Experience level. Consider the length of time an employee has been in
a particular job and how well he or she has mastered its basic requirements. The most effective technique for measuring the performance of
experienced employees may not be the same one you would use for beginners.

Growth considerations. Small and mid-sized companies should bear in
mind that, just as with a salary administration program, their performance
appraisal system should be flexible enough to expand as the company
grows. A small but rapidly growing company would very quickly out-
grow the ranking performance appraisal system and have to replace it
with a more sophisticated program.

Performance Appraisal Forms

A well-designed appraisal form can greatly facilitate the performance appraisal process; a poorly designed or misused form can render the appraisal system virtually useless. Performance appraisal forms are used for:

- Recording appraisal information
- Helping managers organize their thoughts about the employee's
  performance before the face-to-face interview takes place
- Helping human resources ensure consistency between evaluations
  and salary increase recommendations
- Making decisions about promotions, transfers, demotions, and ter-
  minations
- Helping resolve disciplinary matters
- Meeting specified performance goals and objectives
- Documenting the need for training

The time and energy required to design an effective performance appraisal form is an important investment in any organization's future. For
this reason, using another organization's form for your own is not recommended, no matter how similar the other organization may be in composition, size, goals, and so on. Your company's form should reflect your
company's unique environment.

If you wish to adapt an existing form, question how every item relates
to performance of the jobs within your organization, and eliminate criteria

or performance areas that are not job specific. Of course, the form you use will also depend on which performance appraisal system you have chosen.

Performance appraisal forms should be used for three primary purposes:

1. To highlight an employee's performance from the last review to the present, in relation to established goals and objectives
2. To discuss areas requiring improvement and agree on methods for improvement
3. To establish new goals to be met by the time of the next performance appraisal review

Unfortunately, many forms try to go beyond these three areas. One common tendency is to include a list of personal characteristics. More often than not, the terminology is subjective and irrelevant. For example, trying to evaluate an employee's attitude on a scale of 1 to 5 simply cannot be done objectively. Trying to define the term "attitude" objectively merely serves to complicate matters further. Only those factors that are measurable or can be described in tangible terms should be part of a performance appraisal form. For example, job knowledge, skill, decision making, communication, leadership, productivity, quality of work, quantity of work, and attendance and punctuality can all be defined objectively; they are measurable and tangible.

One of the most common errors organizations make in designing their performance appraisal forms is not to give adequate, clear instructions to the evaluator. Written instructions accompanying any performance appraisal form should include the following information:

- The purpose of the performance appraisal
- How the form is to be used
- The respective roles, responsibilities, and relationships of everyone concerned in the performance appraisal process
- The exact period of time the appraisal is to cover
- Specific definitions of rating terminology
- Whom appraisers can go to with questions

In addition to written instructions, training should be offered to all managers and supervisors who are responsible for conducting performance appraisal interviews. Even the most clearly written set of instructions is not adequate preparation for a manager conducting a review. The opportunity to ask questions and actually fill out practice forms is essential for the successful use of any organization's performance appraisal form.

There should be as much room for the employee's comments on a performance appraisal form as for the appraiser's comments. Unfortunately all too often the employee is offered the opportunity to write a response to the appraisal, only to find a limiting one or two lines for this purpose. Employees who have more to say than will fit in this space are sometimes encouraged to write on a separate piece of paper and attach it to the formal form. Most employees react negatively to the idea that their comments serve as an addendum to their own performance appraisal. Not wanting to seem pushy or overly conspicuous, they may write few or no comments and depart a review session feeling disheartened. This can have a negative impact on their future productivity, as well as on their working relationship with their manager or supervisor. Hard feelings can be avoided by very simply allowing the employee the space and opportunity to write comments on the same form the appraiser used.

Some performance appraisal forms rely too heavily on numerical ratings. These ratings are easy for appraisers to use. Numbers ranging from 1 to 5 are found on many forms, and evaluators know that the highest possible rating should be reserved for outstanding employees and the lowest possible rating should be reserved for very poor performers. Hence many evaluators play it safe and go down the middle, checking off a series of 3's. Or, as mentioned earlier, they may give in to the halo or horns effect, and check off a series of 1's or 5's. This is rarely an accurate portrayal of an individual employee's actual performance. Depending on numerical ratings without accompanying supportive statements provides an incomplete picture.

To illustrate this point, let us say that the factor being evaluated is productivity—the quantity of work produced. The numerical ratings range from 1 to 5:

   1 = far exceeds the required quantity of work
   2 = exceeds the required quantity of work
   3 = meets the required quantity of work
   4 = needs to improve the quantity of work
   5 = produces an unsatisfactory quantity of work

If the evaluating manager believes that the employee far exceeds the required quantity of work, then he or she should supplement the number 1 rating with specific examples. Room for comments should be provided for every factor being evaluated, not just at the end of the entire form.

Some performance appraisal forms also use adjectives too casually. Many forms include lists of adjectives such as:

ambitious	overly emotional
argumentative	receptive
contrary	reliable
cooperative	responsible
dedicated	results oriented
energetic	trustworthy
flexible	uncooperative
hardworking	unresponsive
lazy	unyielding

The evaluator is asked to choose the most applicable term from a group of five or so adjectives listed for each actor being evaluated. Some adjectives are positive and some negative. Of course, the key problem with this system is that the appraiser is forced to select a term even if none of them really applies. In addition, this system may put ideas into the appraiser's head that are not completely accurate. Also, most of these terms are highly subjective, so their usefulness is questionable on this basis alone.

Misuses of the Performance Appraisal Form

One of the most common misuses of the performance appraisal form occurs when the appraiser completes the form and submits it to personnel without discussing the contents with the employee. The employee may informally be told that the overall evaluating was good or otherwise. However, he or she never gets the chance to discuss in detail the various categories being evaluated or to review means for improving performance. In addition, the manager and the employee do not have a chance to set performance objectives together for the next review period. This renders the appraisal useless for several of its intended purposes and represents a major opportunity lost for the employee, the manager, and the company.

To prevent this, the form should have a line for the employee's signature. This signature should mean that the employee has read and understood the contents, although he or she may not necessarily be in agreement. There should also be a line for the manager's signature, and personnel should return any forms submitted without both signatures intact.

Another misuse occurs when the manager meets with the employee to discuss his or her performance with a blank appraisal form on the desk between them. The manager reviews the various categories of the form, commenting verbally on the employee's performance in each. Although the employee may be encouraged to comment, nothing is written. Sometime after this meeting, the manager completes the form (generally by just checking off boxes and not writing comments) and then submits it to personnel for filing. This approach seriously undermines the detail and accuracy of the performance appraisal form. Once again, having a line for the employee's signature can help prevent this problem.

A third misuse of the performance appraisal form occurs when the manager completes the form and submits it to the employee to review, comment on in the space provided, and sign. There is no face-to-face discussion between the two parties. The form is sent to personnel and processed accordingly. Even if the employee agrees with all the comments and evaluations made by the manager, the process can be very frustrating, since the employee is not given an opportunity to discuss them. Face-to-face interaction between the employee and the manager is essential for maintaining a positive working relationship, planning objectives for the next review period, and encouraging career development.

A fourth common misuse occurs when the manager changes his or her comments after meeting face to face with the employee. Rarely are these changes for the better; they often occur when the employee says something during the interview that makes the appraiser think he or she was too generous with the rating in the first place. Sometimes merely by disagreeing with the manager's overall rating, the employee angers the manager and inspires this form of retaliation.

Changing a performance appraisal rating after meeting with the employee, without the employee's consent or knowledge, is both unprofessional and dishonest and must not be permitted in any environment. One way to safeguard against this practice is to require supporting statements for every numerical rating, so that an appraiser cannot arbitrarily check off a number indicating that an employee's performance is below average without providing specific examples.

Limitations of Forms

Sample performance appraisal forms appear in Appendixes H and I. Before looking at them, however, note that no matter how well a form is designed, it cannot create a successful performance appraisal system by itself. Although the form is an important aspect of a performance appraisal program, its primary use should be to facilitate the face-to-face interview between the appraising manager and the employee being reviewed. No form can guarantee a successful performance appraisal if the manager's skills are inadequate.

Also remember that once the performance appraisal form is completed and the interview is conducted, the process is far from over. Coaching and counseling for performance improvement are ongoing managerial responsibilities, not a once-a-year occurrence. Managers should remember that employees who perform well are entitled to positive coaching (stroking) just as poor performers require coaching for improvement.

Performance appraisal forms may be designed with a specific appraisal technique in mind. Many growing organizations prefer to use a more general type of form, conducive to changes in methods for evaluating standards of performance. These organizations generally design one form for exempt or professional employees and a second form for nonexempt employees, using a combination graphic rating scale and essay evaluation method for evaluating standards of performance.

Preparing for a Performance Appraisal Meeting

Before meeting with an employee to discuss the performance appraisal, managers should make certain their evaluation is fair and objective, particularly if the appraisal is unsatisfactory. Accordingly, managers are advised to consider these questions concerning the employee's job:

- Is there a proper match between the employee's skills, knowledge, and interests and the position?
- Is there a match between the intangible factors, such as management style or personality, of the employee and myself?
- Does the employee have a clear understanding of the job duties and scope of responsibilities?
- Have I worked with the employee long enough (at least three months) to be able to evaluate his or her performance?
- Have I objectively measured the employee's work record against the requirements of the job?
- Have I evaluated the employee's entire performance and not just focused on positive or negative factors?
- Has the employee been provided with sufficient instructions and work tools?
- Has the employee been encouraged to ask questions or seek clarification regarding his or her work assignments?

If your answer to any of these questions is no, an employee's unsatis-factory performance may have nothing to do with ability. Additionally, an unsatisfactory evaluation may be due to an evaluating manager's failure to:

1. Set mutually agreed-upon meaningful objectives
2. Accurately measure accomplishments against the agreed-upon objectives
3. Examine personal attitudes that may interfere with an objective measurement of performance

Before meeting with an employee, the manager should also have conducted a thorough review of the employee's work record, including any accomplishments; considered what improvements are needed and how they may best be accomplished; and anticipated the feelings and reactions of the employee. Additionally, employees should be given several days' notice to prepare for the meeting and perhaps be asked to prepare a self-evaluation to be discussed at the meeting.

Managers should plan an employee's written evaluation several weeks in advance, to allow time to review overall performance, evaluate specific accomplishments, assess areas requiring improvement, and consider potential. Contents of the written evaluation should meet the following guidelines:

- Use only statements that are objective, factual, job related, specific, and/or instructional.
- Use language that will be clearly understood by the employee.
- Avoid absolutes such as *always* or *never.*
- Consider the employee's job description.
- Consider all aspects of the employee's work record.
- Use examples to support your praise or criticism.

Conducting the Performance Appraisal Meeting

The core of any performance appraisal system is the face-to-face meeting between the managers and the employee to discuss how the employee has been performing on the job, how a high level of performance can be maintained, or how performance can be improved in the future. If a manager has been doing a satisfactory job as a coach and counselor throughout the year, nothing that is said during the evaluation should come as a surprise to the employee.

The manner in which this appraisal meeting is conducted can have a great impact on an organization's entire appraisal program. It is these qualities exhibited by the manager, as opposed to the system and type of forms used, that will ultimately result in changes in employee behavior.

This is not to say that the entire burden of improved performance rests on the shoulders of the appraising manager. The employee must have both the motivation and the ability to improve. Similarly, a well-planned and effectively conducted interview cannot compensate for a poor working relationship between manager and employee that existed throughout the rest of the year. In addition, there must be a match between an employee's skills, knowledge, and interest with the job in order for any performance appraisal system to operate effectively.

The environment in which the performance appraisal meeting takes place should be private and comfortable, with a minimum number of distractions and interruptions. These conditions are essential if employees are to be encouraged to talk freely. They must believe that the discussion is private and confidential. Employees should feel at ease and comfortable with the location of the meeting. Accordingly, some managers prefer to conduct performance appraisals in the employee's office or work space.

In order to ensure that a performance appraisal interview is conducted as smoothly as possible, managers should apply the following interviewing skills and techniques:

1. *Establish a format* reflecting your own personality and style that incorporates the necessary components of the performance appraisal interview, including discussing past performance, setting mutually agreed-upon performance objectives, discussing areas requiring improvement, and discussing means for achieving improvement.

2. *Use icebreakers* at the beginning of the meeting to establish rapport. The more neutral these icebreakers are, the better. Their sole purpose is to put the employee at ease before discussing the review.

3. *Begin the core of the discussion* by asking the employee to restate each performance objective that was agreed upon at the last evaluation meeting, explaining the results attained, or reviewing each category on the appraisal form, describing your assessment regarding each area.

4. *Actively listen* to what the employee has to say approximately 50 percent of the time. Periodically summarize what the employee has said to ensure accuracy.

5. *Observe the employee's body language,* looking for changes in patterns. Beware, however, of assigning specific meaning to a given movement or

gesture until you can be fairly certain that you are correct. Be careful, too, not to interpret an employee's body language according to your own patterns.

6. *Encourage the employee to talk.* Use repetition (repeat the last few words of an employee's statement and let your voice trail off as a question mark); summarization; open-ended questions; silence accompanied by positive body language such as nodding, smiling, direct eye contact, and leaning forward; and words of encouragement and understanding, such as, "I see" or "How interesting!"

7. *Make certain the employee understands what is being said* by allowing ample opportunity to ask questions, observing changes in body language patterns and periodically asking the employee to summarize what has been said thus far.

In discussing specific performance objectives, ask the employee for an assessment of performance. Share your data as well as your reactions to the employee's self-assessment. If you must criticize, criticize the person's performance, not the person. Explain why you assessed the performance as you did, providing examples as often as possible. Then summarize the results of your joint analysis, and together develop a plan of action that includes specific techniques or approaches that may help the employee improve his or her performance. Managers are reminded that their role at this stage is that of a coach.

Before concluding the performance appraisal meeting, managers should summarize what was discussed, review the agreed-upon action plan, and set follow-up dates to review progress. The meeting should always end on a positive note with praise for work well done and encouragement for the attainment of mutually agreed-upon goals.

Here are some typical pitfalls that managers should avoid when conducting performance appraisal meetings:

- Avoid superficial discussions.
- Avoid becoming defensive or argumentative.
- Avoid dwelling on past deficiencies.
- Avoid discussing personality traits and attitudes.
- Avoid dwelling on weaknesses, faults, or shortcomings.
- Avoid dwelling on isolated incidents.
- Avoid comparing the employee with another or with oneself.
- Avoid statements such as, "If I were you . . ."
- Avoid leading questions, such as, "Don't you think . . . ?"
- Avoid solving the employee's problems for him or her.

- Avoid interrupting the employee as long as he or she is saying something relevant.
- Avoid talking down to the employee.
- Avoid talking about yourself.
- Avoid excessively positive evaluations for fear of disagreement or argument over honest, partially negative appraisals.
- Avoid opinions, impressions, and feelings. Stick with facts.

360-Degree Performance Appraisals

When properly administered, the performance appraisal approach described is reliable and effective. For employers seeking a more innovative approach, however, there is a relatively new way: the 360-degree appraisal, consisting of feedback from a number of people dealing with an employee on a regular basis and having useful information on how the employee performs the job. This includes employees from within the organization, such as the appraising manager, members of senior management, representatives from other departments, peers and subordinates, as well as others from outside the company: clients, customers, suppliers, and consultants.

Generally companies using 360-degree appraisals select between five and ten raters. The criteria or questions used are based on areas familiar to the raters. Often, in the case of external clients, quantifiable measures of performance are used—existing customer satisfaction data, for example, in place of a formal appraisal. When an appraisal form is used, simplicity is the guideline: a one- to two-page form with five to fifteen questions and room for additional comments. The data and perspectives are then pooled, resulting in a final written evaluation, usually by the employee's manager. If there are discrepancies in the raters' feedback, the manager returns to the original raters for clarification or may seek input from new raters. Finally, the manager conducts the face-to-face appraisal meeting with the employee.

This method of appraisal certainly provides a comprehensive view of an employee's performance. It also makes an employee more accountable to all internal and external relationships since these raters now have appraisal power. However, many raters, such as peers or clients, may be reluctant to provide feedback, either because they lack the appropriate skills or in anticipation that it will strain their relationship with the employee. There is also the problem of varying expectations by the raters: some rate low, while others are generous in evaluations. Also, the input of the raters should not necessarily be weighted equally, in view of their different levels of knowledge about the employee. Additionally, culling data from as many as ten raters is a time-consuming and complex process.

Companies interested in 360-degree appraisals should proceed only after receiving full support from senior management and providing training to employees as to how the process works. It is also a good idea to measure the success of the program in other companies. Digital Equipment Corp., in Maynard, Massachusetts, Johnson & Johnson Advanced Behavioral Technology based in Denver, Colorado, and Hamilton Standard Commercial Aircraft in Colorado Springs, Colorado, are a few of the organizations currently using 360-degree appraisals.

Summary

An effective performance appraisal system is job related, reliable, valid, standardized, consistent, practical, workable, and acceptable to all concerned. It requires the cooperation and input of human resources specialists and managers. Among managers' most important responsibilities are coaching and counseling; in this way, nothing that is said during the formal appraisal meeting will come as a surprise to the employee.

Employers may choose from numerous performance appraisal methods, keeping in mind that even the best system is likely to fail if it is not effectively implemented and monitored. And a well-designed appraisal form is worthless if the appraising manager is not well prepared for the face-to-face meeting with the employee and fails to practice effective communication skills during the evaluation.

8

Benefits Administration

A benefits package with a slight edge over the competitors' could result in attracting and retaining qualified employees who might otherwise opt to work elsewhere.

Over the past four decades, benefits administration has become an increasingly complex area to develop, implement, and monitor. This is true for several reasons:

- Categories of mandatory benefits have increased.
- Benefits beyond basic protection levels have expanded.
- Legislation governing both mandatory and flexible benefits has become more stringent.
- Organizations must actively compete with one another by offering the most comprehensive benefits package in order to attract and retain qualified employees.

Proposed full health care reform is expected to increase the linkage between organizations, health-care providers, and insurance companies.

Since the benefits provided for employees represent a substantial expense for a company, the various components of benefits administration should be thoroughly assessed before developing any kind of a program:

- The primary objectives of benefits programs
- Key benefits-related legislation
- Benefits trends over the past thirty-five years
- Costs of benefits
- Choosing an insurance carrier
- Workers' compensation

- Unemployment compensation
- Occupational Safety and Health Act of 1970 (OSHA)
- Pension plans
- Leaves of absence
- Preretirement programs
- Holidays
- Vacations
- How to develop a benefits plan
- Ongoing benefits planning
- Health care reform

This chapter will discuss all these areas.

Primary Objectives of Benefits Programs

Most organizations, regardless of size, offer their employees benefits beyond those required by law. This is done for six primary reasons:

1. *To attract qualified employees.* If salaries are comparable, applicants frequently decide between employment opportunities on the basis of the benefits offered by each organization. Consequently companies do all they can to promote their benefits packages in their recruitment efforts. For example:

- Advertisements for available positions often carry lengthy descriptions of the company's benefits.
- Employment agencies and search firms are given detailed accounts of a company's benefits so that these may be passed on to prospective employees.
- During campus recruiting, job fairs, and open houses, organizational representatives distribute literature describing their firms' benefits packages.
- Human resources representatives describe benefits to applicants who come for interviews.

Whatever a company's methods of recruitment may be, a comprehensive description of its benefits will be included. A benefits package with a slight edge over the competitors' could result in attracting and retaining qualified employees who might otherwise opt to work elsewhere.

2. *To maintain a favorable competitive position.* In order to maintain a competitive position in any field, management must strive continuously

to enhance the benefits offered its employees. This means keeping up to date on current trends in benefits packages as well as finding out what competitors are offering. The latter is not as difficult as it might sound initially. Benefits specialists may belong to organizations specifically for individuals in the benefits field. These organizations hold meetings during which benefits information is exchanged between members. In addition, benefits specialists from various organizations frequently conduct both formal and informal surveys. (Of course, you must be willing to provide benefits information about your company in order to receive information about the benefits offered by other companies.)

By recognizing the important role that benefits play in an employee's career with your company, and by keeping abreast of benefits trends as well as the specific benefits offered by competitors, your organization should be able to maintain a competitive benefits program.

3. *To enhance an employee's image of the company.* People who work for large organizations that are household names, such as IBM or General Motors, need not concern themselves with explaining who their employer is or the nature of their business. This is not the case with most small and mid-sized companies that are not as well known as their big-name competitors. Consequently employees of lesser-known companies, when asked where they work, probably feel compelled to offer a brief descriptive statement. For example, an employee working for XYZ, Inc., might add, "We lease cars." In addition, employees usually hasten to add a brief statement about what it is like to work there. If the company offers a comprehensive benefits package, they might say something like, "The company really looks out for its employees; you should see the benefits we get!" This kind of statement may lead other people to seek employment with your organization.

4. *To improve employee morale.* Employees need to be reminded that their employers have a continued interest in their growth and development. There are many ways to demonstrate this, such as job postings, workshops and seminars, on-the-job training, and regularly scheduled performance appraisals and salary reviews. The organization's benefits program may be added to this list. By striving to maintain the best, most comprehensive benefits plan possible, management demonstrates that it is concerned with the well-being of its employees. Even if there are specific elements of a benefits program that do not suit everyone, a bona-fide effort by management positively affects morale and helps motivate employees to do the best job they possibly can. Of course, an increase in employee

morale and motivation means greater job satisfaction, which ultimately results in an increase in productivity.

5. *To maintain a union-free environment.* It is commonly known that one of the primary reasons employees become interested in joining unions is that they are dissatisfied with company benefits. Clearly, then, one way to prevent unionization is to offer employees a comprehensive benefits plan.

6. *To reduce turnover.* Reducing turnover should be an ongoing goal for any organization. One way to do this is by offering your employees a benefits package with a slight edge over those of your competitors. This will make employees who are essentially satisfied with the other elements of their jobs, such as the working conditions and relations with their managers, less likely to seek employment elsewhere.

Key Benefits-Related Legislation

Over the past eighty-five years or so, various laws have resulted in numerous changes in benefits administration. Even though workers' compensation, unemployment compensation, payment of half of employees' social security taxes, and, in many states, disability insurance are, technically speaking, the only benefits employers must provide their workers, many organizations now also offer such benefits as medical and dental insurance and pension plans. This section highlights some key legislation that either led to or regulated many of these benefits.

State Workmen's Compensation Laws of 1910

In 1910 New York State enacted the first workers' compensation law, and several other states followed soon after. The original purpose of these laws was to promote the general welfare of employees by providing compensation for accidental injuries or death suffered during the course of employment (that is, to protect workers suffering occupational disabilities).

It is significant to note that under current legislation, employers may also be liable for injuries incurred during nonwork activities if these activities are in some way related to the job, such as injuries received while attending a company picnic.

Additional information on workers' compensation will appear later in this chapter.

Social Security Act of 1935

The original purpose of social security was to ensure a continuing income when earnings either stopped or were reduced because of retirement or disability. In 1939 the law was expanded to also pay survivors when the worker died, as well as certain dependents when the worker retired.

When it originated, social security covered workers only in industry and commerce. However, during the 1950s coverage was extended to include most self-employed persons, state and local employees, household and farm employees, members of the armed forces, and members of the clergy.

In 1972 additional legislation was enacted to guarantee the automatic increase of social security benefits in relation to the cost of living. Today the financial soundness of the program is questionable, largely because the proportion of the population over age 65 is increasing.

Keogh-Smathers Act of 1962

This act pertains to owners of nonincorporated and self-employed businesses, professional practitioners, sole proprietors, or members of a partnership. It allows them to contribute annually a certain dollar amount or specific percentage of earned income, whichever is less, to a private retirement fund. No taxes are paid on the income, or the interest it earns, until the funds are withdrawn when the employee retires. Benefits are paid on retirement, on permanent disability, or to a named beneficiary on death.

Civil Rights Act of 1964

The Civil Rights Act of 1964 has had a significant impact on benefits by requiring that all benefits be made available on a nondiscriminatory basis. This means that equitable benefits must be provided regardless of race, color, religion, sex, or national origin. To illustrate, if insurance coverage is available for the wives and children of male employees, it must be offered to the husbands and children of female employees. Insurance coverage may not limit maternity benefits to married women only. Also, eligibility for insurance and disability programs may not be based on head-of-household status.

Health Maintenance Organization Act of 1973

This act emphasizes maintaining good health and preventing illness. It requires that employers of twenty-five or more employees that are subject to the minimum wage provisions of the Fair Labor Standards Act of 1938, and that offer traditional health insurance, must offer their employees the option of membership in a health maintenance organization (HMO) if their location is served by a qualified HMO and if a qualified HMO approaches them with proposals. It is important to note that employers are not required either to form or to seek out an HMO.

To meet the standards of the law, the HMO must provide certain specified services to its members, including physician services, inpatient and outpatient hospital services, emergency health services, and mental health services.

Employee Retirement Income Security Act of 1974 (ERISA)

The primary purpose of ERISA is to protect the rights of participants in employee benefits plans, as well as their beneficiaries, by ensuring the equitability and soundness of retirement income plans. The term "retirement income" refers to any plan providing deferred income to participants. Hence individual-account plans, defined-benefit plans, multiple- or single-employer plans, pensions, excess-benefits plans, stock-allocation plans, deferred profit-sharing plans, and retirement plans must conform to ERISA standards.

ERISA permits employers to integrate social security into their pension plans so that projected pension benefits are offset by projected social security benefits. However, in January 1986 (*Dameron* v. *Sinai Hospital of Baltimore, Inc.*), a federal district court ruled that the employer may be held liable if the social security projection is too far off. The court determined that the total pension benefits may be offset only by the actual amount of social security benefits, and not by an estimated amount if the estimated amount is considerably higher than the actual income.

Calculations of this sort are best handled by actuaries and other professionals who administer pension plans.

ERISA protects employees' benefits in several important ways. It provides:

- Rules to ensure that participants are provided with information regarding the operation of their plans.
- Standards of fiduciary conduct for those individuals responsible for

managing and operating pension plans. This helps to protect plan assets against misuse.

- Minimum standards that pension plans must meet in matters of participation, vesting, joint and survivor protections, benefits accrual, and funding.
- A program of plan termination insurance that essentially ensures that participants in defined-benefit plans will receive a designated part of their vested benefits in the event their plan terminates.

ERISA is administered and enforced by three different units:

1. The Office of Pension and Welfare Benefit Programs (a section of the Department of Labor's Labor-Management Services Administration), which is responsible for the reporting and disclosure requirements as well as the fiduciary standards
2. The Internal Revenue Service, which oversees the minimum standards provisions required of pension plans
3. The Pension Benefit Guaranty Corporation (PBGC), which is responsible for administering the plan termination insurance program

Additional information regarding ERISA may be obtained by writing to:

Office of Pension and Welfare Benefit Programs
Labor-Management Services Administration
Room N-5471
U.S. Department of Labor
Third and Constitution Avenue, N.W.
Washington, D.C. 20216

Pregnancy Discrimination Act of 1978

According to this act, pregnancy is a temporary disability, so pregnant women may not be singled out for special treatment. Generally benefits must be the same for pregnancy as for all other disabilities. If special rules regarding pregnancy are established, organizations must be prepared to prove that they are dictated by business necessity or related to issues of safety or health. Pregnant women must be permitted to work as long as they are able to perform the essential functions of their jobs. Therefore, arbitrarily set dates for beginning maternity leave are not permitted. Company policies must allow each woman to tailor her schedule to her own physical condition. Physicians' statements regarding a pregnant woman's health and ability both to continue working and to return to work after childbirth may be required.

It is significant to note that a January 1987 Supreme Court ruling (*California Federal Savings and Loan Association v. Guerra*) determined that states may require employers to grant special job protection to employees who are physically unable to work because of pregnancy. Readers are urged to follow new developments in this area to determine how they are likely to affect their organizations' benefits programs.

Age Discrimination in Employment Act of 1967 (ADEA), Amended in 1978

This federal act protects workers over the age of 40. According to current ADEA guidelines, it is unlawful for employers to discriminate on the basis of age in matters of benefits. On the other hand, employers are not required to adjust work schedules to accommodate wage-earning restrictions.

Effective January 1, 1987, it became illegal to force most employees to retire because of their age, even at age 70. The amendments, which apply to businesses employing twenty or more workers, also require employers to continue group health insurance for workers over 70. Some groups of workers, such as air traffic controllers, may still be subject to mandatory retirement.

Individual Retirement Account (IRA)—Established by ERISA

Workers may set aside a portion of their pay in an IRA and pay no tax on that income, or on the interest it earns, until the funds are withdrawn on retirement. Therefore, IRAs are tax sheltered, as opposed to tax free.

Consolidated Omnibus Budget Reconciliation Act of 1985 (COBRA)

COBRA requires employers to offer extended health care benefits to former company employees who fit into any of a number of different categories. The law applies to private employers with twenty or more employees. With plan years that began after July 1986, health insurance must be made available to the following:

- *Employees who are terminated or laid off.* Such employees must be allowed to continue in an employer's health insurance plan for a period of eighteen months. However, employees who are terminated for gross misconduct are not entitled to continued health insurance.

- *Spouses and dependents of former employees.* The spouses and dependent children of former employees are entitled to continued coverage, generally for a period of thirty-six months.
- *Divorced spouses.* The former spouse of an employee is entitled to coverage, generally for a period of thirty-six months after the divorce.
- *Dependent children who "age out."* Dependent children who reach the maximum allowable age for coverage are also entitled to continue coverage for a period of eighteen months.

COBRA contains many other provisions, including the following:

- The annual termination-insurance premium that employers with defined-benefit pension plans must pay to the PBGC is increased, retroactive to January 1, 1986.
- It is now more difficult and expensive for companies to terminate underfunded pension plans. Most companies have to pay all guaranteed benefits before they can terminate a plan. Financially distressed companies are still allowed to terminate an underfunded plan, but their liability to the PBGC is higher than under previous law.
- Many changes in Medicare are made. Among those that affect employee benefits are these: Employers have to give employees and spouses age 70 and older the option of enrolling in their group health insurance plans instead of Medicare to receive their primary health care coverage. Medicare coverage is extended to all state and local government employees. Medicare payment is denied for failure to obtain a second surgical opinion for certain procedures.

Failure to comply with COBRA provisions can result in not only the loss of all federal tax deductions for *all* of an employer's health care plan expenses, but possible civil and equitable damages under ERISA.

The Budget Reconciliation Act of 1986 made some technical corrections to COBRA. Because of the complexity and importance of these laws, it is imperative to seek the advice of a benefits specialist to be sure that your company is in compliance with their requirements.

Americans with Disabilities Act of 1990

Under the provisions of the Americans with Disabilities Act of 1990 (ADA), employers providing insurance or other benefit plans to their employees must provide the same coverage to employees with disabilities. However, employers do not have to offer greater insurance coverage to workers with disabilities than they offer to workers without disabilities. Additionally, employers cannot deny insurance to an individual with a disability or subject someone with a disability to different terms or conditions of insurance, based on disability alone, if the disability does not pose increased insurance risks. Furthermore, an employer cannot terminate or refuse to hire an individual with a disability because the employer's current health insurance plan does not cover the individual's disability, or because the individual may increase the employer's health care costs.

The ADA does allow employers to provide insurance plans that comply with existing federal and state insurance requirements even if those provisions have an adverse effect on those with disabilities, provided that the provisions are not used as a subterfuge to evade the objectives of the law. Employers may offer insurance policies that limit coverage for certain procedures, treatments, and drugs, even if such restrictions adversely affect individuals with disabilities, as long as the restrictions are uniformly applied, without regard to disability.

Employees injured on the job and awarded workers' compensation benefits are not necessarily protected by the ADA. In most cases, the term *disability* carries a different definition under state workers' compensation laws than it does under the ADA.

The ADA supersedes any conflicting state workers' compensation laws. A worker filing a worker's compensation claim is not prevented from filing a disability discrimination charge under the ADA as well.

Additional information regarding workers' compensation and health insurance coverage under ADA may be found in the *Technical Assistance Manual* on the employment provisions (Title I) of the act. The manual may be obtained by contacting the Equal Employment Opportunity Commission.

Family and Medical Leave Act of 1993

In compliance with the Family and Medical Leave Act of 1993 (FMLA), all employers are required to maintain an employee's coverage under any group health benefits plan provided before the granting of leave under the same conditions as if the employee had been continuously employed during the entire leave period. If an employer provides a new health plan or changes health benefits while an employee is on FMLA leave, the worker is entitled to the new benefits as if still working.

Employees are responsible for continuing to pay any share of health plan premiums that were required before the leave commenced. If the FMLA leave is substituted for paid leave, the employee's share of premiums must be paid by the method normally used during any paid leave—generally as a payroll deduction. If the leave is unpaid, the employer may require that the payment be made either to the employer or to the insurance carrier. Other payment options may be exercised, including prepayment of premiums through increased payroll deductions before the leave begins. If the employee's premium payment is more than thirty days late, an employer's obligations to maintain health insurance coverage ceases. However, the employer must restore to the returning employee the equivalent coverage and benefits that would have been earned had the leave not been taken and the premium payments not missed.

Revenue Reconciliation Act of 1993

The Revenue Reconciliation Act of 1993 is a major tax reform measure. Title XIV contains significant provisions affecting employee benefits including:

- Employer-provided educational assistance
- Repeal of limitations on the amount of wages subject to health insurance employment tax
- Reduction in the deductible portion of business meals and entertainment
- Disallowance of deductions for certain employee remuneration
- Reduction in compensation taken into account when determining contributions and benefits under qualified retirement plans

Additional Legislation

The summary of benefits-related legislation provided in this section is not all inclusive. Several other acts, notably the Tax Reform Act of 1986 (TRA), the Tax Equity and Fiscal Responsibility Act of 1982 (TEFRA), and the Multiemployer Pension Plan Amendments Act of 1980 (MEPPAA), have had major impact on benefits administration. A good source of further information on benefits-related legislation is the International Foundation of Employee Benefit Plans, 18700 West Bluemound Road, P.O. Box 69, Brookfield, WI 53005.

Benefits Trends Over the Past Thirty-Five Years

The prevailing attempt to offer competitive employee benefits and still keep costs under control began during the 1960s. Some of the features of benefits plans during that decade included:

- Retirement programs with increased funding by employers
- More protective medical benefits
- Life insurance at least equal to an employee's annual salary
- Improved vacations, holidays, and sick leave

Organizations struggled to keep up with inflation and to exceed the pay and benefits offered by their competitors. However, many businesses were able to pass along the increased costs of benefits programs to their clients and customers.

Matters began to change in the 1970s, as U.S. businesses started to face growing competition from abroad. At the same time, human resources costs became a major expense that increasingly eroded the financial success of organizations. On the other hand, it became apparent that improperly designed benefits programs could lead to dissatisfaction within the workforce. Unlike the previous era, when workers often devoted an entire career to one company, the 1970s saw employees become more loyal to their personal career goals, more mobile, and more willing to risk changing jobs in order to further their careers. During the 1970s, then, benefits trends included these:

- A younger, more professional workforce was more concerned with immediate benefits and less interested in retirement plan improvements.
- Problems with the country's social security system became apparent.
- Health and dental coverage became more important.
- Flexible benefits plans became more popular.
- Containing the cost of benefits became a major business concern.
- Employers tried to respond effectively to employees' changing benefits needs.

The priorities of the workforce continued to change during the 1980s. Employees wanted freedom to select different types of benefits beyond a basic protection level and the option of cash compensation instead of benefits. However, the priority of corporations continued to be cost containment. Specific characteristics of benefits during the 1980s included these:

- Employees were being asked to pay for more of their own benefits to meet cost-containment concerns.
- Retirement plans were closely studied for ways to reduce benefits (to cut back on costs) without adversely affecting employee morale.
- Businesses tried to simplify benefits in order to save administrative costs.

Meanwhile, benefits trends for the turn of the century are already starting to become evident. Experts predict the following changes:

- Social security benefits will be reduced substantially by Congress.
- The eligibility age for retirement under social security will be raised.
- Employees will be asked to pay for larger portions of their own benefits, creating a partnership between employers and employees.
- Flexible benefits will be primarily employee-funded.
- Fixed-benefit retirement plans will gradually diminish.
- Profit-sharing plans will become more prevalent as retirement-funding vehicles.
- Full health care reform is likely to affect employers with fewer than 5,000 employees.

In addition, an increase in some specific benefits is almost certain, although employees will probably have to pay for many of these themselves. These benefits include dental care, vision care, health and wellness programs, prescription drug plans, group homeowners' insurance, group auto insurance, life insurance for dependents, care for children and other dependents, adoption benefits, legal counseling, and financial counseling.

Cost of Benefits

According to the Business and Legal Reports (BLR) 1993 Survey of Employee Benefits, more than one in three employers reported increased employees' contributions to health care premiums as a cost-control measure, and one in four reportedly increased workers' copayments. The survey also revealed a greater financial burden on employees for dependents' health insurance than in past years, with about 43 percent of the nearly

3,000 survey respondents reporting deductibles of $400 or more under family plans. Employers also have decreased the percentage paid in premiums for employee dependents. In prior years, more than half of BLR's survey respondents reported paying 80 percent or more of premiums for employees' dependents; the 1993 survey reported only about 37 percent as paying 80 percent or more.*

Benefits dollars are typically spent on:

- Legally required benefits, such as workers' compensation, unemployment compensation, social security, and, in many states, disability insurance
- Agreed-on benefits, such as insurance and pensions
- Time not worked, such as vacations and holidays
- Bonuses, profit sharing, and other "extra" benefits

Attempts to curb expenses range from wellness and fitness plans, which reduce insurance claims and sick leave, to cost sharing by employees. In addition, many organizations are exploring health care delivery systems such as HMOs, which lower costs by reducing the use of traditional health care services, and preferred provider organizations (PPOs), in which a group of doctors and hospitals agree to provide services at a reduced fee in exchange for guaranteed higher volume and prompt payment.

With the continuing emphasis on containing health care costs, many organizations are using these cost-containment programs:

- Mandatory second surgical opinions
- Increased deductibles or copayments
- Incentives for outpatient surgery and testing

Increasingly, organizations are setting up cost-containment programs. In planning one for your company, be sure to include a balance of short- and long-term strategies. Take a careful look at the incentive structure that guides employees and providers in making health care decisions. The program selected should suit your specific organizational needs.

Choosing an Insurance Carrier

Companies offer numerous types of insurance to their employees. The five most commonly offered forms of health insurance are hospital insurance,

---

*As reported in *HR Manager's Legal Reporter* (May 1993), p. 5.

surgical insurance, regular medical insurance, major medical insurance, and loss-of-income protection. In addition, many companies offer dental coverage, accidental death and dismemberment insurance, group term life insurance, group survivor benefits, short- and long-term disability insurance, and business travel accident insurance. With the soaring costs of these services, selecting the best insurance carrier is of vital importance to everyone. This is true whether you are selecting a carrier for the first time or changing carriers.

The financial arrangements and administrative services offered by different carriers will vary, so the first step in selecting an insurance carrier is to determine which factors are important to your organization. Once these factors have been selected, ask insurance companies to bid against one another. Unfortunately, all too often the only factor considered in comparing one bid with another is cost—that is, the premium rate to be charged for each line of coverage. It may be, however, that the quoted cost is not the most significant factor. For example, some insurance carriers offer lower premiums to companies that file fewer than the average number of claims over a period of time. Premiums for such companies are based on administrative expenses plus the number of future claims projected from that company's past history. However, if your company is too small to qualify for this, your premium costs will play a more significant role.

Questions to Ask Carriers

Evaluating the bids of several different insurance carriers is critical. These seven questions will help you:

1. Are you willing to guarantee premium rates for more than one plan year? If so, for how long and at what additional cost?
2. Does your company use a customary-charges schedule? If yes, how is the schedule developed? How frequently is it updated? What percentage of charges is reimbursed? Can the schedule be customized to reflect our actual experience?
3. What administrative services are included in your regular fee? What additional services are available, and at what additional costs?
4. What is your claims turnaround time?
5. Please provide a brief description of your claims administration and control procedures.

6. Please attach a description of the cost-containment services you provide.
7. If we terminate our policy "off anniversary" (before the plan year ends), what happens to any surplus premiums that have accumulated toward the current policy year?

Workers' Compensation

Workers' compensation laws were developed to promote the general welfare of workers by providing compensation for accidental injuries or death suffered during the course of employment. Workers' compensation is legislated and administered by the individual states, and schedules of benefits are established by statute.

Over the past several years, workers' compensation costs have increased dramatically. In 1991, businesses spent approximately $62 billion nationwide on workers' compensation, representing 2.1 percent of payroll, according to the Bureau of Labor Statistics. This is three times as much as was paid just a decade ago.

Compensation-related medical fees alone are rising 14 percent annually, compared to 8 percent for medical costs outside the compensation system. This is due, in part, to an upsurge of claims by disabled workers seeking compensation for alleged mental injuries—for example, physical-mental claims involving a physical injury's causing a disabling mental or emotional condition, such as brain damage resulting from a head injury; mental-physical claims involving physical disabilities' arising in response to mental stresses, such as cardiovascular disease; and mental-mental injuries in which both the cause of the injury and the injury itself are entirely mental in character (many states do not recognize mental-mental claims; others limit the scope of compensability).

Many employers are responding to this rise in compensation-related medical fees by embracing a managed-care concept, whereby employers are able to control costs through medical fee schedules, limited choices of doctors, and monitoring the appropriateness of treatment. Other cost-cutting medical trends include prohibitions barring doctors from referring workers' compensation patients to any specialty service clinics in which the doctors have financial interests, and limiting the range of compensable injuries. Enlightened employers use preloss management techniques, such as safety programs, along with postloss strategies, such as injury management, to control costs.

Experts suggest that the most common error committed by companies with exorbitant workers' compensation costs is the improper management of their programs. Too many companies sit back and assume they can do nothing instead of availing themselves of some of the options. Another problem is a company's failure to follow up on injured workers after they become disabled. Employers tend to assume that the worker's doctor will advise when the employee is able to return to work. However, this approach fails to consider that the doctor may not know of the employee's modified duty program or that the job might be changed to accommodate the worker's medical or physical restrictions. These same employers generally fail to contact the employee as well. Without contact, the employee may lose the necessary incentive and motivation to return to work and become "psychologically disemployed."

Unemployment Compensation

Unemployment compensation was established to provide some measure of protection for employees who lose their jobs involuntarily. As with workers' compensation, each individual state is responsible for developing and administering criteria for determining eligibility. Costs are shared by the state and the company. Most states require that an individual must have worked a minimum number of weeks in covered employment at a specified average minimum wage or that the worker earned wages in a "base period" within the calendar quarter.

There are four primary instances in which employees are not eligible to collect unemployment compensation.

1. *Willful misconduct.* Employees who are discharged because of willful misconduct are ineligible for unemployment compensation if the employer can prove the charge. In order to prove a willful misconduct charge, employers must show that (1) they had a rule or past practice forbidding the act committed, (2) the employee knew about the rule, (3) the employee actually violated the rule, and (4) the violation was the actual cause for the discharge.

2. *Refusal to accept suitable employment.* The law requires recipients of unemployment compensation to look for jobs and to accept any "reasonable" offer. If they do not, they may lose their benefits.

3. *Voluntary termination of employment.* Employees who leave work voluntarily are not eligible for unemployment compensation, with certain exceptions. For example, employees who quit their jobs because their spouses are being relocated have usually been found eligible. Also, em-

ployees who quit after working conditions deteriorate drastically are usually found eligible.

4. *Labor stoppage.* Employees who are out on strike are ineligible for benefits in all but a few states. An important distinction should be made between being "out on strike" and being "out of work because of a strike," however. In many states, employees who are laid off because their work is dependent on strikers' work *are* eligible for benefits, as long as their union is not participating in the work stoppage. Similarly, employees who are laid off before the strike are usually eligible, unless they walk picket lines or otherwise participate in strike-related activities.

Occupational Safety and Health Act of 1970 (OSHA)

OSHA sets standards for the maintenance of safe and healthful working conditions. The law sets specific standards that must be observed; requires employers to keep records and file reports of work-related illnesses, injuries, hazards, and deaths; and provides for inspections. All employers engaged in a business affecting commerce are covered by OSHA.

Numerous standards covering a broad spectrum of occupations have been developed. For the most part, the standards are based on those adopted by the American Standards Institute and the National Fire Protection Association. Some are general, outlining housekeeping responsibilities, fire protection measures, sanitary facilities, and so on. Others are very specific and regulate particular industries, processes, and equipment.

OSHA has developed a voluntary safety and health-protection program for companies that have historically had superior safety records and programs. Participants are subjected to less intense and less frequent inspections by OSHA than other companies.

Inspections may be made routinely, or to investigate a specific health- or safety-related incident. Sometimes OSHA initiates a specific program geared toward examining a particular industrywide problem.

The federal Occupational Safety and Health Administration periodically makes known its list of most frequently issued citations. Recently, it revealed that violations of the federal hazard communication standard, commonly known as the employee right-to-know law, continues to top the list of citations. The agency reports that in a twelve-month period, it issued more than 19,000 citations for violations of the general industry standard and nearly 17,000 citations for violations of the construction standards. Right-to-know violations have headed this list since the hazard communication standard took effect in 1985. Organizations that have maintained compliance typically enlist employees' help by alerting them to the need to report missing documentation or to request additional training if needed. Communication, then, is the key to avoiding this particular OSHA citation.

Employers are responsible for keeping abreast of and complying with all changes in OSHA regulations. For example, in 1992, OSHA issued a final rule designed to prevent catastrophic chemical explosions. The standard, which primarily affects petrochemical and chemical firms, requires covered employers to analyze possible hazards at each step in their chemical process as well as take action to prevent releases and explosions. Companies are required as well to provide written operating procedures for their safety systems and operations.

Pension Plans

Pensions emerged when employers could not afford to pay employees much money and instead gave them deferred payments for service. These programs entail systematically setting money aside to provide determinable benefits at retirement age. Typically they involve an insurance contract or a trust fund, either of which may be designed with a number of variations. The choice of such a plan or combination of plans will vary with the specific characteristics of an organization, including its size. Smaller companies, for example, may find it best to opt for an individual-policy pension trust or group permanent pension plan, since neither approach requires a minimum number of participants. Your company should investigate the availability of retirement programs through a special-interest group that may provide wider benefit options at a considerable savings.

There are two additional kinds of pension plans: profit sharing and stock bonuses. In a *profit-sharing retirement program,* a company establishes a trust fund into which it contributes, according to a prescribed formula, a share of profits for accumulation and investment to be distributed to employees at the time of retirement. No payments are made into the fund unless the specified profit levels are met.

Stock bonus programs are similar to profit-sharing plans in that all contributions are made by the employer, usually from profits. The difference is that, instead of contributing cash, the employer sets aside shares of stock for each eligible employee according to an established formula. Retirement income then takes the form of dividends or the sale of stock.

The administration of pension plans is extremely complex. Employers must be aware not only of the federal laws discussed earlier in this chapter but of accounting regulations set by the Financial Accounting Standards Board (FASB). These regulations change periodically, so it is critical to consult an accountant when planning and implementing a pension plan.

A growing number of companies are redesigning and simplifying their pension plans to meet the needs of a changing workforce. In part, this means making the pension plan portable: that is, allowing employees to take their retirement income when they leave the company and roll it over into a new employer's savings plan or IRA. Through this type of plan, those employed at several different companies throughout their careers will have a retirement income that is similar to the income of employees working at the same company throughout their entire careers, provided the income levels at retirement are similar.

This approach makes sense for many businesses, such as high technology, electronics, and biotechnology, where employees are more mobile and less likely to remain at a company long enough to benefit from traditional pension plans. On the other hand, workers still tend to stay for many years in certain industries, such as manufacturing, in which case there may be no reason to change prevailing pension plan structures.

Employers who opt for portable pensions may choose from such alternatives as 401(k) and cash-balance plans, pensions that rely more on age and final pay than tenure, and variations of defined-benefit or defined-contribution plans.

Leaves of Absence

There are several different types of leaves of absence; traditionally, the most common have been maternity, military, sick, and personal. It is important for organizations to have clearly defined policies regarding leaves of absence. The policies should cover the following areas:

- Circumstances under which various types of leaves will be granted
- Whether various types of leave will be paid
- Length of service required before a leave of absence will be granted
- Maximum duration of a leave of absence
- Number of leaves of absence that may be granted during any calendar year
- Relationship of unused vacation and personal days to leaves of absence
- Procedure to be followed by employees applying for a leave of absence

- Managerial guidelines for deciding whether to grant a leave of absence
- Effects on job status, including seniority and benefits

Note that specific federal legislation and, in some instances, state laws govern certain types of leave. For example, the Pregnancy Discrimination Act of 1978 prohibits mandatory pregnancy leave of any duration unless a similar requirement is imposed on male employees with temporary disabilities that impair job performance. If an employer insists on establishing special rules for pregnancy, such rules must be dictated by business necessity or be related to issues of safety or health. The act further stipulates that an employer must permit an employee on maternity leave to return to her job on the same basis as other employees returning to work following an illness or disability leave. Reservists as well have certain employment rights, outlined by the Office of Veterans' Reemployment Rights and provided by the National Committee for Employer Support of the Guard and Reserve (800/336–4590).

Perhaps the most significant form of leave governed by legislation is the Family and Medical Leave Act (FMLA), described in Chapter 3. The act mandates employers to permit workers time off from work to tend to certain family matters without being penalized. Additionally, employees are guaranteed reinstatement and continuation of health insurance benefits. Guidelines include affording a total of twelve weeks of intermittent, unpaid leave during any twelve-month period to employees who have worked for at least twelve months or not less than 1,250 hours in the past year. Employers may require that employees substitute paid time off, such as vacation and personal and sick days, for unpaid FMLA leave.

Some HR experts recommend integrating existing maternity and personal leave practices into the FMLA policy. In so doing, employers must avoid imposing more onerous requirements for FMLA leave than for other forms of leave. For example, provisions for continuation of benefits, other than medical benefits, during the leave period must be the same under FMLA and other leave policies. This "forced" consistency among leave policies will serve to reduce the chances that an employee will challenge an employer's leave practices as discriminatory.

Preretirement Programs

Retirement programs have been in existence for many years. However, most firms were not actively interested in them until the passage of ERISA in 1974 and the amendment of ADEA in 1978. ERISA requires companies to communicate the details of their pension plans "accurately and comprehensively" to employees. ADEA emphasizes the need for employers to do something positive for older workers. Consequently corporations have turned to retirement-preparation programs as a means of satisfying these specifications.

Some employers limit their involvement in retirement preparation to periodic mailings describing the company pension and benefits plan, with an added note to call personnel for additional information. Others provide employees and their spouses with personal counseling on legal and financial matters. Many organizations have developed programs offering general information about the variety of problems and opportunities employees are likely to encounter in making the transition from full-time employment to retirement. These programs make participants aware of their options and encourage them to explore the pros and cons of each alternative available fully. They also encourage participants to develop realistic goals and attitudes.

A typical retirement-preparation program might consist of eight to ten group sessions, with each session lasting approximately two hours. Each meeting is devoted to a specific topic of interest and concern to preretirees. These topics may include benefits, budgets, taxes, legal matters, income, investments, meaningful use of time, health and nutrition, and alternative living arrangements. Recent popular additions to this list include facts and myths about aging, the meaning of work, changing family relationships, and second careers in retirement.

Holidays

The average number of paid holidays granted to employees annually increased to ten in 1993. The actual cost of holidays has increased since the institution of Monday holidays, which ensure that holidays are not "lost" when they fall on weekends. The trend of granting an increased number of paid holidays to employees is expected to continue until many of the so-called minor holidays are included as well.

Because of this trend, it is important for organizations to have clearly defined policies regarding holidays. These policies should cover the following points:

- Eligibility for paid holidays
- Amount of pay to be received for holiday work

- Relationship of holidays to absences on the day before and/or after a paid holiday
- Relationship of vacations to holidays
- Relationship of sickness or disability to holidays
- Relationship of various forms of leave to holidays

Vacations

In most organizations, the amount of vacation time granted employees varies according to length of service and/or level of position. For example, nonexempt employees might start out receiving two weeks of vacation per year, increasing to three weeks after five years of employment, and to four weeks after ten years. Exempt employees, on the other hand, might be granted three or four weeks of vacation at the time of hire. It is an accepted practice to provide more vacation time to employees with greater responsibility, since managers and other professional employees often work extra hours without additional financial compensation.

Company vacation policies should include such factors as:

- Eligibility
- Carryover of unused vacation time from one calendar year to another
- Payment instead of vacation
- Scheduling
- Unused vacation at the time of termination

Note that some companies are moving toward comprehensive leave policies, which designate a certain amount of paid time off each year. Employees then take the time as they wish, for vacations, personal days, and so on.

How to Develop a Benefits Plan

The increase in legislation affecting benefits, coupled with an ever-expanding array of benefits from which companies may choose, has raised some questions about how to establish a comprehensive yet affordable benefits plan. To eliminate some of the confusion, consider the following guide to developing a benefits plan.

Categories of Benefits

These seven primary categories of mandatory and flexible benefits may serve as a framework for the specific employee benefits coverage in your organization. In formulating a package, take into account such factors as cost, likelihood of return on investment, overall appeal to employees, and manageability.

Income Stabilization

Most income-stabilization policies, such as workers' compensation, unemployment compensation, social security, and, in many states, disability insurance, are part of the mandatory core of benefits. These policies provide assurance of income flow in the event of personal injury or death.

Term life insurance is not legally required, but it is provided by most organizations. Employees are frequently given a choice between lower-cost term insurance or lesser coverage of higher-cost equity insurance, depending on individual needs.

Job-Loss Protection

Job-loss protection is provided by basic and supplemental unemployment insurance. In addition, the 1974 Trade Adjustment Assistance Act established layoff and cutback protection in industries affected by foreign imports.

Health and Accident Insurance

Health and accident protection is commonly offered through a combination of basic health care and major medical insurance or a combined comprehensive plan. HMOs and PPOs also provide additional outpatient and clinical services.

Employers often provide minimum medical coverage with additional options based on employee choice and shared expense. Other available coverage includes deferred postretirement coverage; various coverages for dependents; and vision, hearing, and dental care.

Flexible benefits plans are attractive to both employees and employers. Employees have the option of choosing the most appropriate health care package for them, and many companies believe that allowing employees to put together their own benefits package forces them to evaluate the costs involved. This will compel them to keep health costs down, which continue to escalate in disproportion to other benefits costs.

Deferred Income

Sections 125 and 401(k) of the Internal Revenue Code allow varying types of payroll deductions for present or deferred stock or trust accounts, in addition to the traditional company-provided retirement programs. This lets a broad range of investment alternatives qualify for flexible choice and tax deferral. The majority of companies with 401(k) plans offer or soon intend to offer added incentives to employees who want to participate.

Personal-Loss Protection

Group insurance policies for automobiles, homes, and other high-value property can normally be offered at 10 percent to 20 percent savings over individually written policies.

Paid Time Off

Most companies provide their employees with paid time off for ten to fourteen national or state holidays, and for vacation, usually ranging from one to four weeks on the basis of position and tenure. Some companies allow a partial vacation "buy-back" for employees who prefer the additional cash to time off. Many companies also provide paid time off for one to twelve sick days, one to four personal days, jury duty, voting, and attendance at professional or business-related meetings and seminars.

Employee Services

Many companies provide various employee services, such as:

- On- or off-site facilities for child care or elder care, or both
- A cafeteria
- Educational services, including partial or full tuition reimbursement
- On- or off-site physical fitness facilities and programs
- Subscriptions to professional journals

• Membership in professional or recreational organizations
• Financial, legal, or tax counseling services

Several of these types of employee services are discussed further in Chapters 1 and 12.

Types of Flexible Benefits Plans

The seven categories of benefits already described may be incorporated into three different flexible benefits plan designs: core cafeteria, buffet, and alternative dinners.

Core Cafeteria Plan

Under this concept, all employees have an identical minimum level of benefits in each of several areas. These benefit levels are the lowest the employee will allow each employee to accept. For example, coverage might consist of $5,000 of group life insurance, a short-term disability income plan, a one-week vacation, and a minimum level of hospital and medical coverage for the employee only. Beyond the core of minimum coverage, employees have a choice of additional life insurance, more vacation, better health insurance for themselves, health insurance for dependents, long-term disability coverage, dental coverage, and any other plan options within their flexible benefits allowances. They are able to "buy" these benefits with the flexible benefits allowance and, if necessary, with payroll deductions.

The core cafeteria plan offers employees a wide range of choices, thus enabling them to tailor their benefits to suit their specific needs.

Buffet Plan

Under the buffet plan, employees have the option of retaining exactly the same coverage they had prior to the introduction of flexible benefits. However, they may now choose lower benefits such as less vacation, a lower amount of life insurance, or a higher deductible in the hospital/ medical plan. By choosing lower benefits, an employee accumulates credits that may be used toward the purchase of other benefits, such as dental coverage and long-term disability.

As with the core cafeteria plan, there is a minimum benefits level below which the employees may not go. The buffet also offers many choices to employees and gives them the opportunity to individualize their benefits coverage.

Alternative Dinners Plan

The alternative dinners plan represents some degree of choice for the employee but does not provide a wide-open selection. Rather, the employer designs a set of benefits packages aimed at target groups of employees. For example, one package might be aimed at the employee with a nonworking spouse and children, another might be aimed at the single employee, a third at the single parent, and a fourth at the employee with a working spouse and no children. The employee may choose one of these packages.

The advantages of the alternative dinners plan are simpler administration and communication. The disadvantages are a limited choice of options and possible adverse reactions by employees who cannot get the exact combination of benefits they want.

Each of these three plans is designed to be of equivalent value; that is, the cost of each "dinner" is roughly equal, and any employee contributions required are also equal.

In addition to incorporating many of the flexible benefits described above when determining the best plan for your organization, it is also important to keep up to date on recent benefits developments and include these changes into your program as needed.

Ongoing Benefits Planning

The average employer spends an additional 30 percent of payroll on such benefits as pensions; health, disability, and life insurance; various thrift and stock plans; social security; workers' compensation; and unemployment compensation. Paid time off for vacation, holidays, and sick leave represents an additional 10 percent of payroll costs, bringing the total benefits expenditure of the average employer to 40 percent of payroll. Accordingly benefits planning must be a thorough and ongoing process, which should include these six steps:

1. Set short- and long-range objectives beneficial to both management and employees.
2. Gather relevant information about benefits offered by other organizations of comparable size, location, and services.

3. Determine your firm's strategy for approaching, analyzing, and comparing the bids of various insurance carriers.
4. Consider recent developments in benefits legislation.
5. Provide employees with the opportunity to choose a benefits package likely to suit their particular needs.
6. Encourage feedback and suggestions from employees regarding future additions to and changes in the existing benefits plan.

Because benefits planning is so complex, many organizations employ the services of consultants who are experts in this field.

Health Care Reform

At this time no one can predict with any certainty the direction of health care reform in the future. Although President Clinton's plans for comprehensive national health care legislation have been temporarily stymied, many experts predict full health care reform before the turn of the century. Meanwhile, individual states are attempting to implement their own health care measures. To accomplish this, however, a congressional exemption from a long-standing ERISA preemption barring states from regulating or taxing self-insured corporate benefit plans is needed.

As of December 1994, legislation has been introduced that would grant Florida, Oregon, Hawaii, Maryland, New York, and Washington federal waivers to expand health care coverage and tax currently exempt companies, as well as provide $50 billion to implement local reforms. There is a great deal of opposition to this move by businesses, since most corporate health plans are self-insured. Additionally, multistate employers fear having to write a different health plan for each state in which they operate. An increase in employee challenges to corporate benefit packages is also of concern to employers. According to Chris Bowlin, a health care expert with the National Association of Manufacturers, "Granting an ERISA exemption to these states could be disastrous for all employer-sponsored health care plans."[*] But state officials argue that since Congress has not been able to pass national reform legislation to date, they must go ahead on their own. "If the federal government can't lead, then I wish they'd get out of the way and let us solve our own problems,"[†] complains Nelson Sabatini, head of Maryland's Department of Health.

[*]*HR Focus* (December 1994), p. 1.
[†]*HR Focus* (December 1994), p. 8.

Because the future of health care reform is uncertain, employers are advised to prepare their HR information systems for change. Specifically, employers should prepare for health care reform in the following ways:

- Adopting software for a probable linkage between themselves, their health care providers and insurance companies
- Making the administration and enrollment systems for benefits more cost-effective and more user friendly
- Making statistical data easier to obtain and analyze
- Showing that managed care linked to flexible benefits works and is cost-effective, even for smaller employers
- Automating to be able to handle employee benefits allowed under future health care and tax laws and to be able to send information electronically whenever requested

Summary

The area of employee benefits has grown significantly in scope and complexity. It has also become increasingly expensive to administer. More and more employees expect to be able to choose options suited to their particular needs from a flexible benefits plan. Accordingly, employers are urged to review their objectives carefully and examine benefits trends before implementing a new benefits program or revising an existing one.

9

Employee Relations

As an organization grows in size, the uniform interpretation of management objectives becomes increasingly important. Nowhere is this more significant than in matters directly affecting the employer-employee relations of an organization.

In small and mid-sized companies, the term *employee relations* (ER) generally encompasses several facets of human resources management. For example, career development and employee assistance typically fall under the general heading of employee relations. The responsibility for ER is usually assigned to a human resources generalist with experience in various categories of human resources management derived from a similar workplace environment.

Exactly what is included as part of employee relations depends on the amount of work each respective area generates. EEO and affirmative action, for instance, were traditionally tossed into the employee relations pot. Over time, however, with the enactment of additional legislation and the development of more EEO-related policies and procedures, the legal side of human resources has increasingly been removed from ER and delegated to EEO specialists.

While it may be tempting to place "miscellaneous" aspects of human resources under the catchall heading of employee relations, growing companies are cautioned against allowing this category to become overloaded with too many functions. Each company must consider its size, projected growth, and goals, as well as other factors, before deciding what areas belong under the ER umbrella. Periodic review of human resources staffing needs will indicate the necessity for revamping this area.

The categories discussed in this chapter are those that are typically included in employee relations in small and mid-sized companies:

- Human resources planning
- Career development
- Manager-employee counseling
- Employee assistance programs
- Grievances
- Disciplinary proceedings
- Alternative dispute resolution
- Union and labor relations
- HR policies and procedures manuals
- Employee handbooks
- Attitude surveys

Human Resources Planning

Human resources planning enables HR specialists to achieve a broad overall view of the direction in which the organization is heading and to help it get there. The basic goals are to estimate future human resources requirements and to develop strategies to ensure that these requirements will be met, both by hiring people from outside the organization and by more fully developing the organization's present staff.

Although each organization should tailor its human resources plan to its own particular needs, the following general, sequential process may be modified to suit most organizations.

1. *Collect data for planning.* In order to develop an effective plan based on projected needs, human resources specialists must properly identify and analyze the goals of the organization. In addition, they must measure various aspects of the external environment, such as general economic conditions, societal norms and values, the political and legal climates, and the size and competition of the labor supply.

All these data are input into the planning system and form the foundation for the forecasts themselves.

2. *Analyze current skills.* The second phase of the planning process concerns analyzing the availability of internal employees. This process should result in a detailed inventory of employees' skills, levels of performance, potential, salaries, and levels of productivity. The number of workers at various levels and in various departments and locations is also important.

Such an inventory can help an organization better understand its existing human resources status and more effectively plan for the future.

3. *Forecast future needs.* Once the organization's goals have been identified, the external environment has been examined, and the existing skill levels of current employees have been determined, planners can begin to synthesize all this information into forecasted requirements for various time periods. Both short and long time periods should be included. Planners can then develop budgets that reflect the costs of hiring or training the workers necessary to meet the organization's goals.

4. *Implement the plan.* Once the forecasts for future needs have been made, the plan is ready to be implemented. This may involve:

Recruiting people to fill vacancies

Appraising current employees' performance to determine their strengths, areas requiring improvement, and potential for promotion

Training and developing employees to meet future needs

Making transfers, promotions, terminations, and other changes in status to maximize the best possible match between job requirements and workers' abilities

5. *Evaluate and redesign the plan.* The plan must be continually monitored and evaluated to ensure its ongoing effectiveness. Carefully assess whether it is still attaining stated objectives, and redesign it if necessary.

Career Development

Most human resources professionals agree that career development benefits the organization overall, as well as its individual employees. Many employers are becoming actively interested in career development because there is increasing evidence that it benefits them financially, especially when the kinds of training offered are clearly related to the goals of the organization.

Experts agree that career development should begin with entry-level employees. All employees should know that the organization is concerned with every worker's growth and development. The way this concern is shown varies from company to company. Large, technically oriented companies, for example, may be able to offer elaborate, multifaceted career development programs. Most small and mid-sized businesses can adopt more modest but equally effective career development strategies for their employees.

Career counselors are being increasingly utilized, both informally on the job and through more structured arrangements. This one-on-one approach is time-consuming but can yield excellent results.

Conducting careful follow-up interviews when candidates apply for a posted job is also a good career development technique. Instead of merely notifying applicants via a form letter that they were not selected for a given job, a human resources representative might sit down with each applicant and describe exactly what kinds of skills, training, and education would be needed to qualify for a similar position in the future; how and where these skills and knowledge can be obtained; and what assistance the company can offer.

Follow-up interviews to unsuccessful job posting applications, and counselor-employee relationships, can clearly produce beneficial career development results. However, in order to extend career development options to all employees and to accomplish faster results on a wider scale, an organization needs a more comprehensive system. A structured career development program less elaborate than those in large corporations may be adopted by any small or mid-sized organization. The key to success is commitment to tailoring the career development system to meet the needs of each particular employee. Individual career growth is a personal matter; a career development plan should guide and assist each employee toward the achievement of his or her goals.

The five steps described in the following career development model are simple, allowing ample room for modification to suit a particular company's needs. It is strongly recommended that the person in charge of developing and monitoring the program be skilled in a wide range of HR-related areas, such as interviewing and performance appraisals.

1. *Keep an up-to-date record of the skills, interests, and knowledge of each employee.* This may be accomplished in a number of ways, including:

   Periodically distributing "information update" forms to be completed by each employee.
   Arranging regularly scheduled meetings with each employee to keep abreast of recent work-related accomplishments.
   Informing employees, via a memo or a message in their employee handbook, that they are responsible for keeping the human resources department advised of any interest in changing their present status

Periodically meeting with each employee is considered ideal, but this is impractical if your organization has more than 100 employees. A questionnaire designed to obtain information about each employee's interests and abilities is best for most mid-sized companies. Leaving it up to the employee to contact personnel is the least reliable method.

2. *Assimilate the data submitted by each employee.* Speak with employees to get clarification or additional information as required. It is important that you clearly understand the career development objectives from the employee's perspective before proceeding. Do not discourage employees or think in terms of whether their goals are practical or realistic, given the present organizational structure. Your sole objective at this stage is to interpret employees' interests and aspirations accurately.

3. *Integrate the employee's goals into organizational goals.* Consider the company's present status, and its short-term and long-term objectives. Take into account past patterns of the organization's success in achieving set goals, and review management's overall philosophy, including its position on risk taking and flexibility. Then look for compatibility between organizational and individual goals. Where there appears to be a conflict, look for ways in which the employee might modify his or her plans without making any major changes.

4. *Map out a career plan for each employee.* The plan should reflect the individual's goals, outline steps toward accomplishing them, and identify a realistic target date for each step. Steps might include additional formal education, attending workshops or seminars, an apprenticeship program, or job rotation. As part of this process, be prepared to inform the employee of any assistance the organization is prepared to offer, like tuition reimbursement or payment of membership dues.

As each step is accomplished, the employee should be encouraged to discuss his or her feelings about wanting to continue with the plan. Sometimes, once the actual effort of working toward a goal begins, the employee decides it is not really what he or she wants to do. Should this occur, be careful not to be judgmental; rather, work with the employee to develop a new direction.

Note that not all growth is upward. Today there is less of an emphasis on vertical mobility and more emphasis on horizontal movement, with a reward system based on flexibility and breadth of knowledge rather than depth of knowledge. Employees who enjoy their current work should be encouraged to explore their interests while remaining in that job. Others may be uninterested in promotions but interested in lateral transfers or job rotation.

5. *Make career development a team effort.* Just as a career development plan must be personalized to be effective, it must also be a team effort.

This means support from human resources and senior management, as well as cooperation and encouragement from an employee's manager.

If this process is initiated when an organization is relatively small (fewer than a few hundred employees), its upkeep is more manageable and its results are more beneficial to all concerned. However, it is never too late to begin a career development program.

Manager-Employee Counseling

Effective counseling by a manager about a specific work-related issue should enable the employee to examine his or her behavior objectively, explore much desirable ways of behaving, and review the problem consequences of each alternative course of action. The counseling process allows the manager to help the employee bring about change himself or herself. Ideally employees will behave differently not because they feel they have to change but because they want to change.

Counseling may be preventive or corrective. In either instance, the ultimate goal is for employees to function more effectively on the job and to pursue their career goals successfully. The counseling process may run more smoothly if the following sequence of steps is followed:

1. *Prepare for the meeting.* Managers are encouraged to plan carefully and consider exactly what they want to discuss during a counseling interview. Informing the employee of the meeting's topic in advance allows him or her ample time to give the situation some thought. In preparing for counseling meetings, it is important for managers to rid themselves of excessive emotions or biases that might interfere with their objectivity.

2. *State the purpose of the meeting.* At the outset of a counseling session, the manager should inform the employee why the meeting is being held. Clearly stating the purpose of the meeting will help both parties focus on the critical issues at hand.

3. *Define the problem.* After stating the purpose of the meeting, the manager should immediately define the problem. It should be outlined in an objective, factual, and nonjudgmental manner, focusing on behavior and providing specific information. Personal feelings about what has happened are not relevant at this stage.

4. *Listen to the employee's side.* Because it is the employee who must ultimately behave differently in order for the problem to be resolved, it is critical that the employee be permitted to state his or her perception of what the problem is and what is causing it. The manager should listen

patiently while the employee speaks. By asking open-ended questions, remaining silent, indicating understanding, and periodically summarizing what the employee has said thus far, the manager is likely to gain a clear understanding of the employee's perception of the situation and convey that understanding to the employee.

5. *Help the employee develop a solution.* The manager cannot solve the problem for the employee but can help the employee develop possible solutions. This step encourages the employee to develop a series of possible alternatives. Together the manager and the employee can select the most feasible alternative and define a specific course of action, outlining exactly what the employee plans to do, how he or she plans to do it, and within what time period.

6. *Follow up.* Once the employee has outlined a specific course of action, the manager should follow up to see how he or she is doing. Informal follow-up might consist of periodic encouraging words or comments. A more formal follow-up might include setting a specific date to get together and review how the employee is progressing.

Even though this counseling procedure is the responsibility of the managers in a company, it is up to the human resources department to make certain that the process functions smoothly and effectively, to the mutual benefit of all concerned.

Employee Assistance Programs

Employee assistance programs (EAPs) originally focused on alcohol and drug issues, patterned after the concept of occupational alcoholism programs developed in the 1940s. They increased in popularity following enactment of the Drug Free Workplace Act of 1988, with many companies providing EAPs in an attempt to comply with the act's requirement that federal employees and employees of firms under government contract must have access to EAP services. Today EAPs are available to employees needing help with a wide range of concerns: family and work problems, legal and financial difficulties, mental health issues, and substance abuse. When properly managed, EAPs may prevent an increase in absenteeism, tardiness, sick leave abuse, health insurance claims, disability payments, employee theft, litigation, and turnover.

The cost of an EAP depends on a number of variables, such as size and scope of services, but most run about two to three dollars per month per employee for an off-site program (most small and mid-sized companies opt for an off-site program, while large corporations usually retain

EAP personnel on staff). According to EAP experts, a well-run EAP will minimally return three dollars for every dollar spent on the program.

In searching for the most appropriate off-site program, or EAP vendor, Employee Assistance Professionals Association (703/522–6272) recommends that the following questions be asked:

- What is the vendor's reputation among its clients and among EAP professionals?
- Does the vendor have offices in all or most of the locations in which your company needs services?
- What kinds of employee problems can the vendor service?
- What services are offered?
- Is access by telephone, face to face, or both?
- What hours are services available?
- How are the counselors trained and supervised?
- Is the vendor's EAP compatible with your company's health care benefits?
- How does the vendor deal with confidentiality?
- What is the cost of the program?

It is also advisable to select an EAP that covers employee dependents, since often the dependent is the person having the problem or is the source of the employee's problem.

Employers are advised to ensure that EAP policies and procedures clearly comply with all relevant state and federal laws and regulations, such as those concerning confidentiality of client records. In addition, all program personnel should be covered by professional liability insurance.

Grievances

The three primary purposes of an employee grievance policy are to ensure prompt and equitable treatment for all employees, help eliminate causes of job dissatisfaction, and resolve job-related problems so that productive work relationships may be resumed or maintained.

The filing of grievances should be permitted for any condition of employment thought to be inequitable. An employee should be permitted to initiate a grievance procedure with any one of four parties:

1. His or her immediate supervisor
2. The immediate manager of the employee's immediate supervisor, if the grievance concerns the immediate supervisor

3. The human resources manager, if the subject is sensitive and the employee is reluctant to speak to management directly
4. The company's EEO officer, if the grievance concerns allegations of discrimination

Formal grievances should be submitted in writing directly by the employee, and not anonymously or by a third party. The manager or officer receiving the complaint should attempt to resolve the situation and render a decision in writing as promptly as possible—usually within five working days.

Employees may generally appeal the decision within ten working days of receiving it. The appeal should be in writing and submitted to any of the parties mentioned above. Within a reasonable period of time— usually ten working days after the filing of a written appeal—a formal hearing is held by a grievance committee. The grievance committee usually consists of one representative of senior management, a lower-level manager, and a personnel representative. None of the members of the committee should have had any involvement, to date, with the issue of the grievance. The decision reached during the hearing should be final, and the employee should be notified in writing, usually within five working days of the hearing.

Managers should comply fully with their organization's grievance procedure. No record of any grievance filed should be kept in an employee's personnel file. No employee should be subjected to retaliation for having used the grievance procedure—nor should a bias be shown *toward* any employee who files a grievance. Neither filing nor appealing a grievance should affect an employee's future opportunities for promotion, transfer, training, salary increases, or performance evaluation.

The Disciplinary Process

Disciplinary action might be brought against an employee for any one of a number of reasons, including:

- Repeated or excessive tardiness
- Repeated or excessive absenteeism
- Interfering with the work of other employees
- Abusive or inconsiderate treatment of customers or fellow employees
- Insubordination

- Failure to meet required work standards
- Tending to personal matters during working hours
- Theft, destruction, or abuse of organization property
- Falsification of records
- Threats or actual acts of physical violence

Having an established disciplinary procedure to be followed for infractions like these is essential for effective employer-employee relations within any organization. Although the exact nature of the infraction will determine the severity of discipline, here are some general guidelines that can be modified to suit your company:

1. "Back documentation" should not be permitted. Documentation and discipline should occur at the time of the infraction in order to be valid.
2. The degree of discipline to be administered should depend on such factors as the seriousness of the offense; the frequency of its occurrence; its effect on productivity, other employees, and the organization as a whole; and the employee's overall employment history.
3. Avoid acting hastily. Administering discipline is a very serious matter, and all the facts must be gathered and objectively evaluated before you decide on a course of action.
4. Any type of disciplinary action taken against an employee should be based on a real infraction that was the employee's fault.
5. Employees should not be disciplined for violating rules or regulations with which they were unfamiliar.
6. The disciplinary procedure must be applied uniformly and without bias.
7. The sequence of disciplinary steps outlined below must be for a repeat of the same infraction, not an unrelated one.

Disciplinary Steps

The following steps are intended as a guide for most kinds of infractions (such as excessive tardiness or absenteeism). Certain serious occurrences, such as acts of physical violence, may warrant suspension without pay pending an investigation or immediate dismissal; issuing a verbal warning followed by two written warnings would not pertain to them.

1. *Verbal warning.* Verbal warnings should always be conducted in private and should serve as an opportunity to clarify misunderstood directions, eliminate incorrect assumptions, and resolve any conflicts.

2. *First written warning.* If the same problem recurs after a verbal warning, the employee should be issued a written warning. This is a statement of what has occurred, who was involved, when and where the unacceptable behavior took place, why it warrants disciplinary action, and what improvement is expected in the future. The employee should be given an opportunity to read the written warning and make comments, both verbally and in writing. Then the employee should be asked to sign the written warning, indicating that he or she understands its contents. A sample of a first written warning appears in Appendix J.

3. *Second written warning.* If the problem is repeated or continued, it may result in a second written warning. Should this occur, the guidelines described under Step 2 above should apply again. A sample second written warning appears in Appendix K.

4. *Suspension.* If the problem continues, suspension may be warranted. Suspensions are usually for a period of one to three working days, without pay. The employee should be informed of the suspension, told of the reasons for the suspension, and warned that failure to improve in work or conduct could result in termination.

5. *Termination.* After a verbal warning, two written warnings, and suspension, termination for repeated or continued infractions may be called for. A written statement summarizing the reasons for termination should be placed in the employee's personnel file.

Alternative Dispute Resolution

Increasingly, companies are seeking nonlitigious, more expeditious, and less costly ways of defending themselves against wrongful discharge and discrimination charges. One such means is alternative dispute resolution (ADR), a process that encourages the settlement of employment-related complaints before they reach the courts by means of either internal personnel or external parties. ADR differs from the traditional grievance procedure described earlier by focusing on issues headed for court. With discrimination cases taking years to resolve, only to result in legal awards as high as seven figures, and court costs for a jury trial averaging from $50,000 to $100,000, employers are strongly motivated to try the ADR approach.

Companies approach ADR in a number of different ways. Some rely on external arbitration or mediation, which may be internal or external. Costs for arbitration and external mediation procedures range from $2,000 to $3,000, including administrative fees of up to $1,000, and hourly fees negotiated with the arbitrator or mediator. Others designate a peer review panel coupled with an internal complaint resolution process. Generally complaints can be heard and decided within six weeks. An employee dissatisfied with the decision may later file a formal complaint with the EEOC. The EEOC, however, may be less inclined to pursue a complaint that has already been resolved by ADR. Still other employers establish a "company court" with a designated person rendering a decision, usually within two weeks of the hearing.

There are many advantages to ADR. Besides the financial savings, the process allows employers to focus on trouble spots in the company without publicity. In addition, it sends a message of fair dealing and trustworthiness to employees. Employees also appreciate not having to wait months or years for resolution.

Successful ADR programs adhere to the following guidelines:

1. The ADR process should be carefully explained to prospective employees during the application and interview process.
2. The employee handbook should clearly describe ADR, including its purpose and uses.
3. Employers should make certain their ADR agreements are enforceable under state arbitration statutes, modeled after the Uniform Arbitration Act, which is applicable in about two-thirds of the states.
4. The process should be well publicized at the outset and receive senior management's support.
5. All complaints should be treated confidentially, with concessions and admissions leading to settlement without outsiders' becoming aware of the details.
6. Psychologists and other persons with special expertise in these matters should be brought in to assist in the process as appropriate to ensure that employees' feelings are considered in addition to the complaint itself.

Employers are advised to consult with an attorney specializing in labor and employment law before establishing an ADR program.

Union and Labor Relations

Human resources practitioners should be familiar with three important laws concerning labor-management relations.

National Labor Relations Act of 1935 (Wagner Act)

This act is based on the premise that employees who are not organized are at a disadvantage because they do not enjoy benefits comparable to those of management. In addition to establishing employees' right to organize and the employer's obligation to bargain, it created the National Labor Relations Board (NLRB), outlines procedures for the NLRB to review complaints, invests the NLRB with investigatory and enforcement powers, and affirms employees' right to strike.

Labor Management Relations Act of 1947 (Taft-Hartley Act)

This act defines and outlines unfair labor practices by both employers and unions, imposes specific restraints on the activities of both, and requires labor to maintain a reporting relationship with the secretary of labor. It declares unions able to sue and be sued, prohibits secondary boycotts, and affirms the right of states to legislate against union shops.

The essential philosophy of this act is represented in section VII, as follows:

> Employees shall have the right to self-organization, to form, join, or assist labor organizations, to bargain collectively through representatives of their own choosing, and to engage in other concerted activities for the purpose of collective bargaining or other mutual aid or protection, and shall also have the right to refrain from any or all such activities except to the extent that such right may be affected by an agreement requiring membership in a labor organization as a condition of employment as authorized in Section VIII(a)(3).

Labor-Management Reporting and Disclosure Act of 1959

This act directly affects organizing in four provisions:

1. "Hot-cargo" clauses are made illegal; Title VII makes illegal any disagreement requiring that an employer refrain from handling

unfair or struck work. An exception is made for the garment industry.

2. Picketing for both organizational and recognition purposes is sharply restricted.
3. Economic strikers are given the right to vote for a period of up to one year from the commencement of a strike, at the discretion of the NLRB, if a representation election is held.
4. Conduct of representation elections is delegated by the NLRB to regional directors.

The legislation described above essentially established the framework for labor-management relations. This framework may be summarized as follows:

- Employees have the right to form collective bargaining units.
- Employers must recognize unions that meet established criteria.
- Employees and unions must recognize employee rights, bargain in good faith, and refrain from engaging in unfair labor practices.
- Commerce must be protected from disruption caused by the actions of employers and/or unions.

The NLRB is a powerful influence in all matters of labor relations. It has full powers to investigate charges of unfair labor practices and to enforce its decisions. Charges of unfair labor practices may be brought by employees, employers, or unions. Once a ruling has been made, the NLRB has the power, if required, to obtain a court order to enforce its judgment.

Effects of a Union

Many people view unions in a very positive light. Over the years, unions have been responsible for increasing the wages of their members, bringing about much-needed improvements in working conditions, and expanding employee benefits. They can also provide workers with a sense of job security and protection. In addition, union representatives are available to listen to employee complaints and represent them in grievance proceedings. This can reassure employees that their interests are being taken seriously and that they will be fairly treated—even if management believes that these things are true without a union.

On the other hand, many view unions negatively. Some possible disadvantages to employees are that:

- Employees may lose direct contact with managers.
- The union steward can essentially become another boss.

- Employees are required to pay dues, fees, fines, and/or assessments.
- Unions can compel reluctant members to participate in activities that they do not support, such as strikes.
- Strikes can have a devastating financial and emotional impact on employees and their families.

Managers are affected by unions as well. They must deal with a union steward as opposed to interacting directly with employees whom they may have communicated with effectively for years. The atmosphere can become charged with a "them against us" feeling. More time may be devoted to grievances, relations with employees may become more formal and strained, and restrictions are placed on how managers may accomplish their work.

In addition, the overall company is affected by unions. It may be burdened with excessive additional costs for attorneys, consultants, and executive time spent in negotiations, grievances, and arbitrations. Productivity is often adversely affected. Bad publicity may result from strikes, and customers or clients may resist dealing with an organization with union problems.

Recognizing Union-Organizing Activities

These signs usually indicate that union-organizing activities are taking place:

- Employees are asking a lot of questions about union-related matters.
- Discarded authorization cards are found on the premises.
- Strangers are found loitering about employee exits at quitting time.
- Employees are evasive when communicating with managers.
- Small groups of employees not normally friendly with one another are found to be gathering together.
- Intense conversation among a small group of employees abruptly terminates at the appearance of someone in management.
- One employee seems to move from one group of employees to another.
- The same complaint, as experienced by several different employees, is presented to management.
- Employees discuss a complaint that affects one or more employees and is of an emotional nature but that has not been filed as a formal grievance.
- Employees dig up and rehash age-old complaints.

If any of these occurrences is observed, careful notes accurately describing all the facts involved should be maintained and submitted to senior management. No direct action should be taken except as directed by senior management.

Preventing Unionization of Your Company

Clearly the introduction of unions to an organization irrevocably alters its employer-employee relations. Employers who wish to avoid unionization should consider why most employees set out to organize. Since unions attempt to magnify areas of worker dissatisfaction, employers should make every attempt to provide a work environment in which employees do not feel the need to seek external assistance. Simply translated, this means:

- Developing, establishing, and maintaining fair and impartial personnel practices and work standards
- Implementing sound management practices
- Offering a competitive compensation system
- Providing a comprehensive benefits package
- Eliminating arbitrary employment practices
- Offering opportunities for growth and development
- Practicing open two-way communication

In addition, whenever possible, employees should be involved in the development of those policies and procedures that directly affect them.

HR Policies and Procedures Manuals

As an organization grows in size, the uniform interpretation of management objectives becomes increasingly important. Nowhere is this more significant than in matters directly affecting the employer-employee relations of an organization. For this reason, growing companies should translate company goals and objectives into specific policies, programs, and procedures. The result of this process is a human resources policies and procedures manual: an essential managerial tool.

HR policies and procedures manuals should provide complete, current, and easily interpreted information about all aspects of employer-employee relations, including recruitment, selection, hiring, working conditions, benefits, compensation, training, career development, promotions, transfers, performance evaluations, and termination of employment. Of course, the specific contents should reflect each organization's philosophy, objectives, and needs.

Specific revisions and additions to the manual should be made as required. In addition, the entire manual should be reviewed annually to ensure continued overall appropriateness.

It is strongly recommended that organizations provide their managers with training in the effective use of the HR policies and procedures manual, as opposed to merely distributing it to them. This will help ensure the uniform interpretation and implementation of the manual's content.

It is also critical that managers and human resources representatives understand the correlation between the language in an HR policies and procedures manual and charges of wrongful discharge. An employee may interpret certain language in the manual as representing an employment contract—for example, that termination will occur only under certain circumstances. If a manual clearly states that employees may be terminated "for just cause only," and a worker is discharged for other reasons (such as a reduction in force), the result may be a charge of wrongful discharge.

Employees can claim that an HR policies and procedures manual represents a contract between an employer and an employee only if they received a copy of the manual. Also, the employer must be located in a state that has not ruled that such manuals are not valid contracts.

Figure 1 shows an excerpt from an effective HR policies and procedures manual of a company with approximately 500 employees.

Employee Handbooks

An HR policies and procedures manual is a tool to be used by managers and the human resources department. Employees also need a tool—a single source of information about what the organization expects of them and what they can expect from the organization. This source of information is the employee handbook.

Figure 2 shows the table of contents from an employee handbook of an organization with approximately 1,500 employees. In contrast, some employee handbooks are set up in two parts. In such a case the first part generally outlines company rules, regulations, and policies, and information of general interest. The second part is usually devoted to benefits: medical and other forms of insurance, and other benefits including holidays, vacations, personal days, and tuition aid.

Figure 1. Excerpt from an HR policies and procedures manual.

Section: Employment/Selection Practices

Subject: Job Posting

Policy

In keeping with the policy of this company to help employees with career development, both exempt and nonexempt positions will be filled with existing staff wherever and whenever feasible. Positions advertised via job posting will be offered to those employees interested in making lateral moves as well as those interested in promotions.

Procedure

Whenever a position becomes available—either through a vacancy created by a terminating or transferring employee, or because of an addition to complement—the opening will be posted. Posted bulletins will be placed in convenient and readily accessible locations throughout the organization. Employees will be given up to five working days to apply for any position posted. The procedures noted in the job-posting bulletin must be adhered to.

Managerial Responsibilities

Managers should encourage employees for whom they are responsible to apply for positions compatible with their skills, interests, abilities, and potential. Employees who are "held back" will not feel motivated, and productivity is certain to be adversely affected.

Outside Recruitment

Continued rapid expansion and demands for highly skilled and trained employees in certain areas sometimes require recruiting individuals from outside the organization. This will be done, however, only after employees have had ample opportunity to apply for such positions, and their skills and potential have been fairly evaluated by the human resources department and the respective department manager.

Frequency of Job-Posting Applications

There is no limit to the number of jobs an employee may apply for or the number of times he or she may apply. Rejection for one position must not be used in any way against an employee applying for a similar or different position in the future.

Job-Posting Stipulations

In order for an employee to be eligible to apply for a posted job, he or she must have been employed by this company for at least six months, and have been in his or her present job for at least the same period of time. In addition, the employee's most recent performance appraisal must reflect a satisfactory or better overall rating.

Notification of Job-Posting Results

All employees who apply for posted positions will be notified in writing about the decision reached. A copy of this notification will be kept in the employee's personnel file.

Figure 2. Table of contents from an employee handbook.

Like the HR policies and procedures manual, the employee handbook should be maintained and kept up to date. Changes and/or additions should be distributed promptly to all employees.

As with an HR policies and procedures manual, it is imperative that managers and human resources representatives understand how the language in an employee handbook may result in lawsuits for wrongful discharge.

The handbook, like the manual, may be considered an employment contract. Employees hired at will may claim that the at-will status changed when they received a handbook outlining specific conditions of employment. For example, if a company's employee handbook states that the company will resort to dismissal for just and sufficient cause only, then an employee terminated for other than "just cause" or without being given the opportunity to correct his or her behavior may, on the basis of that statement, sue for breach of contract in some states.

Figure 3 shows an excerpt from the employee handbook of the same 1,500-employee organization mentioned above.

Attitude Surveys

Attitude surveys should be conducted periodically to help improve employee motivation, morale, job satisfaction, performance, and productivity. Often they succeed in eliminating conditions that might otherwise lead to an employee grievance. At the very least, they demonstrate management's interest in the opinions, ideas, and problems of employees, thereby improving goodwill and communication throughout the organization.

Figure 3. Excerpt from an employee handbook.

Employee Referrals

You are encouraged to recommend suitable candidates for employment with this organization. In keeping with this practice, we will offer cash payments to employees whose referrals are hired.

The recommending employee will receive a $250 payment when the new employee has received a "satisfactory" or better evaluation during his or her first formal performance appraisal after six months of employment.

If you wish to recommend someone for hiring consideration, contact your human resources representative.

In order to be successful, an attitude survey program must be well planned, publicized to employees, and conducted carefully and openly. The answers should be analyzed honestly and thoroughly, and announced to the participants. Most important, corrective action that is called for must be taken promptly. This last point is where many attitude surveys break down: Many companies want to know what their employees are thinking but fail to follow through on suggestions. This often causes more harm than good.

Properly conducted, however, an attitude survey can be extremely helpful toward improving employer-employee relations. The following sequence of steps may serve as a guide in conducting an attitude survey:

1. Identify clear and specific objectives for conducting the survey.
2. Obtain senior management's approval and commitment prior to the initiation of the survey.
3. Decide how, when, and where the survey will be conducted, as well as the target population and the size of the survey sample. (For small companies, the entire population should be surveyed.)
4. Determine specifically what is to be measured.
5. Design the questionnaire.
6. Announce and explain, to both managers and employees, the purposes of the survey and how the information will be used.
7. Distribute the questionnaires, with explicit instructions on when they are to be returned and to whom.
8. Tabulate, analyze, and evaluate the questionnaire results.
9. Prepare a summary report of findings and recommendations.
10. Develop an action plan for implementing recommendations as approved by senior management.
11. Announce the survey results, what action will be taken, and within what time frame.
12. Thank the employees for their participation.

Most companies conducting attitude surveys do not require employees to identify themselves by name or unit. This way, employees are more likely to be honest in their comments.

Each company's questionnaire will specifically reflect its own particular environment, but most surveys ask questions about the following areas:

- Satisfaction with the content of job tasks
- Full utilization of employees' skills and abilities

- Opportunities for challenge, initiative, and growth on the job
- Opportunities for promotion and advancement
- Scope of responsibilities on the job
- Clarity of job responsibilities
- Sufficient resources with which to perform the job
- Managerial fairness in managing, planning, and scheduling work
- Technical competence and job knowledge of managers
- Managerial concern for employees
- Working conditions
- Adequacy of pay
- Adequacy of benefits
- HR policies and procedures
- Fairness of performance appraisal system
- Training opportunities
- Hours of work
- Philosophy of management

Summary

Determining those human resources functions to be included in a company's employee relations function depends largely on an organization's size, projected growth, and goals. This chapter discussed eleven categories that may be considered for inclusion in your company's employee relations unit: human resources planning, career development, manager-employee counseling, employee assistance programs, grievances, disciplinary proceedings, alternative dispute resolution, union and labor relations, HR policies and procedures manuals, employee handbooks, and attitude surveys.

10

Training and Development

Whether an employer's focus is on skills and technical training or management training, the emphasis of training overall is increasingly on high-performance work.

Training and development should contribute to the attainment of short-term and long-term goals, for both the company and its individual employees. In order to be effective, a training and development program requires the full commitment and support of senior management, and it must reflect the overall philosophy of the organization.

Training and development should be established as a separate function in a mid-sized company's human resources department, headed by a specialist in the field. A small company should make certain that the human resources generalist in charge of its training and development has appropriate skills and knowledge; these will be discussed later in this chapter.

Whether you are establishing a training and development function for the first time or revising an existing one, you should consider these factors:

- The overall role of training and development—what it should and should not be expected to accomplish, and the respective responsibilities of all concerned.
- How to analyze the organization's needs to identify specific goals and objectives.
- The availability of both skills training and management training
- The focus on high-performance training
- The components of the training and development process, and various training techniques
- Guidelines for starting a program

- How to evaluate the program's effectiveness
- Selecting appropriate trainers
- Assessing training costs
- Tuition aid for employees wishing to pursue formal education related to their jobs
- Training trends

This chapter will discuss all these facets of a comprehensive training and development program.

The Role of Training and Development

Training and development may be appropriate when new skills are required or existing skills are deemed deficient. Before deciding to train, however, ask the following questions:

- Would better methods of recruiting, interviewing, and selection result in more qualified employees being hired?
- Have the job requirements been appropriately defined?
- Are the working conditions suitable to the work required?
- Is there a more effective way to utilize existing skills?
- Would the introduction of new technology and automation make a difference?

The answers to these five questions should yield important information and help you determine whether training is the solution you are seeking.

Training may be appropriate when:

- There is a proven need for a specific skill that does not currently exist in the workforce or is not available in sufficient numbers.
- There is a proven need for a specific standard of skill performance, and it has been shown that workers are not performing up to that standard.
- There has been a change in technology, methods, or required behavior that renders current skills obsolete.

The existence of one or more of these conditions does not necessarily mean that training is the solution to a problem. It is important to consider realistically what training and development programs can and cannot accomplish. Consider the following examples of situations in which training would not be helpful:

- If employees work in an environment that does not warrant or permit the use of the skills acquired during training
- If the change in behavior brought about by training cannot be identified or measured in tangible terms
- If employees are unmotivated to meet performance standards, even though they are capable of doing so
- If organizational goals and objectives can be met more effectively through other means
- If the resources required to conduct effective training are insufficient or ill suited

Once you have determined that training is an appropriate solution to a given problem, consider the respective responsibilities of all concerned:

Trainers: Responsible for clarifying training objectives, developing appropriate training materials consistent with those objectives, presenting the information in the most appropriate manner possible, and following up to ensure that the training objectives have been met.

Managers: Responsible for identifying employees who require training, providing support and encouragement to employees participating in training programs, allowing employees to use newly learned skills on the job, and encouraging continued growth and development.

Trainees: Responsible for approaching the training process with an open mind and a positive attitude, actively participating in the training program by asking questions and making comments, seeking clarification as needed, and applying newly learned skills to their jobs.

Successful training depends on a cooperative effort.

Needs Analysis and Goal Setting

Before planning your training program, you must thoroughly assess your organization's needs and the current levels of employee performance. The design, methods, cost, and time frame of a training program all depend on this assessment. The process involves these five steps:

1. Analyze the organization's objectives to determine its short- and long-term goals and needs.
2. Translate these goals into the performance and skill levels of people required to meet them.
3. Determine the tasks required to achieve the necessary levels of performance and the important dimensions of those tasks.
4. Measure current performance levels of workers by using some sort of appraisal technique in order to pinpoint any deviation from the standards identified and to note precise areas of performance deficiency.
5. Design and conduct specific training and development programs to meet these deficiencies.

An important aspect of this process is to identify workers whose skills are becoming obsolete and to begin cross-training them as soon as possible. Cross-training programs are designed to increase the number of skills held by an employee (as opposed to upgrading the skills he or she is already using). This can help the company immediately by providing a reserve workforce in the event that a particular specialist becomes unavailable. In the long run, cross-training acquaints employees with the concept of ongoing training, helps them develop new skills, and prepares them to transfer when new jobs arise.

Unfortunately, many training programs fail because trainers seem more interested in conducting the training program itself than in first assessing the needs of their organization and its workers. Training is useless to the organization unless employees learn skills that are genuinely needed.

Skills and Technical Training

Skills and technical training programs are designed to compensate for deficiencies in employees' skills or knowledge. This may involve training newly hired employees; correcting deficiencies in current employees' performance caused by inadequate skills or knowledge; or teaching current employees to operate new equipment, use new procedures or techniques, or create new products. Generally skills and technical training programs employ direct, hands-on experiences using equipment and tools identical to or comparable with those found on the job.

The four most common forms of skills training are apprenticeship training, on-the-job training, vestibule training, and classroom training.

Apprenticeship Training

Apprenticeship training is a long-term process requiring continual supervision; this makes it one of the most expensive forms of skills training. Apprenticeship programs are used to train people in certain crafts, such as machinists, electricians, and carpenters.

Apprenticeship programs are generally administered by joint labor-management committees for each craft, which determine the criteria for admittance to the programs. These committees are also responsible for the content of training programs, in accordance with the general guidelines established by the government under the National Apprenticeship Act of 1937. The committees decide on course agenda, method of instruction, and amount of time devoted to group instruction and on-the-job training.

Apprenticeship training has several advantages. Apprentices are trained in the production environment by skilled workers who are acquainted with the processes and procedures currently being used by the employer; this makes the training directly applicable to the job. The system also provides an excellent opportunity for labor, management, and educators to work cooperatively in meeting the needs for a skilled labor force. Finally, the ultimate skill level produced in apprentice training can be greater than in any other training system.

On the other hand, after a long period of apprenticeship is completed, there is no assurance that apprentices will remain with the firm that trained them.

On-the-Job Training

The second primary form of skills training, on-the-job training, is the method most widely used. It can vary from an extremely structured program to a very informal one. Formal on-the-job training involves the careful selection of trainees and a listing of the skills that will be taught during the training period. In the informal mode, new employees are turned over to experienced employees, who are instructed to teach them how to do the job.

Whether on-the-job training is formal or informal, the job to be learned must be broken down into specific processes and steps. In addition, a timetable reflecting the amount of time required to master each step should be provided.

On-the-job training is considered especially appropriate for certain industrial and factory jobs. In addition, clerical jobs and many mechanical occupations rely heavily on on-the-job training to produce the required skills. Among the advantages of on-the-job training are:

- No special equipment is required.
- The skills learned during the training are immediately transferable to the actual job.
- The trainee can immediately practice what has been learned.
- The trainee is likely to be highly motivated since he or she is working in an actual job situation, as opposed to preparing for future employment.
- Any unusual or difficult situations that may be present on the job are also present during the learning process.

Some disadvantages of this method are:

- The instructor must be highly skilled for training to be effective.
- Since training takes place within a real work environment, a trainee's slowness and errors may disrupt productivity.
- The one-to-one ratio required between trainers and trainees is more expensive than a classroom situation, where one trainer can teach numerous trainees simultaneously.
- A great deal of time and space are generally needed.

Vestibule Training

In vestibule training, the production system is duplicated in a separate area, where the actual processes, procedures, and equipment used are approximated as closely as possible. Trainees are not under any pressure to maintain a standard rate of production.

Vestibule training is most appropriate when the job to be learned involves the operation of a single piece of equipment or regular, repetitive processes. It is very useful when large numbers of employees must be trained quickly, such as when the start-up of a new plant requires training a complete workforce. It is also appropriate when the job to be learned is normally performed in an area filled with distractions or safety hazards.

This form of training is considered by many to be superior to on-the-job training for the following reasons:

- The instructors have training as their primary task, so it does not take time away from other duties.
- The learning process does not jeopardize normal production.

- Training methods that would not be appropriate during actual on-line production can be used.
- The learning environment is free from the pressures of production and the demands of meeting standards for quantity and quality of work.

On the other hand, there are some disadvantages that should be considered before using vestibule training:

- The cost of a training facility can be high.
- The process can be economically impractical if only a small number of people are trained simultaneously.
- Workshop equipment and processes must constantly be updated to reflect changes made in the actual workplace.
- The absence of production pressure may make it more difficult to adjust to the real job.
- Supervisors may unrealistically expect trainees coming from the vestibule environment to be fully qualified in all aspects of the job.

Classroom Training

Classroom training may take place either in-house or at a vocational or technical trade school (or some other institution outside the organization). Subjects offered and skills taught vary considerably, depending on specific interests and needs. The best classroom training establishes explicit goals, breaks the subject down into bits of logically sequenced knowledge, requires active participation by the learners, allows them to set their own pace, and provides immediate reinforcement of learning through feedback of results.

The impact of rapid technological changes on existing skills and jobs is one reason classroom training is so popular. Ongoing programs that retrain employees for new occupations in the same organization are becoming increasingly necessary. For example, as more and more repetitive, routine, and clerical jobs are replaced by data processing installations, some of the workers who would otherwise be displaced can be retrained with new appropriate skills.

Management Training

There are three forms of management training. The first utilizes internal professional trainers who either purchase commercially available training packages or develop their own programs. The second involves outside consultants who are brought in-house. The third sends the managers to outside seminars and workshops conducted by professional trainers and training organizations.

In-house training programs are the most widely used, particularly for supervisors and lower-level managers. This may be the most cost-effective means for management training, but it is usually considered the least productive by those who have attended both in-house workshops and outside seminars. Being sent to an outside program is a form of special recognition. It is a tribute to a person's importance, and may encourage managers who are on their way up in the company. In addition, an outside program offers the valuable stimulation of association with people from other companies. This in itself is bound to heighten a manager's sense of professionalism.

Bringing outside consultants in-house is also advantageous because the material presented is often custom designed and targeted for a particular group of managers. Since hiring consultants can be costly, it is important that businesses hire an expert who suits their particular needs. In this regard, the ideal consultant will listen to the concerns and objectives expressed by the employer, will work closely with a designated company representative to ensure that the agreed-upon goals are being met, will provide progress reports for long-term training projects, and will evaluate the end result of a training assignment to determine whether the program delivered was what was promised.

From this information, then, it would appear that ideal management training is conducted by an outside consultant, either in-house or off company premises. However, each organization must select its own management-development program to suit its own climate, the level for which training is required, the particular characteristics of the managers to be developed, their specific developmental needs, and the availability of funds.

A wide range of topics may be encompassed in management development. Some of the most popular include:

Effective employer-employee relations	Perception and image projection
Communication	Full utilization of skills
Decision making	Building confidence
Problem solving	Business writing
Teamwork	Delegation
Motivation	Coaching and counseling

Career planning   Time management
Behavior modification   EEO and affirmative action
Goal setting

High-Performance Training

Whether an employer's focus is on skills and technical training or management training, the emphasis of training overall is increasingly on high-performance work. The exact composition of high performance is different for each company, but there are certain common characteristics, according to economist Anthony Carnevale:

1. Work is performed by customer-focused teams.
2. Employees are able to perform a variety of skills.
3. The company is actively involved in managing change.
4. Collaboration, both inside and outside the company, is the norm.

Carnevale then sets out four key factors that are needed for an organization to meet high-performance standards:

1. Flexible technologies
2. High-performance organizational formats
3. Highly skilled workforce
4. Collaborative labor-management relations*

A *Training and Development* magazine survey, described in the December 1994 issue, reveals that more companies are involved in performance-related training than ever before: 22 percent more businesses are conducting change-management training; 19 percent more are teaching basic skills; 18 percent more are providing customer service training; and 17 percent more are doing team building or team management.

Self-Directed Learning

High-performance training also places a heavy emphasis on learning, with the focus shifting away from isolated skill building and information provided by the instructor, toward the direction of performance improvement by the learner. This is self-directed learning (SDL), also known as

*Patricia A. Galagan

individualized instruction or prescriptive learning. Essentially, it is a process in which trainees work at their own pace, generally without the aid of an instructor, but under the guidance of a facilitator, to achieve predetermined goals. To be successful, an SDL program should begin with a thorough four-step analysis process:

1. Analysis of the trainees' jobs, identifying all the tasks to be mastered
2. Analysis of where SDL will take place—at a central self-directed learning center or at multiple work sites
3. Analysis of the format, identifying the media resources to be used for SDL
4. Analysis of the SDL facilitator's tasks and responsibilities

Following the analysis process, employers may proceed to create a specific SDL package. In doing so, employers are advised to make certain the programs developed are sufficient in terms of meeting trainee objectives, practical, usable, up to date, and effective.

Computer-Based Training

Computer-based training (CBT) enables employees to conduct training sessions whenever needed. The courses can be viewed repeatedly in their entirety, or selected modules may be provided. Since most modules are approximately twenty or thirty minutes in duration employees can take frequent "CBT learning breaks."

Although computer training may stand on its own, CBT is sometimes used to enhance traditional classroom training. CBT trainees are often tested on their knowledge and certified upon satisfactory completion of the course. Since the process is geared toward self-study at each user's pace, CBTs are particularly useful when the workforce is diverse, multiple skills are required to do a job, and job skill requirements continually change.

Many companies purchase off-the-shelf CBT packages; others prefer to author their own. If you choose to author your own CBT program, strive for standardization for maximum effectiveness. If there are several courses in a training curriculum, each course should meet certain guidelines:

• *Organization.* Each course should provide directions on how to use the CBT system, identify course objectives, describe the contents of the course, provide a summary, and list references to supporting materials, such as workbooks and users' guides.

• *Screen composition.* Each course should contain one main idea per screen, bulleted lists of ideas, paragraphs of no more than six to eight lines, boxes containing instructional information of the same size and in a consistent location on the screen, and typing directions in the boxes.

• *Text placement.* When placing words on the screens focus attention on one idea at a time, keep sentence length short, use one- and two-syllable words, use the second person (*you*), and be consistent in your use of command syntax.

• *Feedback to users.* When designing CBT program feedback to users as they make choices, use nonjudgmental words; make the feedback format consistent in locution, punctuation, and so forth; explain why an answer is incorrect and provide the correct answer; and reinforce correct answers by restatement in slightly different terms.

CD-ROM

CD-ROM (compact disk–read only memory) is a take-off from the technology that produces compact disks used for recordings. A CD-ROM can hold the equivalent of more information than 470 high-density floppy disks. In addition, it can sort, organize, or search through this information in a matter of seconds. With sound and video added, CD-ROM becomes a valuable multimedia resource for trainers.

Color, animation, and sound, as well as interactive indexes and reader participation opportunities, transform traditional presentations into lively learning experiences. Indeed, there is an increase in the number of companies taking videotape training programs and placing them on interactive CD-ROM disks. The technology is easy to master, is relatively inexpensive (it costs only 5 percent more to produce a CD-ROM disk instead of a videotape), and is projected to become standard equipment on any PC. According to the Optical Publishing Association in Columbus, Ohio, $1.7 billion was spent on CD-ROM disks in 1994, representing a 30 percent increase over the previous year.

Businesses interested in CD-ROM are advised to view it as they would any other new technology. Visit computer stores, attend conferences or seminars designed to explain how CD-ROM can help your company, and compare costs. Business information publishers produce CD-ROM ranging from a low of $50 to as much as $10,000. Discounting is a common practice for quantity purchases. Also, talk to colleagues from other companies currently using CD-ROM training and inquire how employees respond to CD-ROM versus videotapes. Ideally, CD-ROM can be used to supplement or enhance instructional training and is excellent as a "personal refresher" for employees with desktop or laptop computers.

Training Components and Techniques

Whether using SDL, CBT, or CD-ROM, a successful skills-training or management-development program must have three primary components:

1. *Practice:* Performing tasks after learning them, in order to improve proficiency. Ideally practice should be distributed over a period of time, as opposed to taking place all in one session. It should also require trainees to respond to stimuli other than those encountered in the training program, to generalize the scope of their learning.

2. *Feedback:* Knowledge of the results of one's efforts is essential to successful training. Feedback may be either positive or negative; in either event, trainees need to know where they stand and whether they are on the right track. Feedback may be provided in a variety of formats, including formal and informal evaluations by trainers, and trainees' observing their own performance via videotape.

3. *Reinforcement:* The positive consequence of one's behavior, which strengthens the probability of that behavior's being repeated. For example, if a trainee who performs a new task correctly is praised by a trainer, then the trainee will associate correct performance of this new behavior with a pleasant outcome, and probably do it again.

A number of different training methods may be employed in order to facilitate learning, and to underscore the three components of practice, feedback, and reinforcement. Different techniques have varying degrees of effectiveness, depending on the training objectives, backgrounds, and attitudes of the trainees, and the skill level of the instructor. It is also important to note that any single training program may employ many different training techniques; their skillful combination contributes to the program's overall success.

Here are some specific training methods that may be incorporated into the design and implementation of an in-house training program. Most programs use a combination of information-processing and simulation techniques.

Information-Processing Techniques

In addition to SDL, CBT, and CD-ROM, these techniques are useful for conveying information to trainees. They do not involve trainees as actively as the simulation techniques discussed later.

Lectures

Lectures can provide a great deal of information in a relatively short period of time. In order for lectures to be effective, the speaker must be both interesting and well informed. Anecdotes, quotations, and illustrations enliven the presentation. It is also recommended that lecturers permit questions both during and following the lecture, in order to maintain a high level of trainee interest.

If training programs are to rely on lectures as their primary method of training, there should be more than one speaker.

Panels

In panel presentations, a limited number of speakers express their views in a series of short lectures. Normally these presentations are followed by a discussion in which the panelists exchange ideas with one another or react to questions from the trainees.

This training technique can bring a variety of viewpoints or specializations to the trainees relatively quickly, and the interaction among the speakers can make panels more exciting than straight lectures. As with lectures, however, it is imperative that the panelists be both knowledgeable and interesting. In addition, it is important to follow up with a question-and-answer session.

Films and Slides

Films and slides can be a primary instructional medium or can be used to strengthen and clarify verbal presentations. Most programs are accompanied by a comprehensive guide for discussion leaders that provides material for stimulating, challenging discussions and/or project sessions.

Videotape

Preprogrammed videotapes may be shown, or blank tapes may be used to record trainees' activities during a workshop. The tapes can then be viewed and discussed by participants.

Videotape allows for close-ups of specific operations or skills, and the instructor can stop the tape anywhere to emphasize a particular point. Videotaping trainees as they participate in role-playing or other types of group exercises, and then providing feedback as the tape is replayed, can be a very valuable source of learning. However, encourage participants to ignore the camera and not "act."

Overheard Transparencies

Overhead transparencies may be prepared in advance and projected onto the screen, or they may be written and projected as an instructor talks during the program. They are useful in emphasizing key points simultaneously being made by the instructor, and are a helpful note-taking guide for trainees. Generally no more than twenty-five characters should appear on each overhead.

Handout Materials

Handout materials are printed documents supplied to each trainee, containing a summary of the ideas to be covered during the training program. Handouts may also be used for enrichment as related reading assignments. They should only be used if they relate directly to a specific objective.

Assignments

Assignments may be completed before, during, or after classroom hours. They should be accompanied by a follow-up in which all trainees can ask questions or comment about the ideas included in the assignment.

All assignments should be directly related to an immediate learning objective. Most assignments should be relatively short.

One-to-One Instruction

This mode of instruction is based on the "tell, show, do" approach to learning. A trainer and a single worker meet in a designated area so that the instructor can teach the employee certain procedures, methods, skills, or techniques. The worker then returns to the workplace and puts the learning into practice. The instructor remains accessible, to review the employee's performance, discuss any uncertainties, and make corrections as needed.

Simulation Techniques

These techniques are more participative than the information-processing techniques just described and can be used to represent real on-the-job situations.

Exercises and Project Sessions

Exercises and small-group project sessions reinforce specific points presented by the trainers. Workshop attendees are given assignments, instructed to work together during a specified time frame, and then invited to present their findings to the rest of the group. A discussion of each group's findings then takes place. At the end of an exercise or group project session, the original point is stressed once again.

Trainers should note that the process involved in a group project session, including the interaction among participants, is more important than the actual results.

Role Playing

In role playing, trainees enact situations that let them apply principles learned during a training workshop. The most effective role playing is informal, followed by immediate feedback and discussion. This feedback should not evaluate the performance of the players; rather, it should analyze the effectiveness of the behavior shown.

Because role playing can make trainees uneasy, it is best to start with multiple, simultaneous role plays, so that no individual or small group of trainees is subjected to a critical analysis by the rest of the class. In addition, it is best if the trainer participates in the first series of role plays, in an impromptu manner.

In-Basket Exercises

An in-basket exercise is a simulation in which the trainee is given a number of notes and memos similar to those found in an in-basket during a typical day on the job. The trainee is then asked to deal with each of the items in one of two ways: as he or she has been taught during training, if the exercise is being used for evaluation, or as he or she would normally deal with these items, if the exercise is being used as a diagnosis before the training begins.

All items included should be realistic and representative of a real on-the-job situation. Feedback following the exercise is essential.

Brainstorming

Brainstorming is an unstructured form of discussion in which trainees generate as many ideas as possible on a given topic, without judging whether the ideas are right, feasible, or of high quality. This method stimulates creative thinking.

Effective brainstorming brings about highly participative discussions in which every member contributes, thus inspiring ideas that might not otherwise have developed.

Case Studies

Case studies are detailed written descriptions of an actual or imaginary situation related to the objectives of the training program. Small groups read the case and then analyze it for specific considerations as instructed.

When using case studies, make sure that the situations contain sufficient information from which to draw conclusions. The cases should be described in clear, concise language. Allow adequate time for discussion.

Games

Most games used during a training program are simulations augmented by competition among several teams. Given basic data about a situation, participants are instructed to make key decisions and follow their decisions through to the next consequence, when they are again asked to decide what to do. The cycle continues until the trainees have learned what the game is designed to teach.

Games provide an interesting way of learning new concepts. They are particularly helpful in courses involving planning, organizing, controlling, decision making, team building, problem solving, and organizational development. For maximum effectiveness, group size should be limited to five or six members.

Start-Up Guidelines

Many small and mid-sized organizations wait two or three years after establishing the initial components of their human resources department before adding a training function. By that time, they should have a clear sense of the identity of the department, the needs of the various divisions of the organization, and support from senior management.

Here are ten suggestions for starting a training and development program. These recommendations will also prove helpful if you want to revamp an existing training and development function.

1. Know your company's history, present status, projected goals and objectives, and philosophy.

2. Staff the training function with qualified individuals possessing "expandable skills" so that their talents may evolve as the needs of the training function change.

3. Conduct a thorough needs analysis before conducting any training. Include an assessment of needs perceived both by management and by staff.

4. Become thoroughly familiar with the various functions performed by employees throughout the organization. It is best to do this firsthand, by spending time in the various departments observing workers and talking with them about what they do.

5. Gain support from senior management, if at all possible. Sometimes this support will develop gradually once the process begins. If it is not available at the beginning, do not become discouraged; rather, keep senior management apprised of your progress, and remain persistent.

6. Make certain that the first training program is likely to appeal to most of the participants. This will be far more effective than making the first program remedial or one to which employees are sent, as opposed to invited. If you want a training function to succeed, it has to be interesting and attractive to the participants.

7. Be realistic in your expectations of the training function. As discussed earlier in this chapter, training is not a panacea for all that ails an organization. Offering skills and technical training to employees does not necessarily mean that they will embrace them; offering management-development skills to supervisors and managers does not mean they will apply them. The training process is ongoing, and perseverance and repetition are the keys to success.

8. Educate managers about what training can and cannot be expected to accomplish. Specifically, tell them that some performance problems cannot be corrected by training. The environment in which employees work, the specific responsibilities they are expected to carry out, interrelations with coworkers and management, and the appropriateness of the job they are performing are all possible factors contributing to poor performance.

9. Market the training function effectively. As you develop programs, prepare printed material for distribution to all employees, including brief descriptions of the courses, how often they will be offered, eligibility for attendance, and so on. Make this material attractive and interesting so that employees will want to attend.

10. Continually evaluate everything you do. This includes gaining feedback every time a training program is run and assessing the responses so that any valid suggestions may be incorporated into the next program. Also, examine the results of each training program to see how closely it is meeting your short- and long-term goals.

Evaluating the Effectiveness of Training and Development Programs

Surprisingly few organizations attempt to evaluate their training programs, often because it is assumed that the assessment of whether training has actually strengthened job performance is difficult. Indeed, studies show that only about 15 percent of companies measure trainees' training transfer: that is, the actual application of knowledge and skills acquired in training programs. Evaluation often consists of merely asking trainees whether they have learned anything. Although trainee feedback is valuable, it is not a sufficient gauge for determining a program's overall effectiveness.

Measuring the effectiveness of training requires focusing on the training outcome, measured by changed behavior. One method is to solicit feedback from trainees' supervisors. Another is to have trainees develop action plans with follow-up to gauge how well these plans have been implemented. Most organizations would do well to follow D. L. Kirkpatrick's four levels of traditional evaluation procedure: reaction, learning, behavior, and results.*

Reaction may be defined as what the trainees thought of a particular training program. In order to gauge participants' reaction effectively, pre-

*As reported in Richard W. Beatty and Craig E. Schneier, *Personnel Administration* (Reading, Mass.: Addison-Wesley, 1981), pp. 338–339.

pare a questionnaire on program development, format, methods, and content. It should be designed so that the responses may be tabulated easily.

Additional space should be given for opinions about items not directly covered in the questionnaire. The information trainees volunteer here often provides the basis for developing new training programs in the future.

To encourage honest opinions, trainees should be permitted to submit the questionnaires anonymously.

Learning is the successful absorption of the principles, facts, and techniques that were specified as training objectives. One measure of learning is the paper-and-pencil test. The measures used should be quantifiable indicators of what was learned during the training program.

Ideally, learning should be assessed both before and after the training program in order to measure any changes effectively.

Behavior refers to actual changes in job performance. It is often measured by such performance appraisal techniques as the behaviorally anchored rating scale (BARS). As described in Chapter 7, the BARS technique identifies the primary duties and responsibilities of a specific job or job family, as well as the most effective and least effective ways for accomplishing these functions.

For maximum effectiveness, performance levels should be measured before and after training to see whether learning has transferred to job performance.

Results refer to a program's effects on various facets of an organization's environment (such as productivity) and on certain employee factors (such as turnover, absenteeism, grievances, and morale).

The effectiveness of training should be evaluated throughout the actual training program, at its conclusion, and at periodic intervals after it has ended. To make certain that a thorough analysis has been conducted, consider the following questions:

- Can the individual trainees now perform the specific tasks identified as objectives of the program?
- Can the trainees sustain learned behaviors on the job?
- Do the learned behaviors and tasks produce the desired operational results?
- Does the monetary value of these results exceed the costs of the training?

The value of the information gathered at each level increases as the evaluation moves from measuring reaction to measuring results. Results evaluation is considered to be the most intensive level. Unfortunately, many organizations do only reaction-level evaluations.

Selecting Trainers

Whether you employ in-house trainers or hire outside consultants to conduct your training programs, all trainers should possess certain traits. These include:

- Highly developed presentation and platform skills
- Group-dynamics skills
- The ability to convey enthusiasm for the subject matter
- Team-building skills
- A high level of interest in training
- A high level of skill and experience in using a variety of instructional techniques
- A high level of skill and knowledge in the subject matter
- An understanding of how people learn
- Effective communication skills
- Flexibility
- A high level of skill in leading discussions
- The ability to serve effectively as a role model
- The ability to adjust instruction to the needs of the trainees
- Highly developed coaching skills

If the trainer is also responsible for designing the program, he or she must also possess excellent course-development skills.

Any organization that is establishing or revamping its training function should select one or more trainers who have demonstrated these capabilities and who have also proved that they can conduct learning experiences in an empathetic, facilitative way.

Training Costs

Training costs range from absolutely nothing to several thousand dollars a day. Free programs offered at local schools and universities may be suitable for certain employees; these are usually single-session courses, lasting a couple of hours, that provide an overview of a given topic. Various training and consulting organizations offer workshops and seminars to all interested companies. These workshops usually last from half a day to a week and cost anywhere from $100 to $500 per day per participant. In-house consultants who custom-design training workshops to suit the needs of an individual organization usually charge from $350 to $3,000 per day. For this amount most consultants will train up to twenty-five employees in one session. Some consultants, on the other hand, prefer to charge "per head"—from $40 to $150 per trainee. These figures often preclude program development costs.

  Companies interested in consultants or training organizations should shop around. Compare costs, services provided, and the skills of the trainers. Do not hesitate to ask about evaluations provided by former trainees, or to request some of their names and telephone numbers. Be careful not to assume either that cheaper is better or that more expensive means higher-quality services. Neither statement is necessarily true.

  Companies that prefer to hire their own trainers should note that the salaries vary considerably, depending on such factors as geographic location, the size of the organization, the exact nature of the training, and the degree of experience required. Check the classified sections of newspapers and trade journals, and talk with representatives from qualified agencies, to determine ballpark figures for the kind of person you are seeking before launching a recruitment drive. In order to do this effectively, of course, you should have a comprehensive job description.

Tuition Aid

Most employers offer some sort of tuition aid to employees who want to attend outside seminars, workshops, or courses related to their jobs. This means that part or all of the cost of tuition, books, and supplies will be paid back to the employee on satisfactory completion of a course. In some companies the policy is quite restrictive and covers only those courses directly related to the employee's present job. Other companies take a more liberal position and are willing to pay for general education.

  Figure 4 is an example of a typical tuition aid policy in an organization with approximately 1,400 employees.

Training Trends

Increasingly, training is being viewed as a vital part of the human resources function. The Clinton administration has proposed a mandate that organizations spend a percentage of company payroll on training or do-

Figure 4. Sample tuition aid policy.

As an extension of our training and development policy, this organization supports self-development via the pursuit of outside courses. We therefore will reimburse employees for all successfully completed job-related courses at accredited schools and colleges. Successful completion is defined as:

> Attaining a grade of C or better in a graded course
> Attaining a grade of "pass" in a pass/fail course

Eligibility

To be eligible for tuition aid, an employee must:

> Be a permanent, full-time employee
> Have a minimum of one year's service
> Have an overall rating of satisfactory or better on the last performance appraisal
> Maintain a performance rating of satisfactory or better while undertaking course work

Reimbursement Schedule

Reimbursement will be based on the following schedule:

Grade	Percentage of Tuition Reimbursement
A− or better, or Pass	100%
B−, B, or B+	75%
C−, C, or C+	50%
Below C−	0%
Fail	0%
Incomplete	0%

Reimbursement is for tuition only. Books, registration fees, and other related costs will not be reimbursed.

Procedure

On completing registration, employees must submit a bursar's receipt to the human resources department via their manager. After successfully completing courses, employees must submit an official school record to human resources. Reimbursements will be made according to the schedule above within approximately 30 days of submission.

nate a portion to a national training fund. The business response to this proposal is split, but this recognition that training is important sends a strong message to companies that dismiss the need for ongoing training and development.

As we approach the twenty-first century, it is expected that the emphasis on high-performance training will continue, with a steady shift from isolated skill building and information transfer to performance improvement and support. Learning will be much more integrated with the actual work being performed. Additionally, employees will be encouraged to interact more with others, putting a greater emphasis on those group training events used to motivate and generate teamwork. Small businesses are projected to rely increasingly on partnerships with other small companies, community colleges, and government and civic organizations to meet training needs. Furthermore, technologies that change how, when, and where people work will also change how they learn.

Even the language used to describe various aspects of training points the way to the future: "lifelong learning" is replacing "school-age education"; "process reengineering" is substituting for "quality improvement"; "organized learning" is referred to instead of "teaching"; and in some organizations "employees" are now referred to as "performers."

Training between companies is also more common. For example, if one organization excels at particular skills and another does particularly well in some other area, employees may be swapped for a period of time. In this model, trainees may become trainers for a time, and vice versa.

Increasingly, companies are moving away from the concept of training as a one-way transfer of information by a training expert, to multiple kinds of learning, encompassing both skills enhancement and problem solving by training professionals as well as nonprofessionals. "Learning facilitators," such as line supervisors and managers expert at performing specific tasks, will be increasingly relied on to help others learn innovative ways of dealing with short- and long-term situations. This shift has the potential of making a significant impact, since training professionals often are not viewed as being as knowledgeable about organizational matters as are managers and consequently lack the credibility needed to address complex issues. Training and development professionals may then focus more on program design and facilitation.

Summary

Serious thought should be given to the role of training and development and what it may realistically be expected to accomplish. The company's needs should be analyzed to identify specific objectives before any training takes place. When training is deemed appropriate, it should be made available to all employees, in the form of both skills and management training, with added attention paid to high-performance training methods such as self-directed learning, computer-based learning, and CD-ROM. In addition, an ongoing system of measuring the effectiveness of each program should be implemented. Trainers should be carefully selected on the basis of platform skills and the ability to integrate various training methods and techniques. Companies using outside consultants or training organizations should carefully compare the costs and services of various options.

In addition to providing in-house training and development programs, many companies also offer tuition reimbursement to employees wishing to pursue formal education.

Employers are urged to keep on top of training trends, noting particularly the increased use of managers and supervisors as learning facilitators to supplement the information imparted by training and development professionals.

11

Records Maintenance and Information Management

A well-planned human resources information system will automate procedures, serve as an electronic filing system, and provide information to a wide range of nontechnical managers with numerous requirements.

The area of human resources records maintenance has expanded considerably over the past several years. This is not surprising, considering the increase in HR-related legislation. Records must now be maintained to meet various legal requirements, such as those pertaining to EEO and OSHA. In addition, employers keep records of nearly all aspects of an individual's employment to use in human resources planning, to serve historical needs and to provide a database for research. The result is a myriad of records, forms, and reports that must be retained, and, in some cases, submitted to the government.

Several federal labor laws also require employers to post various official notices.

One of the positive offshoots of this increase in records maintenance and posting requirements has been the computerized human resources information system (HRIS). Computer-based systems have virtually freed human resources staff from having to assemble manually the required data for various records, forms, and reports. Even a small company—with fewer than 100 employees—may now have an automated records maintenance system.

In addition, a growing number of small and mid-sized companies are using an HRIS to support a broad range of information management needs in the human resources area. The final section of this chapter will outline several aspects of HRIS.

Federal Record-Keeping Requirements

The following section summarizes the key aspects of the record-keeping requirements of various federal laws. Readers are urged to consult with the appropriate agency or legal counsel for any changes that may have occurred since this book was published. Furthermore, the information in this chapter is not intended to be all-inclusive; some companies may be responsible for records, forms, and reports not described here. Nor is this chapter to be considered legal advice.

Employers are required to prepare and retain certain records in accordance with the following federal laws:

> Fair Labor Standards Act of 1938
> Walsh-Healey Act of 1936
> Davis-Bacon Act of 1931
> Title VII of the Civil Rights Act of 1964
> Executive Order 11246 of 1965
> Age Discrimination in Employment Act of 1967
> Rehabilitation Act of 1973
> Vietnam Era Veterans' Readjustment Assistance Act of 1974
> Employee Retirement Income Security Act of 1974
> Landrum-Griffin Act of 1959
> Occupational Safety and Health Act of 1970
> Toxic Substances Control Act of 1976
> Immigration Reform and Control Act of 1986

Fair Labor Standards Act of 1938

According to this act, payrolls, individual contracts or collective bargaining agreements, sales and purchase records, and basic records containing various employee-related information must be retained for three years. In addition, information about employment and earnings, wage and salary rates, work schedules, additions to or deductions from wages paid, and the payment of any wage differential to employees of the opposite sex in the same establishment must be retained for two years.

No specific form of retention is required. Microfilm may be used if the employer agrees to provide transcripts as needed. Punched tape is also acceptable if records can be easily converted to reviewable form.

Walsh-Healey Act of 1936

This act requires employers to retain certificates of age for all minors for as long as these minors are employed. Employment records containing the following information must be retained for three years from the date of the last entry:

> Name and address
> Sex
> Occupation
> Date of birth of each employee under 19 years of age
> Wage records for each employee
> If a union is involved, the identifying number of the contract worked
>   under by each employee

Annual summaries of occupational injuries and illnesses must also be kept for three years following the end of the year to which they relate. (Note that this is superseded by the OSHA requirement that the log and summary of occupational injuries and illnesses be kept for *five* years.)

No particular form of retention is required.

Davis-Bacon Act of 1931

This act requires employers with public contracts to keep payroll records that include the name, address, correct classification (of each laborer and mechanic), rate of pay, number of hours worked (daily and weekly), all deductions made, and actual wages paid.

Records must be retained for three years from the date of completion of a contract. No specific form of retention is specified.

Title VII of the Civil Rights Act of 1964

Title VII stipulates that employment records relevant to hiring, promotion, demotion, transfer, layoff, termination, rates of pay or other terms of compensation, and selection for training or apprenticeship must be retained for six months from the date of making the record or taking the HR action involved, whichever occurs later. In addition, HR records regarding charges of discrimination or action brought against the employer must be retained until final disposition of the charge or action. These records may include the human resources files of the charging party and other employees in comparable positions, and the completed application forms and tests of unsuccessful candidates for a given position.

Companies with apprenticeship programs must keep a chronological list of the names and addresses of all applicants, their dates of application, their sex and minority group identification, and other relevant records such as test scores and interview notes. This information must be retained for two years or the duration of the successful applicants' apprenticeship, whichever is later.

Employers with 100 or more employees must submit the EEO-1 Employer Information Report. Employers with more than one establishment need not file separate EEO-1 Reports for their plants with forty-nine or fewer employees. Current EEO-1 Reports must be retained indefinitely.

Records reflecting racial or ethnic identity may be obtained via the maintenance of posthire documentation, as dictated by state law. Such records should be kept separate from the employee's HR file.

Executive Order 11246 of 1965

This order requires federal contractors and subcontractors to retain written affirmative action statements and all supporting data indefinitely. Other records relating to compliance with applicable affirmative action requirements—including documents regarding the use, validation, and results of tests—must also be retained for an unspecified period. No specific form of retention is required.

Age Discrimination in Employment Act of 1967

To comply with this act, employers must keep payroll records containing each employee's name, address, date of birth, occupation, rate of pay, and weekly earnings. These records must be retained for three years. In addition, HR records relating to job advertisements or other notices regarding employment opportunities, job applications, resumés, tests, physical examinations, promotions, demotions, transfers, selection for training, layoffs, recalls, and terminations must be retained for one year from the date of the HR action to which the record relates. (An exception is application forms and other preemployment records of applicants for temporary jobs, which require a retention period of only ninety days.)

Records relevant to employee benefits plans, seniority systems, and merit rating systems must be retained for one year beyond the time the plan or system is in effect. Also, all documents relating to an enforcement action against the employer must be retained until the matter is resolved.

There is no specified form of retention for any of these records.

Rehabilitation Act of 1973

This act stipulates that federal contractors and subcontractors must retain complete and accurate employment records for all applicants and employees with disabilities for one year. Records regarding complaints and actions taken under the act must also be retained for one year. There is no specified form of retention.

Vietnam Era Veterans' Readjustment Assistance Act of 1974

This legislation also applies to certain federal contractors and subcontractors; it requires that records regarding complaints and action taken under the act must be retained for one year. No specified form of retention is required.

Employee Retirement Income Security Act of 1974 (ERISA)

ERISA specifies that records providing the basis for all required retirement plan descriptions must be kept for at least six years after the filing date of documents based on them. In addition, the records determining what benefits are due to each participant in the plan must be kept for as long as they are relevant.

Although no specific form of retention is required, the information must appear in sufficient detail so that the documents may be verified, explained, clarified, and checked for accuracy and completeness.

Landrum-Griffin Act of 1959

This act requires employers to retain records concerning all required reports of payments, agreements, or arrangements—including vouchers, work sheets, and receipts—for at least five years after the filing date of the documents based on them. No particular form of retention is required. However, as with ERISA, the information must appear in sufficient detail so that the documents may be verified, explained, clarified, and checked for accuracy and completeness.

Occupational Safety and Health Act of 1970

In accordance with OSHA, both summaries and details of occupational injuries and illnesses—including the extent and outcome of each incident and summary totals for the calendar year—must be retained for five years following the end of the year they concern. Complete and accurate records of all required medical examinations must be kept for the duration of employment plus thirty years, unless otherwise specified. In addition, records of any personal or environmental monitoring of exposure to hazardous materials must be kept for thirty years.

OSHA Form 200 (or a private equivalent) must be used for the overall summary of occupational injuries and illnesses; OSHA Form 101 (or a private equivalent) is required for records containing more detailed information for each occurrence of injury or illness. There is no specified form required for medical examination records or records about exposure to hazardous materials.

Toxic Substances Control Act of 1976

Section 8(c) of this act requires employers to keep records of "significant adverse reactions" to health or the environment that may indicate "long-lasting or irreversible damage, partial or complete impairment of bodily functions, impairment of normal activities which is experienced by all or most of the persons exposed at one time, and impairment of normal activities which is experienced each time an individual is exposed." Such records must be retained for thirty years in cases of employee health-related allegations arising from any employment-related exposure; and five years for all other allegations, including environmental or consumer charges.

Records must contain the original allegation, the name and address of the plant site that received the allegation, the date the allegation was received, identification of the implicated substance, a description of health and environmental effects, the results of any self-initiated investigation of the allegation, and copies of any other relevant reports or records. Allegations must be in either signed written or recorded oral form.

Federal Posting Requirements

Several federal laws require the posting of official notices in the workplace, the following for businesses with more than fifty employees:

> Americans with Disabilities Act
> Age Discrimination in Employment Act of 1967
> Title VII of the Civil Rights Act of 1964
> Minimum wage effective April 1, 1990, and the Fair Labor Standards Act
> Williams-Steiger Occupational Safety and Health Act of 1970—OSHA
> Employee Polygraph Protection Act of 1988
> Family and Medical Leave Act of 1993

Employers with fewer than fifty employees are not required to post a notice regarding the Family and Medical Leave Act of 1993.

For convenience, these federal laws have been consolidated into one poster (the "5-in-1" for businesses with fifty or more employees and the "4-in-1" for companies with fewer than fifty employees). Individual posters are also available. For information on obtaining these posters write or call:

> Equal Employment Opportunity Commission (EEOC)
> 1801 L Street, N.W.
> Washington, D.C. 20507
> 800/669-EEOC

The consolidated posters are available from the EEOC free of charge. G. Neil Companies, a firm specializing in labor law posting requirements, may also be contacted, at 800/999-9111, for posters meeting all federal standards and registered with the U.S. Copyright Office at the Library of Congress. The 5-in-1 and 4-in-1 posters from G. Neil range in price from $6.99 to $29.99, depending on paper, lamination, and framing preferences.

Notices must be posted prominently and conspicuously in places easily accessible to employees as well as job applicants, including those having physical, visual, and other disabilities. Accordingly, notices should be posted low enough to be read by people with mobility impairments, made available on audiocassettes, or read to persons with vision impairments. The EEOC has audiocassette recordings of its poster, available to employers free of charge in limited quantities. In addition, if an employer's workforce comprises a significant portion of workers not literate in English, notices must be posted in their languages. Reproduced posters must be at least 8½ inches by 11 inches and must contain fully legible text.

Any employer willfully violating the federal posting requirements may be assessed fines up to $7,500.

In addition to federal labor laws, your company also must comply with state laws. If the company has locations in several states throughout the country, there must be compliance with the posting requirements in each state. Such requirements may include workers' compensation, child labor, unemployment insurance, and sexual harassment. With regard to the last, the EEOC recommends displaying a sexual harassment poster, even if posting is not required in your state.

Recommended Forms

Every aspect of the human resources function has a potential form to go along with it. From recruitment through termination, forms may be used to record a variety of data. Some of these forms are mandatory: the W-4 is required by the Internal Revenue Service for payroll deductions; the I-9 is required of all employers for every new hire to comply with the Immigration Reform and Control Act; and the annual EEO-1 report is required of all private employers with 100 or more employees and certain federal contractors (state and municipal government employers are required to file the EEO-4 report). Others, like the employment application form, are vital sources of work history and educational information. However, there are certain forms that are not necessarily useful to small and mid-sized organizations. For example, a small company probably will not need a separate form designed to track an employee's attendance history, yearly absenteeism, or tardiness record, and a form devoted to vacation requests and approvals is a bit excessive for a business employing fewer than 100 employees.

The specific forms that a small or mid-sized company will probably find useful are as follows:

- *Job requisition form.* Serves as the foundation for a job, outlining requirements and primary duties
- *Job posting notice.* Describes available positions to employees
- *Job posting application.* Official application form used by employees interested in making internal job changes
- *Employment application form.* Critical for making effective hiring decisions and useful in matters of salary review, job posting, transfers, promotions, disciplinary matters, grievances, termination, and references
- *Affirmative action voluntary information form.* Helps businesses comply with EEO, affirmative action, and ADA regulations
- *Job descriptions.* Helpful in every stage of employment—recruiting, interviewing, selecting, orientation, performance appraisals, salary increases, promotions, transfers, demotions, grievances, disciplin-

ary action, termination, and references; also helpful in discrimination matters

- *Employee summary form.* Contains entries for all key employee data so employers can discern certain information at a glance
- *Employee status change notice.* Helps keep employee changes such as title, position, department, or salary up to date
- *Time sheets.* Keeps records of an employee's regular and overtime hours
- *Performance appraisals.* Essential for evaluating the job knowledge, skill level, and work-related goals of all exempt and nonexempt positions
- *Warning notice.* Formalized document for lending uniformity to disciplinary matters
- *Accident report.* Critical for OSHA insurance purposes and company records

Samples of many of these forms appear in the appendixes at the end of this book.

Human Resources Information Systems

Computerized data systems have been used to assist human resources functions since the 1950s. For many years, however, computer applications were restricted to limited areas, such as payroll administration and basic record keeping. By the 1970s, readily available software products offered multifunction capabilities supporting virtually all areas of human resources management. These systems are now referred to as human resources information systems (HRIS). In general, a well-planned HRIS will automate procedures, serve as an electronic filing system, and provide information to a wide range of nontechnical managers with numerous requirements.

Technological advances over the last twenty years have led to the widespread use of HRIS. In particular, the personal computer has made it feasible for small and mid-sized companies to develop an HRIS for complex, sophisticated applications previously used almost exclusively by large corporations.

There are many reasons for developing an HRIS, including:

- The ability to store and manipulate massive amounts of data
- The generation of timely data for management and government reporting

- The reduction in cost and time required to process data
- The ability to respond to "what-if" questions
- The elimination of duplicated data
- The assurance that data are accurate and consistent

While it is beyond the scope of this book to offer detailed information regarding every aspect of HRISs, technology and capability guidelines, system selection, contracts with HRIS vendors, HRIS privacy and security, and software modification follow.

Employers interested in implementing or upgrading an HRIS are advised to review articles regularly published in HR periodicals, as well as the literature supplied by vendors. It is also desirable to talk to human resources professionals with experience in the selection and use of an HRIS before making any purchasing decisions. If no one in your organization has technical expertise *and* an understanding of human resources management needs, it may be wise to use a consultant.

Technology and Capabilities

Today's HRISs rely heavily on desktop personal computers (PCs) linked into client-server networks. The "server" is either a mainframe or powerful personal computer dedicated to storing data in a database; the "clients" are the desktop computers used by individuals to accomplish a variety of tasks, such as succession planning. Together, the client and server are able to process information in a maximally efficient and sophisticated way. In addition, today's PC-based client systems are easier to use than the mainframes in the past.

An example of what can be accomplished by client-server technology is updating employee files. Without computers, this is a tedious, time-consuming, and often flawed task performed by a humans resource representative. With PCs tied in to the database, however, employees can update appropriate portions of their own files at terminals or kiosks, as needed. Putting this responsibility on the individual employee is more likely to ensure accurate and complete data, and frees human resources staff to tend to other matters. Employee PCs might also be equipped with benefits-related software, enabling employees to assess how different benefits choices would affect take-home pay. Electronic forms would enable employees to punch in their selections, and the results would be made available to HR immediately.

Client-server systems can also allow HR to track hiring, firing, and promotion patterns; provide details about how diverse the composition of each department is; provide statutory compliance information; supply benefits and compensation information; and even offer models for change, such as reengineering or downsizing.

The cost of client-server hardware and software can range from $10,000 into the millions of dollars, with software alone costing $30,000 to $100,000. Small and mid-sized companies can implement a comprehensive system at the lower end of this spectrum but should be aware of hidden costs, such as training in the use of the new system and lost work time as employees attempt to make the transition without disrupting work flow. Experts estimate that it typically takes a year or more to install and debug a client-server system.

Selecting an HRIS

Matching the demands of a growing HR department with the most suitable HRIS can be quite a challenge. To minimize the confusion, experts recommend that employers focus attention on a carefully developed request for proposal (RFP). This, it is maintained, will allow focus on the differences between competing software products for selection of those most compatible with a company's requirements.

An RFP should begin with a general description of the company, its current HRIS, and its projected HRIS needs. Next, identify the need for any confidentiality and nondisclosure clauses. The main section of the RFP should be devoted to functional and technical requirements, followed by requests for vendor background information, client reference lists, licensing and maintenance agreements, and product warranties.

Most RFPs do not request a breakdown of fees. Cost summaries are usually submitted separately, following the RFP. This enables the potential client to evaluate the proposal without being influenced by cost. Cost summaries should identify all costs of system acquisition, use, support, and training.

Evaluating the proposals received in response to RFPs is best accomplished by assigning a degree of importance to each of the items, ranging from "critical" to "nice, but not necessary." Making an informed choice is more likely to ensure the best fit between employer and system.

HRIS Contracts

You have isolated the HRIS capabilities needed and selected a supplier. All that remains is signing the HRIS contract, and you are now ready to learn how to implement the system. While it is prudent to retain the services of legal counsel to scrutinize the details of the HRIS contract, employers are advised to keep certain key points in mind:

- Pay close attention to clauses referring to the exclusion of all previous verbal agreements or documents, the reduction or elimination of the usual obligations of the supplier, and the ability of the supplier to alter terms of the contract unilaterally simply by informing the customer in writing.
- Be prepared to hold the supplier liable for any express warranties if promises made by the supplier or specific models or samples were relied upon as the basis for the agreement.
- Have the contract include hardware performance guarantees, if possible.
- Seek fixed hardware and software prices, although it is not unreasonable for the vendor to include a clause allowing for software price variations due to changes in taxation, import duties, or foreign currency fluctuations.
- Require an installation clause, referring to when the system is expected to be operational.
- Include a statement as to what recourse is available if the system does not operate as agreed.
- Payment terms should include a statement that the final payment will not be made until all notified problems are cleared.
- In the event that the vendor ceases to trade, the buyer should require a clause stating that all key documentation and program source codes be deposited with a third party, usually a bank.

Privacy and Security

Today's powerful, high-capacity computer systems allow for the expansion of the amount and type of information that can be filed in an HRIS. Of course, much of this information is job related, such as work, educational and salary histories, performance evaluations, and salary increases. But data pertaining to the employees' personal life are increasingly being placed in company HRISs—for example:

- Marital status
- Number and relationship of dependents
- Test results revealing personality traits, intelligence, and various physical and psychological characteristics
- Medical conditions
- Outside interests and skills

Employers must periodically review the data stored in human resources information systems for two primary reasons: to make certain the contents of these electronic files do not contain unnecessary information and to ensure that the data in the system are adequately secure and protected against theft or damage. Today's technological capabilities allow for virtually unlimited access to HRIS data. The greater number of people having access to private records increases the number of opportunities for privacy abuse.

With a growing number of users on-line and future HRISs expected to allow for even greater data access, employers are advised to develop a data quality policy with procedures covering a broad range of issues, such as:

- Ownership of data elements
- Defining the data
- Entering the data accurately
- Editing the data accuracy and validity
- Placing the data correctly in the system
- Uses of data
- Who should have access to the data
- Restrictions on data access or use

The security policy should be communicated clearly to all system users, both within and outside human resources.

In addition to developing a security policy with related procedures, there are other measures employers should take as well:

1. Ensure that all users are properly trained in the secure use and handling of equipment, data, and software.
2. Ensure that all users sign off before leaving a PC unattended, even for a short period of time.
3. Caution users not to share their password with anyone else.
4. Remind users that they are accountable for all tasks performed with their personal passwords.
5. Change user passwords periodically.
6. Caution users against duplicating both copyrighted programs purchased from vendors and data that are the property of the company, unless to provide necessary backup.
7. Ensure that all software obtained from sources other than vendors be given a clean bill of health by a virus detection program.
8. Ensure that all program copies, data files, software, and printouts

are properly controlled so that only authorized users can access them. ·

Software Modification

Eventually a growing small or mid-sized company's HRIS software will require modification. Software installed in the past may no longer be compatible with new computers or organizational needs. While it is exciting to access a system with new capabilities, there are pitfalls that accompany any major modification. Possible maintenance problems, training, and acceptance of new formats are but a few of the drawbacks. Before proceeding, then, employers are advised to consider three key areas:

1. Identify the capabilities needed from the software. Be realistic and practical, but anticipate organizational changes a few years down the road. You do not want to undergo a major overhaul again a year from now because of short-sightedness.
2. Conduct an in-depth technical evaluation of the capabilities of your existing software, identifying its limitations and capabilities.
3. Examine company policies and procedures to make sure HRIS modification is the best solution to matching user-system needs.

Your goal overall should be to select a system that requires the least amount of modification to meet present and near-future growth needs.

Summary

Not too long ago, organizational record keeping was a relatively simple, manually performed function assigned to the human resources department. Over the years, however, as HR-related legislation has increased and the human resources function has grown in complexity, records maintenance has expanded accordingly. Employees responsible for this area today require extensive knowledge of various legal requirements for retention of records and posting notices.

Even the smallest organizations can now afford to install computerized human resources information systems. Such systems will not only greatly ease the tasks of record keeping but can assist with virtually all aspects of human resources management. Smaller organizations should be able to find an effective packaged system but should recognize that no packaged system will meet all existing and future needs. The secret to implementing a packaged system successfully is to select a program that requires minimum modification to meet current human resources needs and can be further customized in the future.

12

Employee Services
and Activities

The extra employee services and activities provided by a company beyond compensation and standard benefits are a motivating force for improved productivity.

Companies know that employees expect more from their jobs than fair wages and competitive benefits. They recognize that offering a variety of employee services and activities can help improve employer-employee relations, increase motivation, and stimulate productivity. They further understand that people who are weighing several employment possibilities or considering a job change often base their decisions on a company's extra employee services and activities.

In considering which services and activities to offer your employees, be certain to evaluate the need for each activity, the level of employee interest in it, the anticipated extent of its use, its projected effectiveness, and its direct and indirect costs. Also consider the services provided by your competitors. The results of this evaluation process will vary from organization to organization.

Most small and mid-sized companies provide employee communication and publications, suggestion systems, food service programs, and recreational and social programs. They may also provide award programs, and still others are offering innovative services such as humor programs. Let us examine each of these programs in greater detail.

Employee Communication and Publications

Employees need to be kept informed of company matters that affect them both directly and indirectly. In addition, they like to get news about other activities inside—and outside—the company. For these reasons, employee communication is an important aspect of any workplace.

Bulletin Boards

One of the most common sources of employee communication is the company bulletin board. Bulletin boards should be located in areas easily accessible to all employees. Some popular sites include across from elevator banks, in cafeterias, and outside rest rooms. Rules regarding the posting of bulletin board notices should be made available by the human resources department or incorporated in the employee handbook. These rules should include:

- What may be posted
- Where a notice may be posted
- How long a notice may remain posted
- The various forms in which notices may appear
- The maximum size of a notice
- Specific examples of what may and may not be posted
- The procedure to follow when posting a notice

Stress the fact that bulletin boards must not be allowed to become an accumulation of miscellaneous information. They are an important source of communication, and their use should be managed carefully. In small and mid-sized companies, someone in the human resources department should be in charge of reviewing and approving employee notices for posting. Guidelines for approval should include whether the notice will appeal to or benefit a large number of employees. Postings by management or human resources should receive approval from senior management.

It is recommended that most notices remain posted for two to four weeks. This will give employees who are out—on vacation, on leave, or for other reasons—an opportunity to read the most recent postings. Of course, some notices from management should be posted permanently. For example, the notices referred to in Chapter 11 required by federal law should be posted at all times.

Properly monitored bulletin board programs have many advantages:

- They are a fast and accurate medium of communication.
- They allow employees to absorb information at their own pace.
- They can be used equally by management and employees.

- They remind employees, on an ongoing basis, that management is concerned with their interests and opinions.

Bulletin boards usually contain notices regarding a variety of topics, both work related and personal. Consider the following sample of notices appearing on the bulletin board of a mid-sized publishing company. In addition to the permanently posted required notices mentioned earlier, the bulletin board was divided into two primary areas: work-related news and personal news. In the section devoted to work-related news, dubbed "Here and Now," notices included:

- A list of the most recent job openings and guidelines for application
- An announcement describing the latest in a series of lunch-hour career development workshops
- A list of recent promotions and other changes in assignments
- A list of recent retirements, including news of company activities held in retirees' honor
- An update on the company's plans for expansion
- The latest travel discounts available to employees
- New hours for use of the company gym
- That week's cafeteria menu

In the section devoted to personal news, called "After Hours," notices included:

- An announcement about the upcoming company picnic
- Announcements of recent marriages and births
- Notices regarding cars, furniture, and other items for sale
- An ad by an employee looking for someone to share his apartment

Remember to post all notices in places readily accessible to employees with disabilities. In addition, if your workforce comprises a significant portion of workers not literate in English, post these notices in languages in which the employees are literate.

House Organs

The second most common source of employee communication is the house organ, or company newsletter. Like bulletin boards, house organs can be a valuable source of employee communication if properly administered and monitored. The house organs of various companies differ in format and specific content, but most have certain characteristics in common:

- The magazine or newsletter is published for company employees, generally by the human resources or public relations department.
- It contains materials prepared by the human resources or public relations department and information submitted by management and employees.
- The contents reflect a combination of work-related and personal news.
- There is often a message from senior management at the beginning of each publication.
- Creative contributions, reflecting both writing and artistic skills, are encouraged.

Many organizations mail copies of the house organ to their employees at home. This makes certain that all employees receive their own individual copies and allows them leisure time to read and enjoy the contents. (These advantages should be weighed against the cost of postage, however.)

Copies of the most recent house organ should also be prominently displayed in the organization's reception area, where applicants, customers, and clients are likely to wait for appointments. In many ways, the employees' magazine gives a more effective overview of the company than the annual report. It is certainly easier and more interesting to read.

To give you an idea of the varying formats and contents of house organs in different organizations, here are descriptions of three samples.

A manufacturing organization of approximately 1,500 employees publishes its house organ ten times a year, with each edition averaging sixteen pages. The format is similar to a magazine, printed on 8½- by 11-inch paper. Each issue begins with a personal message from the president about a recent accomplishment or goal of the company, accompanied by his picture. Detailed news stories about the overall company are always included. There is also ample room devoted to personal news, such as recent promotions, retirements, marriages, births, and so on.

Various company contests are described, and when they are concluded, winners are announced. The creative talents of employees are displayed in the form of artwork, poetry, and occasionally short stories.

In addition, there is a regular column in which the human resources department answers some of the most commonly asked questions about employee benefits and services. Each issue concludes with a crossword puzzle submitted by an employee, reflecting a specific theme.

A publishing firm with approximately 1,000 employees produces its house organ monthly on 11- by 17-inch paper, in a newspaper format. The average length of each issue is four to six pages. Since the company is growing rapidly, up to a full page is devoted each month to new hires, new assignments, and promotions. Each featured employee's photo appears, along with a brief description of his or her new job and other related information of interest. Articles about recent company developments appear in each issue. Also appearing regularly are that month's birthdays; news of recent weddings, anniversaries, and births; and announcements about upcoming company-sponsored events, such as the annual holiday dinner-dance.

The company is proud of its concern about employee opinions, so its newsletter frequently includes a survey soliciting employee opinions on various company-related matters. The results of these polls are published in subsequent editions.

Appearing monthly is a column on the latest news about benefits and compensation, including the impact of recent legislation on company policies. The newsletter also periodically prints excerpts from the company's employee handbook relating to a matter of recently expressed concern to both managers and employees. Pertinent questions and answers clarify the issues involved.

Another publishing company with approximately 700 employees produces an 8½- by 11-inch newsletter every other month. A recent sample carried a two-column message from the company's president. His positive, upbeat statement was accompanied by his photo and addressed the issue of increased productivity as a way of continuing growth.

The sample newsletter was well organized, with each of its twelve pages headed by a specific caption. Pages under the caption "Business Update" included news about recent promotions and additions to staff, a change in the name of one of the company's publications, the revenue gain of another of its publications, an award issued to a third publication, and the opening of a new sales office.

The "News Briefs" section contained miscellaneous information on such topics as company travel tips, the company's new phone option, and the employee photo exhibit. There were also blurbs about the upcoming Christmas party and blood drive.

The caption "In Good Company" appeared on two pages, with one page dedicated to the operation of the company's printing plant and a second page devoted to the staff of the company's Los Angeles office.

There was also a section called "Sports" that described aerobics classes, volleyball, baseball, and basketball, all available to employees. "Congratulations" listed recent births, marriages, and engagements.

On the back page of the house organ appeared information and photos highlighting the company's child care center. The bottom half of the page was devoted to descriptions of current job openings.

Suggestion Programs

Many human resources experts consider an organization's employee suggestion system to be the best upward communication device management has. Formal suggestion systems are designed to elicit ideas that may improve the cost-effectiveness of operations or enhance general working conditions.

A properly administered suggestion system can benefit everyone. Employees can receive extra cash for each cost-saving suggestion adopted, earn recognition for their knowledge, and increase their visibility and growth opportunities within the company. Managers can receive credit for promoting creative thinking among their employees and will also benefit by increased departmental efficiency. The company is likely to increase productivity, reduce costs, improve operating efficiency, and upgrade product quality. Finally, customers will receive better service and be more satisfied with and confident in the organization.

To accomplish these objectives and operate effectively, a suggestion program should follow certain guidelines:

- Management should provide active and ongoing support for the suggestion system.
- Management should recognize employees' ideas and give full credit accordingly.
- A well-qualified person should be in charge of administering the program.
- A suggestion committee should be established to check the savings and expenses involved in adopting a specific suggestion.
- If the suggestion leads to specific cost reductions, the amount of the award paid should be based on the savings predicted, generally for a year's use of the suggestion. The incentive payoff for a usable suggestion is usually from 15 percent to 20 percent of the calculated first year's savings.
- All suggestions should be acknowledged within a reasonable period of time, usually two weeks.
- Reasons for rejecting suggestions should be provided.

- All employees should be informed of the benefits to be derived from a suggestion that has been adopted.

In spite of the benefits to all concerned, there are certain problems associated with suggestion programs:

- Managers sometimes resent employees who make formal suggestions, fearing that it will make them appear deficient in the eyes of upper management.
- Colleagues may resent the award to a single individual if they feel that the primary impact of the suggestion is to create more work for all of them or that credit for the suggestion should have been shared.
- Specialists may resent other employees' making suggestions in their areas of expertise.
- Employees may become resentful if their suggestions are rejected.
- The routine administrative problems of setting up and monitoring the system can become overly burdensome.

A clearly defined suggestion-system process will help solve the last problem mentioned. These ideas will guide you in setting up a smoothly functioning system.

- Place several suggestion boxes in easily accessible locations throughout the organization, such as near company bulletin boards.
- In clear and definitive terms, post the procedure to be followed for submitting a suggestion, including:

What form, if any, is to be used
To whom the form should be submitted
Any deadlines
Who decides whether a suggestion is to be accepted
When the employee may expect to receive a response
What form the response will be in
Criteria used for accepting or rejecting suggestions
How awards are calculated
What effect, if any, an accepted suggestion will have on an employee's potential for promotion

- Establish a review committee consisting of representatives from management, human resources, and staff.

- Provide the review committee with specific guidelines for evaluating all suggestions. For example, good suggestions:

    Cut costs
    Save time
    Reduce errors
    Improve customer relations
    Increase repeat business
    Improve employee loyalty or morale
    Help avoid conflicts and misunderstandings on the job
    Distribute work more evenly
    Help attract better-qualified employees
    Promote greater interdepartmental uniformity
    Reduce the number of accidents
    Lower absenteeism
    Eliminate waste
    Make more effective use of equipment or human resources
    Prevent equipment abuse
    Simplify present methods
    Result in significant short- or long-term savings

- Develop a reward system that is financially in proportion to the savings or increased profits anticipated as a result of an adopted suggestion.
- Respond to all suggestions, including those to be rejected, within two weeks of each submission date.
- Post all accepted suggestions, giving full credit to the employees who submitted them.

Food Services

Some companies consider employee cafeterias or dining rooms a necessary function. This is usually because the firms are located in areas where restaurants are too far away for employees to get to them and eat within a specified lunch-break time. Other companies believe that an effective food service program enhances employee comfort, convenience, and morale and that these factors have a positive impact on productivity and employer-employee relations.

For locations with fewer than 50 employees, vending machines with coffee, cold drinks, and snacks are usually sufficient. Coffee wagons may also be suitable. Locations with 50 to 100 employees usually add items such as microwave ovens, dollar bill changers, and sometimes hot food and sandwiches. For locations with more than 100 employees, complete lunchrooms are feasible, offering hot foods, sandwiches, beverages, and salads.

If an organization is going to offer any type of food service, it is sensible to make it as effective and appealing as possible. To achieve this, a company must evaluate and choose the best food service program available, monitor the program, and—if a company cafeteria is included—promote it so that is widely used.

Evaluating and Choosing the Best Food Service Program

The first step in establishing or revamping a food service program is to decide what kind of service is best for your particular company, given its location, size, and plans for growth. Next you should consider the offerings of various food service vendors. They may be found via referrals from other organizations, in the Yellow Pages, in professional trade publications, and through direct mail contacts. Some food service companies also make direct sales calls.

Once you have identified approximately half a dozen eligible companies, contact each of them, briefly explaining your goals and objectives. It is very important that each food service company clearly understand both your financial and operational objectives.

If the companies appear able to offer what you are seeking and you are interested in pursuing matters further, invite their representatives to come to your organization to tour the area. Also give representatives general information (preferably in writing) about your organization and the employee population, including:

- Number of shifts worked
- Approximate number of employees who work each shift
- Number of locations
- Total number of employees anticipated in one year and in five years
- Any special functions at which the food service company would be expected to provide services, such as special banquets or special meetings
- Any other information that will give the food service company representative a clear idea as to what your needs will be

Following its on-site survey and an evaluation of the data provided, each food service company should submit a formal written proposal regarding the operation of your food service program. After you receive all the proposals, review their contents and consider which come closest to meeting your overall objectives. The proposals should cover such facets as:

- How the company will physically operate your food service program including cafeteria, coffee wagons, and/or vending machines
- Insurance, licenses, and permit requirements
- Costs and responsibilities of purchasing and installing equipment, furniture, and lighting fixtures
- Responsibility for removing refuse and for any necessary extermination
- Maintenance and cleaning of floors and furnishings
- Handling unexpected costs

Of course, details of these and other areas should be spelled out in the formal contract.

Monitoring a Food Service Program

To monitor any food service program, it is critical to review your food service objectives periodically. They may have changed. If this is the case, then a different program may be needed. It may be, too, that the contractor is not doing all that was originally promised.

Another aspect of monitoring your food service program is to obtain employee feedback. Employees may be asked face to face what they think of the program, or via written surveys.

You should also meet periodically with your food service contractor. Together, review both original and revised goals and objectives, discuss employee feedback, and talk about any other relevant areas.

Finally, monitor the fiscal elements of your food service program. Assess whether the food and labor costs are well documented, reasonable, and justified and whether the reports submitted to you are accurate, detailed, and timely.

Promoting a Food Service Program

The financial success of any food service operation depends on employee acceptance. It is not enough simply to make food available to employees; it must also be appealing. Here are some ways to promote a company cafeteria:

- Display large, attractive signs featuring the specials of the day.
- Post weekly or daily menus on bulletin boards throughout the organization so that employees can make selections before entering the cafeteria.
- Periodically offer "freebies" such as free ice cream with the purchase of a hot meal.
- Have food themes, dedicating each week to a different food, food group, or nationality.
- Promote special holiday meals well in advance.
- Encourage employees with a flair for cooking to bring in samples and offer them to their colleagues.

These techniques will show employees that management is interested in gaining their acceptance and support.

Recreational and Social Programs

Company-sponsored recreational and social activities may serve many purposes, including these:

- They serve as excellent recruiting devices.
- They help retain valuable employees.
- They improve employer-employee relations by demonstrating that management cares about employees' interests outside work.
- They help foster feelings of loyalty.
- They help employees get to know one another better.
- Interacting in off-the-job social and recreational environments can promote better on-the-job teamwork.
- Participation by managers in sporting and entertainment events makes them seem less removed from employees.

Many company-sponsored activities are completely free, such as softball games and other sports events. Activities that are not free may be handled in one of two ways: Either a fee is collected for each specific activity, such as an annual picnic, or annual dues are collected by an employee association, pooled, and dipped into as required.

The employee association, or some other committee in charge of employee recreational and social activities, is vital to a successful program. This committee should be responsible for:

- Exploring all possible community or public recreational facilities and opportunities

- Making maximum use of available community facilities and services
- Basing recreational and social activities on surveys of employee interests, needs, and records of participation
- Encouraging employee participation in managing the program
- Maintaining accurate records of amounts budgeted and expended by the organization, amounts contributed by employees, and the number of employees participating in each activity
- Evaluating these financial and statistical records, along with employee surveys on the effectiveness of recreational programs and activities, in order to plan and prepare for future programs

The list of activities that may be included in a company's recreational or social program is extensive. Exactly what each organization decides to include depends on such factors as cost, management philosophy, human resources available to monitor the program, and level of employee interest. Of course, the size of the organization makes a difference also. For example, a survey of employee recreational facilities in large firms throughout the United States included an auditorium, a country club, a driving range and putting green for golf, racketball courts, and tennis courts. Most small and mid-sized companies cannot offer these. Their recreational and social activities more commonly include:

- *Parties*—during the holiday season, to celebrate the organization's anniversary, in recognition of someone's promotion, or wine and cheese parties for no particular reason at all
- *Dinners*—which are more formal than parties and are for a specific reason, such as awards in recognition of long-term service
- *Picnics*—for Memorial Day, for Independence Day, or just because it is summer
- *Health clubs and gyms,* which may include exercise machines and other equipment as well as a running track
- *Sports activities,* such as softball games and bowling leagues, in which teams from different companies compete
- *Travel services,* whereby company-sponsored discounted trips and tours—for a day, a weekend, or longer—are offered
- *Credit unions,* which offer various "banking" services, often for lower than the prevailing rates. Services may include savings accounts, low-cost loans, and check-cashing privileges.
- *Raffles* for various charities
- *Stop-smoking programs,* some of which include bonuses to employees who stop smoking by the completion of the program

- *Weight-loss programs,* which may also include bonuses to employees who lose and keep off a certain number of pounds during a specified time period
- *Discount tickets for theater, sports, cultural, and public events*

Of course, health clubs, stop-smoking programs, weight-loss programs, and so on accomplish more than just recreation. They may be part of overall wellness programs that provide an important benefit to employees.

Award Programs

Increasingly, award programs are being offered by small and mid-sized businesses as a means of acknowledging exceptional performance and inspiring employees to improve performance. Although these awards are usually for work performed by an individual, they may also be for those in a particular department who, for example, pulled together as a team to meet a particularly demanding deadline.

When employers contemplate awards, they generally think of money. However, experts agree that cash awards amounting to less than 3 percent of an employee's base pay are not likely to be appreciated. Not only that, most employees are inclined to put the money toward paying off bills as opposed to buying something special. Once that is done, there is no tangible reminder of the award, and employees are likely to forget all about it.

Accordingly, employers are advised to offer employees either a mixture of cash and noncash awards or just noncash awards. For example, one organization routinely selects an employee of the month, announces the selection with a notice on its bulletin boards, and treats that employee to a $50 dinner for two at a restaurant of choice, as well as tickets to a movie, or the cash equivalent. Another company has a limousine drive the employee of the month to and from work every day for a week. Yet another employer offers its award recipients a catalog from which the employee may choose a gift, with a maximum dollar value of $100. And one business with both a weight-reduction and a smoke-free program offers employees losing at least two clothing sizes a gift certificate to a local department store worth $75, and a 15-inch color TV to any employee who stops smoking for a minimum of six months.

Awards should be acknowledged and the recipient congratulated publicly, say, at a staff meeting or in the company newsletter. Be sure you explain why the employee is receiving the award.

Jerry McAdams, vice president of performance improvement resources, Maritz Inc. of Fenton, Missouri, says that, according to a new study by the Consortium for Alternative Reward Strategies Research, employers earn an average of $1.34 for every dollar paid to employees through an award program. That is, companies get a 34 percent return on their payouts for awards, in the form of improved performance and productivity.*

Humor Programs

More and more employers are discovering that work is a laughing matter. While it is difficult to assess the full value of humor, we do know of certain physiological benefits. According to William Fry, professor emeritus in psychiatry at Stanford University Medical School, laughter lowers blood pressure and heart rate. In addition, it reduces pain perception, stimulates blood flow, strengthens the immune system, and reduces levels of hormones that cause stress.† These are all factors that have a direct bearing on productivity.

Researchers point to common signs suggesting a need for additional humor in the workplace:

- Increased numbers of people being laid off
- Increased numbers of employees diagnosed as being clinically depressed
- Increased use of sick time
- Increased use of employee assistance programs
- Increased job turnover
- Increased employee complaints about working conditions

Humor consultants suggest that one of the primary barriers to introducing a humor program to the workplace is the misconception that humor, play, and laughter are inappropriate at the office. This is linked to the notion that telling jokes or "fooling around" is childish. On the contrary, humor is reflective of "childlike" behavior, which can often reduce stress and lead to creative thoughts and ideas. Companies are discovering that

*As reported in Bill Leonard, "Big Returns for Awards Bucks," *HR Magazine* (June 1994), pp. 59–60.
†As reported in W. Bradford Swift and Ann T. Swift, "Humor Experts Jazz Up the Workplace," *HR Magazine* (March 1994), pp. 72–75.

working in a relaxed atmosphere where laughter is encouraged results in greater productivity and more teamwork.

Interjecting more humor into the workplace need not be costly, disruptive, or time-consuming. Here are some suggestions for setting up a humor program in your company:

- *Have regularly scheduled "humor breaks."* For five or ten minutes a day, encourage employees to relax in an area set up with games, toys, puzzles, and comic books. If members of senior management take these breaks at the same time as the employees, interaction between the ranks can help improve employer-employee relations as an added bonus.
- *Give "joy grants."* Try doing what Ben & Jerry's Ice Cream Co. does: set up a fund of grants to managers to attend seminars on how to bring more laughter to the workplace.
- *Set up "humor spots."* These might be bulletin boards or a section of the company newsletter devoted to jokes, quips, or cartoons. To be on the safe side, someone in human resources should check the contents and make certain there is nothing that might be deemed offensive.
- *Distribute "stress support kits."* Matt Weinstein, president of Playfair, Inc., Berkeley, California, sells stress support kits that include such items as wind-up teeth, clown noses, and pens shaped like vegetables. He says these items are a big hit with stressed-out executives.
- *Have "funny meetings."* At regularly scheduled staff meetings or anytime during a meeting that tension is starting to build, take a break and have attendees take turns saying something funny.

Humor programs are growing in popularity. Companies such as IBM, AT&T, Du Pont, Wordperfect, Kodak, Ben & Jerry's, Mobil, and the American Institute of Banking have all availed themselves of the services of humor experts in an effort to diffuse stress in the workplace and view matters in a proper perspective.

As Dr. Joel Goodman, director of the HUMOR Project, Inc., Saratoga Springs, New York, says, "In our work what we do is fun but not for fun. [We work] for companies that are interested in adding a little jolt of fun, but not for fun but because there is a serious bottom line. And it is possible for the laugh line and the bottom line to cross."*

*Ibid., p. 75.

Summary

The extra employee services and activities provided by a company beyond compensation and standard benefits constitute a significant lure for prospective employees, as well as being a motivating force for improved productivity by existing employees.

Employers may offer numerous "extras," varying significantly in cost and effort. Most small and mid-sized organizations provide employee communication and publications, an employee suggestion system, a food service program, and different forms of recreational and social programs. Additionally, more companies recognize the advantages of award programs, as well as some innovative means for motivating workers, such as humor programs.

Appendix A:

Job Description Form

<u>*Job Description*</u>

Job title:

Division/Department:

Reporting relationship:

Location of job: Work schedule:

Exemption status: Grade/Salary range:

Summary of duties and responsibilities:

Primary duties and responsibilities:
(E) = essential functions; (N) = nonessential functions

Percentage of time
devoted to each task

        1. ( )

        2. ( )

        3. ( )

        4. ( )

        5. ( )

        6. ( )

        7. ( )

        8. ( )

        9. ( )

Performs other related duties and assignments as required.

Job title:

Division/Department:

Education, prior work experience, and specialized skills and knowledge:

Physical environment/working conditions:

Equipment/machinery used:

Other (e.g., customer contact or access to confidential information):

Job analyst:
Date:

Appendix B:

Sample Job Description

Job Description

Job title: Assistant to the Director of Human Resources

Division/Department: Human Resources

Reporting relationship: Director of Human Resources

Location of job: Headquarters

Work schedule: 9:00 A.M. to 5:00 P.M., Monday through Friday; overtime as required.

Exemption status: Exempt

Grade/Salary range: Grade 14; $38,500–$54,500 (midpoint: $46,500)

Summary of duties and responsibilities: Assists the Director of Human Resources in the HR-related matters concerning the organization's 1,000 employees. This includes the areas of recruitment, interviewing, hiring, benefits, orientation, policies and procedures, job descriptions, compensation, performance reviews, records, EEO and affirmative action, and exit interviews.

Primary duties and responsibilities:
(E) = essential functions (N) = nonessential functions

Percentage of time devoted to each task	
20	1. (E) Recruits applicants for nonexempt positions.
20	2. (E) Interviews and screens applicants for nonexempt positions; refers qualified candidates to appropriate department managers.
8	3. (E) Assists manager with hiring decisions.
8	4. (E) Performs reference checks on potential employees, by telephone or in writing.

8	5. (E) Processes new employees for payroll and benefits; informs new employees of all pertinent information.
8	6. (E) Conveys all necessary insurance information to employees and assists them with questions, processing of claims, and other related areas.
5	7. (E) Helps Director of Human Resources plan and conduct each month's organizational orientation program.
5	8. (E) Assists in the implementation of policies and procedures; may be required to explain or interpret certain policies.
5	9. (E) Assists in the development and maintenance of up-to-date job descriptions for nonexempt positions throughout the company.
5	10. (E) Assists in the maintenance and administration of the organization's compensation program; monitors salary increase recommendations as they are received to ensure compliance with merit increase guidelines.
2	11. (E) Advises managers of schedules for employee performance appraisals; follows up on delinquent or inconsistent appraisals.
2	12. (N) Maintains orderly, systematic employee records and files.
2	13. (E) Maintains all necessary HR records and reports; this includes unemployment insurance reports, flow-log recording, EEO reports, and change notices.
1	14. (E) Assists EEO officer with advising managers on matters of EEO and affirmative action as they pertain to the interviewing and hiring process and employer-employee relations.
1	15. (E) Conducts exit interviews for terminating nonexempt employees.

Performs other related duties and assignments as required.

Education, prior work experience, and specialized skills and knowledge:
Thorough general knowledge and understanding of the human resources function; prior human resources experience, preferably as a generalist or a nonexempt interviewer in an environment similar to this one; demonstrated ability to work effectively with all levels of management and employees; ability to deal effectively with applicants and referral sources.

Physical environment/working conditions: Private office in the Human Resources Department.

Equipment/machinery used: IBM personal computer

Other (e.g., customer contact or access to confidential information): Access to all confidential information regarding employees.

Job analyst: Diane Arthur

Date: May 15, 1995

Appendix C:

Job Requisition Form

Job title: Exemption status:
Division/Department: Reason for opening:
Reporting relationship: Work schedule:
Location of job: Grade/Salary range:

Summary of primary duties and responsibilities:

Education, prior work experience, and specialized skills and knowledge:

Working conditions:

Equipment/Machinery used:

Other:

Signatures:

name (requesting manager)	title
name (department head)	title
name (human resources representative)	title

© 1995 by Arthur Associates Management Consultants, Ltd., Northport, N.Y.

Appendix D:

Job-Posting Notice Form

Appendix E:

Job-Posting Application Form

Job-Posting Application

(Please print or type)

Name:

Date:
Telephone ext.:

Present job title:

Present div./dept.:

Present grade:

Present salary:

Name of present supervisor/manager:

Position applied for:

Job no.:

Job-Posting Eligibility Requirements:

1. You must be employed by XYZ, Inc., for at least 12 consecutive months.
2. You must be in your present position for a minimum of 6 months.
3. You must meet the qualifications/requirements listed on the job-posting notice for this position.
4. Your most recent evaluation must reflect your job performance as satisfactory or better.
5. You must notify your immediate supervisor/manager of your intent to submit a job-posting application.

Job-Posting Application Procedure:

1. Submit the original copy of this form to the Human Resources Department; submit the yellow copy to your immediate supervisor/manager; keep the white copy for yourself.
2. You will be contacted within three working days of receipt of your application.

Appendix F:

Application for Employment Form

Application for Employment

(Please Print)

XYZ, Inc., considers applicants for all positions without regard to race, color, religion, sex, national origin, age, veteran status, non-job-related disabilities, or any other legally protected status.

Date: _____

Name: _____
last   first   middle

Address: _____
number   street   city state zip code

Phone no.: (___) _____ Social security no.: _____
area code

Position(s) applied for: _____

Available to work: (   ) Full-time (   ) Part-time (   ) Temporary
(   ) Days   (   ) Evenings

Referral source: (   ) Advertisement (   ) Employment agency
(   ) Friend (   ) Relative (   ) Other

Have you ever filed an application at XYZ, Inc., before?
(   ) Yes   Date: _____ (   ) No

Have you ever been employed by XYZ, Inc., before?
(   ) Yes   Dates: _____ (   ) No

Do you have any relatives, other than a spouse, already employed by
XYZ, Inc.? (   ) Yes (   ) No

If yes, please list names and positions/departments: _____

Are you above the minimum working age of _____? (   ) Yes (   ) No
If you are under the age of _____ can you furnish a work permit?
(   ) Yes (   ) No
Are you legally eligible to work in the United States? (   ) Yes (   ) No

> If so, will you be prepared to produce proof at the time of hire, in
> accordance with the Immigration Reform and Control Act of 1986?
> (   ) Yes (   ) No

Have you ever been convicted of a felony? (   ) Yes (   ) No
A positive response will not necessarily affect your eligibility to be hired.

> If yes, please explain: _____

_____

_____

_____

_____

Are you able to perform the essential functions of the job for which you are
applying either without accommodation or with a reasonable amount of accommodation? (   ) Yes (   ) No

Have you ever served in any of the U.S. military services?
> (   ) Yes (   ) No

> If yes, what branch? _____
> Briefly describe your duties:

_____

_____

_____

As related to the position applied for, what languages do you speak, read, and/or write?

———————— ( ) Speak	( ) Read	( ) Write	Degree of Fluency ————
———————— ( ) Speak	( ) Read	( ) Write	Degree of Fluency ————
———————— ( ) Speak	( ) Read	( ) Write	Degree of Fluency ————

What professional organizations or business activities are you involved with, relevant to your ability to perform the job for which you are applying?

_____

_____

Employment Experience

Please list present or most recent employer first. If additional space is needed, continue on a separate sheet of paper.

Employer: _____ Phone no.: ( ) _____

area code

Address: _____

number　　　　street　　　　city　　　　state　　　　zip code

Position(s): _____

Immediate Super./Title: _____Start. $:_____ Final $:_____

Dates employed: From:_____ To:_____

mo.　　yr.　　　　　　　　mo.　　yr.

Reason for leaving:_____

_____

Description of primary responsibilities:_____

_____

_____

Employer: _____ Phone no.: (___) _____
                                                                area code

Address: _____
                number   street   city   state   zip code

Position(s): _____

Immediate Super./Title: _____ Start. $: _____ Final $: _____

Dates employed: From: _____   To: _____
                                   mo.   yr.   mo.   yr.

Reason for leaving: _____

_____

_____

Description of primary responsibilities: _____

_____

_____

- -

Employer: _____ Phone no.: (___) _____
                                                                area code

Address: _____
                number   street   city   state   zip code

Position(s): _____

Immediate Super./Title: _____ Start. $: _____ Final $: _____

Dates employed: From: _____   To: _____
                                   mo.   yr.   mo.   yr.

Reason for leaving: _____

_____

_____

Description of primary responsibilities: _____

_____

_____

Education and Training

List all schools attended, including trade, business, or technical institutions, beginning with the most recent.

School Name and Location	*Years Completed; Honors Received; Diploma/Degree*	*Major Course of Study*

Please describe any additional academic achievements or relevant extracurricular activities relative to the position for which you are applying:

Additional Qualifications

Please identify any additional knowledge, skills, qualifications, publications, or awards that will be helpful to us in considering your application for employment:_____

_____

_____

_____

_____

_____

References

Please provide the name, title, address, and phone number of three business references, other than present/former employers, who are not related to you.

1. _____

   _____

   _____

   _____

2. _____

   _____

   _____

   _____

3. _____

   _____

   _____

   _____

Special notice to disabled veterans, Vietnam era veterans, and individuals with handicaps

Government contractors are subject to Section 402 of the Vietnam Era Veterans' Readjustment Assistance Act of 1974, which requires that they take affirmative action to employ and advance in employment qualified disabled veterans and veterans of the Vietnam era; and Section 503 of the Rehabilitation Act of 1973, as amended, which requires that they take affirmative action to employ and advance in employment qualified individuals with disabilities.

Definitions:

1. *Veteran of the Vietnam era* means a person who served more than 180 days of active service, any part of which was during the period August 5, 1964, through May 7, 1975, and who was discharged or released with an other than dishonorable discharge or discharged or released because of a service-connected disability.

2. *Special disabled veteran* means a veteran entitled to compensation for a disability rated at 30 percent or more, or rated at 10 percent or 20 percent if determined to be a serious employment handicap, or a person discharged or released from active duty because of a service-connected disability.

If you consider yourself to be covered by one or both of these acts, and wish to be identified for the purposes of proper placement and appropriate accommodation, please sign below. Submission of this information is voluntary, and failure to provide it will not jeopardize employment opportunities at XYZ, Inc. This information will be kept confidential.

( ) Disabled   ( ) Disabled veteran   ( ) Vietnam-era veteran

Signed _____

Agreement

I certify that the statements made in this application are correct and complete to the best of my knowledge.

I understand that false or misleading information may result in termination of employment.

I authorize XYZ, Inc., to conduct a reference check so that a hiring decision may be made. In the event that XYZ, Inc., is unable to verify any reference stated on this application, it is my responsibility to furnish the necessary documentation.

( ) You may   ( ) You may not contact my present employer.

( ) You may   ( ) You may not contact the schools I have attended for the release of my educational records.

Disclaimer

If accepted for employment with XYZ, Inc., I agree to abide by all of its policies and procedures. If employed, I understand that I may terminate my employment at any time without notice or cause, and that the Employer may terminate or modify the employment relationship at any time without prior notice or cause. In consideration of my employment, I agree to conform to the rules and regulations of the Employer, and I understand that no representative of the Employer, other than the President or Human Resources Officer, has any authority to enter into any agreement, oral or written, for employment for any specified period of time or to make any agreement or assurances contrary to this policy. If employed, I understand that my employment is for no definite period of time, and if terminated, the Employer is liable only for wages and benefits earned as of the date of termination.

I also agree to have my photograph taken for identification purposes if hired.

Signed _____

Date _____

Do Not Write Below This Line

- -

Interviews

Human resources interviewer: _____ Date: _____

Comments: _____

_____

_____

Results: _____

Dept./Div. interviewer: _____ Date: _____

Comments: _____

_____

_____

Results: _____

Dept./Div. interviewer: _____ Date: _____

Comments: _____

_____

_____

Results: _____

<u>Employed:</u>   (   ) Yes (   ) No   If yes:

Title _____   Date of hire _____

Dept. _____   Starting salary _____

An equal opportunity employer M/F/V/D

© 1995 by Arthur Associates Management Consultants, Ltd., Northport, N.Y.

Appendix G:

Interview Evaluation Form

Applicant Evaluation

Applicant:_____ Date:_____

Position:_____

Department/Division:_____

Summary of experience:_____

_____

_____

Summary of education/academic achievements:_____

_____

_____

Relationship between position requirements and applicant's background, skills, and qualifications:

Position Requirements	*Applicant's Qualifications*
_____	_____
_____	_____
_____	_____
_____	_____
_____	_____
_____	_____
_____	_____
_____	_____

Applicant: _____

Position: _____

Additional factors, as relevant:

    Clerical skills: _____

    _____

    Verbal communication skills: _____

    _____

    Writing skills: _____

    _____

    Technical skills: _____

    _____

    Numerical skills: _____

    _____

    Language skills: _____

    _____

Other job-related information: _____

_____

Overall evaluation:
    (   ) Meets job requirements
    (   ) Fails to meet job requirements

Additional comments: _____

_____

              Interviewer: _____

Appendix H:

Nonexempt Performance Appraisal Form

Employee Performance Appraisal (Nonexempt)

Name:_____

Dept./Div.:_____

Job title:_____

Appraisal period:_____to_____

Date of appraisal meeting:_____

Instructions

1. The manager and employee should jointly define specific performance objectives to be achieved during the specified appraisal period.
2. During the appraisal period, progress will be measured against the performance plan developed in Item 1 above.
3. At the end of the appraisal period, the manager will measure the employee's performance against the plan, using the following ratings:

(1) *Outstanding*	Far exceeds expectations in all aspects of the job
(2) *Above Average*	Consistently exceeds expectations in many aspects of the job
(3) *Average*	Consistently meets expectations in all job areas
(4) *Below Average*	Fails to meet expectations consistently in several aspects of the job
(5) *Unsatisfactory*	Fails to meet expectations in most or all aspects of the job

4. During the appraisal meeting, the manager and employee will develop a plan addressing the areas requiring improvement and the employee's goals and interests.
5. Following the appraisal meeting, the form will be signed and dated by both the manager and the employee and forwarded to the next level of management or human resources, as required. The employee should be given a copy of the completed and signed form.

A. *Areas of Responsibility*

Responsibility	*Results Achieved*	*Rating*

B. *Aspects of Performance* (Circle the appropriate rating and support your selection under "Comments.")

1. Knowledge of the job, department/division, and organization
   (1)   (2)   (3)   (4)   (5)

   Comments:

2. Demonstrated skill level
   (1)   (2)   (3)   (4)   (5)

   Comments:

3. Communication
   (1)   (2)   (3)   (4)   (5)

   Comments:

4. Ability to work with others
   (1)   (2)   (3)   (4)   (5)

   Comments:

5. Customer relations
   (1)   (2)   (3)   (4)   (5)

   Comments:

6. Ability to work independently
   (1)   (2)   (3)   (4)   (5)

   Comments:

7. Quality of work
   (1)   (2)   (3)   (4)   (5)

   Comments:

8. Quantity of work
   (1)   (2)   (3)   (4)   (5)

   Comments:

9. Attendance/Punctuality
   (1)   (2)   (3)   (4)   (5)

   Comments:

10. Other (Describe)
    (1)   (2)   (3)   (4)   (5)

    Comments:

C. *Overall Rating*   (Circle the rating that best describes the employee's over-
                      all performance during the appraisal period.)

   (1)   (2)   (3)   (4)   (5)

D. *Mutually Agreed-On Steps to Improve Performance*

Step	*Target Date*

E. *Employee's Goals and Interests*

F. *Comments*
Manager's Comments:

Employee's Comments:

G. *Signatures*   (Note: Employee's signature indicates understanding of contents, not necessarily agreement.)

(Appraising manager)	(Date)
(Employee)	(Date)
(Next level of management)	(Date)
(Human resources representative)	(Date)

Appendix I:

Exempt Performance Appraisal Form

Employee Performance Appraisal (Exempt)

Name:_____ Appraisal period:_____to_____

Dept./Div.:_____ Date of appraisal meeting:_____

Job title
(functional and official):_____

Instructions

1. The manager and employee should jointly define specific performance objectives to be achieved during the specified appraisal period.
2. During the appraisal period, progress will be measured against the performance plan developed in Item 1 above.
3. At the end of the appraisal period, the manager will measure the employee's performance against the plan, using the following ratings:

    (1) *Outstanding*   Far exceeds expectations in all aspects of the job
    (2) *Above Average*   Consistently exceeds expectations in many aspects of the job
    (3) *Average*   Consistently meets expectations in all job areas
    (4) *Below Average*   Fails to meet expectations consistently in several aspects of the job
    (5) *Unsatisfactory*   Fails to meet expectations in most or all aspects of the job

4. During the appraisal meeting, the manager and employee will develop a plan addressing the areas requiring improvement and the employee's goals and interests.
5. Following the appraisal meeting, the form will be signed and dated by both the manager and the employee and forwarded to the next level of management or human resources, as required. The employee should be given a copy of the completed and signed form.

A. *Areas of Responsibility*

Responsibility	Results Achieved	Rating

B. *Aspects of Performance* (Circle the appropriate rating and support your selection under "Comments.")

1. Knowledge of the job, field, department/division, and organization
   (1)   (2)   (3)   (4)   (5)

   Comments:

2. Demonstrated skill level
   (1)   (2)   (3)   (4)   (5)

   Comments:

3. Problem solving and decision making
   (1)   (2)   (3)   (4)   (5)

   Comments:

4. Communication
   (1)   (2)   (3)   (4)   (5)

   Comments:

5. Responsiveness to department/organization needs
   (1)   (2)   (3)   (4)   (5)

   Comments:

6. Leadership
   (1)   (2)   (3)   (4)   (5)

   Comments:

7. Business development
   (1)   (2)   (3)   (4)   (5)

   Comments:

8. Time management
   (1)   (2)   (3)   (4)   (5)

   Comments:

9. Resource administration (staff, budget, and materials)
   (1)   (2)   (3)   (4)   (5)

   Comments:

10. Quality of work
    (1)   (2)   (3)   (4)   (5)

    Comments:

11. Productivity
    (1)   (2)   (3)   (4)   (5)

    Comments:

12. Other (Describe)
    (1)   (2)   (3)   (4)   (5)

    Comments:

C. *Overall Rating*   (Circle the rating that best describes the employee's overall performance during the appraisal period.)

(1)   (2)   (3)   (4)   (5)

D. *Mutually Agreed-On Steps to Improve Performance*

Step	*Target Date*

E. *Employee's Goals and Interests*

F. **Comments**
   Manager's Comments:

   Employee's Comments:

G. **Signatures**   (Note: Employee's signature indicates understanding of contents, not necessarily agreement.)

_____	_____
(Appraising manager)	(Date)
_____	_____
(Employee)	(Date)
_____	_____
(Next level of management)	(Date)
_____	_____
(Human resources representative)	(Date)

Appendix J:

Sample First Written Warning

TO: Kim Sanders/clerk-typist   June 23, 1995
          (Employee's name/title)

FROM: Joyce Appleton/office manager
          (Manager's name/title)

RE: Excessive Tardiness
          (Nature of problem warranting warning)

In accordance with Section 8 of your Employee Handbook, of which you have a copy, all employees are expected to report to work before or at their regularly scheduled starting time. As you are aware, your regularly scheduled starting time is 9:00 A.M. On June 5, 1995, we discussed the matter of your excessive tardiness. Specifically, I pointed out six separate occasions during the preceding six-week period when you reported to work late. They were:

Tuesday, April 18	15 minutes late
Thursday, April 27	20 minutes late
Tuesday, May 2	30 minutes late
Thursday, May 11	25 minutes late
Monday, May 15	25 minutes late
Friday, June 2	20 minutes late

During the above-mentioned verbal warning, you acknowledged these occurrences and stated that you were sometimes having trouble making a certain train connection, which caused you to arrive at work late. You further stated that you planned on making different travel plans to avoid future tardiness.

Since our discussion three weeks ago you have been late on two occasions:

Friday, June 9	25 minutes
Monday, June 12	20 minutes

Failure to correct this behavior may result in a second written warning.

A copy of this first written warning will be placed in your HR file. If no additional instances of tardiness occur over the next 12 months, the warning notice will be removed.

_____   _____
(Manager's signature)   (Date)

_____   _____
(Employee's signature indicating   (Date)
    understanding of contents)

Employee's comments:

Appendix K:

Sample Second Written Warning

TO: Kim Sanders/clerk-typist   Aug. 7, 1995
(Employee's name/title)

FROM: Joyce Appleton/office manager
(Manager's name/title)

RE: Continued Excessive Tardiness
(Nature of problem warranting warning)

In accordance with our meeting and the verbal warning issued on June 5, 1995, and our meeting and the written warning issued on June 23, 1995 (see attached), this constitutes a second written warning.

Over the past six weeks, you have been tardy four times:

Monday, June 26	10 minutes late
Wednesday, July 5	15 minutes late
Thursday, July 20	25 minutes late
Monday, July 31	20 minutes late

Failure to correct this behavior may result in suspension for one to three days without pay.

A copy of this second written warning will be placed in your HR file. If no additional instances of tardiness occur over the next 12 months, the warning notice will be removed.

_____   _____
(Manager's signature)   (Date)

_____   _____
(Employee's signature indicating   (Date)
  understanding of contents)

Employee's comments:

Index